WORKING WITH CHILDREN AND THEIR FAMILIES

Martin Herbert

WORKING WITH CHILDREN AND THEIR FAMILIES

Martin Herbert

Professor of Clinical Psychology, University of Leicester
Director of the Centre for Behavioural Work with Families
Leicester

Published by The British Psychological Society
and Routledge Ltd

First published in 1988 by the British Psychological Society, St Andrews House, 48 Princess Road East, Leicester, LE1 7DR, in association with Routledge Ltd, 11 New Fetter Lane, London EC4P 4EE.

British Library Cataloguing in Publication Data

Herbert, Martin
  Working with children and their families.
  —(Psychology in action).
  1. Welfare work with families with children
  I. Title   II. British Psychological Society
  III. Series
  362.7

ISBN–0–901715–79–4
ISBN–0–901715–80–8 pbk

Printed and bound in Great Britain by The Camelot Press, Southampton. Whilst every effort has been made to ensure the accuracy of the contents of this publication, the publishers and authors expressly disclaim responsibility in law for negligence or any other cause of action whatsoever.

CONTENTS

List of Figures and Tables

Preface

This book is written for the helping professions: those who work with families: parents, adolescents and children. It is about those aspects of helping that are psychological and social in what they have to offer. This means that the book is largely concerned with the personal relationships and interactions that take place within families and the problems to which they commonly give rise – not only for their members, but also for the community in which they reside. Because families are made up of people who are at different stages of development (within individual life cycles), adults and children with different priorities, needs and goals, it is no surprise that family life can generate misunderstanding and conflict.

Leo Tolstoy observed that 'all happy families resemble each other, every unhappy family is unhappy in its own way'. The first part of this quotation may not be altogether true, but the second half certainly is. This means that the reader cannot expect *simple* answers to questions. Every child, every parent and all families are unique, so no *generalized* advice can meet all cases, every circumstance, or a particular individual's special difficulty.

There are no short-cuts to understanding families – so this book has no cut-and-dried prescriptions for immediate application to parents or children in distress. But, hopefully, it does offer a way (the so-called problem-solving approach) of thinking about family problems and of dealing with them.

Part 1 introduces you to the multiplicity of family problems – the difficulties typically presented by parents and children. The reader is provided with a framework for assessing the *specificity* (the 'what', 'where', 'when' and 'how often') of family difficulties, and for estimating their seriousness. It is not possible to cover the entire range of problems, nor to devote an in-depth exploration to everything dealt with in this section. But you will find annotated references to books and articles which will supplement your knowledge base for family work.

Chapters 1 and 2 are essentially about the exploration of the 'what' questions: 'what is going wrong?'; 'under what conditions do the difficulties occur?'; 'what maintains such self-defeating problems?' Chapter 3 deals specifically with the family as a dynamic 'system' – a subject worthy of study in its own right. Chapter 4 asks the 'why' question and puts forward a variety of explanatory 'models', that is, medical and psychological approaches to the understanding of individual and family problems.

In Part 2 – 'Development and Change' – I provide some useful information for those who work with parents and young people. This includes facts and theories about childhood and adolescence and the special life-tasks and problems associated with each stage of development (Chapter 5); also a discussion of the key concept of *responsiveness* in parents and children (Chapter 6). This issue leads to a consideration of *bonding* and the deeply worrying problems of emotional, physical and sexual abuse. Finally there is an introduction to the psychological processes of *loss* and *change* (Chapter 7). These themes lead to a consideration of such topics as divorce, death, bereavement, reconstituted and single parent families; and the perennial concern about the implications of substitute care.

Part 3 is about the professional intervention which brings us to the *how* question: 'How do I best help my clients?' Several broad approaches and specific methods and techniques are described in Chapters 9, 10, 11 and 12. They include giving advice, counselling, communication and parent training, play and family therapy, psychodynamic and behavioural work and finally skills training for better social relationships and effective problem-solving.

In the appendices you will find, among other things, a detailed account of treatment options open to the professional working with child abuse cases. Examples of actual work – a programme for training parents in groups and a vignette of a child abuse case – are also provided.

Throughout the book you will find illustrative case material to highlight the links between theory and practice; I have included flow charts, checklists and proformas to assist you with the 'nuts and bolts' of assessment and the monitoring of your interventions. In order to avoid cluttering the text with distracting references and citations they are collected together at the end of the book together with a chapter-by-chapter *Further Reading* and *Acknowledgements*.

Part 1

Getting to Grips with Problems

❝ *Let us imagine for the moment, and for many it will be close to actual experience, that you are faced with several clients – a family – clamouring for help, with what seems like a very large and very daunting number of what (to them) seem insoluble problems. Everyone is thoroughly miserable, except the teenager who claims to be 'above it all'. The mother feels hemmed in between the demands of Gran (who lives with them) and the commands of a fretful, strong-willed toddler ('my baby'). Father is feeling truly middle-aged, and rather anxious. He faces the possibility of being made redundant, and he feels he gets little sympathy, or for that matter, attention from his wife. ('She's completely wrapped up in the children!') Gran is worried about her health and finds the children noisy and impolite, although she does enjoy making a fuss of the 'little one'. The middle child, aged ten, feels rejected and is having trouble at school; she is beginning to refuse to go – to the concern of her parents. The house is tense; and the atmosphere, particularly in the mornings, fraught with bickering and tears.* **❞**

Given this sort of situation, where on earth do you start? It must be said that this is but one of an immense variety of 'scenarios' which might unfold before the bemused gaze of the social worker, or some other professional who works with parents and children. The problem, indeed, may be a lot worse and more menacing.

Of course, the threshold of vulnerability or annoyance varies from person to person; one individual's 'devastating' life-event has 'nuisance value' only for another hardy being. But everyone deserves at least the dignity of being heard, and attended to with due concern, while the magnitude of their problems and the possible need for an intervention are assessed. And therein lies a difficulty: what *is* a problem, and when can a problem be considered to be serious, especially in the realm of psychosocial events – human relationships and interactions – with which this book is mainly concerned?

There has been a move away from putting certain children with problems into categories with names such as physically handicapped, mentally subnormal, delicate, maladjusted, subject to specific learning

1

disability and so on. The trend today is to assess the needs of individual children relative to their circumstances. *Special needs* – as they are called – are specified in terms of what the child requires above and beyond those requirements normally supplied for all children. Thus they might include psychological or speech therapy, special diets, medication, aids to mobility, physiotherapy and special educational provision. Along with the move goes a trend towards wider integration of disabled children into the community. This concept of community care has required a closer alliance between professionals and parents.

This is not the sort of book to go into the details of different disabilities and the needs and services they generate. There are many excellent guides on this subject (see 'Further Reading'). Rather, it is about problem-solving (and 'trouble-shooting') principles and helping strategies which can be applied to a variety of *potentially* difficult situations. They might involve:

Children
- Children with behavioural (management) problems.
- Children with emotional problems (for example, fears, phobias).
- Children with special needs (disabilities).
- Children who have been fostered or adopted.

Adults
- Parents who cannot cope (for example, who are unskilled or simply demoralized).
- Parents who are unresponsive, unattached to their children.
- Parents who are abusive, who lack self-control.
- Parents who can't get on (for example, marital problems).

In the chapters that follow we shall be considering the following questions:

Question 1. **What**, precisely, is the nature of the problem/s the client/s want help with?

Question 2. **Why** have these problems arisen, and why (with time) have they not gone away?

Question 3. **How** can I help my clients, or better still, help them to help themselves?

All members of the helping professions are faced constantly with *choices* – for themselves and their clients. In this their role is similar to parents and their children. The choices parents make, and the decisions they take, have a potent influence not only on the way their offspring will 'turn out', but also how enjoyable and *relatively* problem-free their journey from childhood, through adolescence, and on to adulthood proves to be.

This book (hopefully) will help you to analyse and decide on choices, and to initiate actions which stimulate change in families that are 'stuck' in self-defeating, unproductive and growth-inhibiting patterns of living. Facts are helpful; and facts about child development and child-rearing (mind you this is *not* a book about baby- or child-care) and family relationships will be provided. But facts on their own are not enough. I hope to provide the kind of facts (based upon many studies) that provide the basis of knowledge and understanding that lead to *practical strategies* for helping parents, and children help themselves.

Chapter 1

Assessment: What Is Important?

One of your earliest choices is where to concentrate your attention in what may present itself as a welter of conflicting claims, complaints and accusations. Some of the problems will reside mainly within an individual (for example, fear) but even then they will have repercussions. The individual's parents (or partner) worry about his or her suffering. Or the problems put constraints on the activities of the family as when holidays are not possible because (say) a mother is agoraphobic, feeling anxious about leaving the house and panicky in a crowded shopping centre.

Other problems arise from the relationships and interactions (such as the give-and-take transactions) between people. For example:

- Mother–Father   For example, disagreements about the chil-
                       dren; quarrels over decisions; other *marital*
                       difficulties.

- Parent/s–Child   For example, management difficulties; disap-
                       pointments over the child's achievements or
                       lack of them.

- Child–Parent/s   For example, resentments about being
                       'babied'; complaints about unfairness,
                       favouritism).

- Child–Child   For example, sibling rivalry, jealousy.

Your client(s) may be one of these persons (a school-refusing child, say), two of them (the embattled parents), or all of them (the family). You might even have to work more widely in the neighbourhood, at the school, or with other agencies in the community. Who the client is, is in fact a vexed question, and one to which we shall have to return. If you work with parents and children, you are quite likely to end up talking to all members of the household.

Some workers like to have all the family present at their interviews,

4

some prefer to see the parent/s first of all, with or without the children present, and then gradually work their way around to talking to other key members of the household. Whichever way you tackle the initial interviews, you are trying to unravel *what* is going on, what the problems are, under what circumstances they occur, and what changes (outcomes) would be desirable for a viable and happier situation to be created or restored.

EXPLORING THE 'WHAT' QUESTION: OBSERVING, ASKING, LISTENING

To explore the 'what' question, you need to have a penetrating, but discreet, look at the significant people who play a part in your client/s' difficulties and setting (*observation*). To this end you conduct a series of guided conversations in which you *ask* questions and *listen* very carefully and sensitively (listening with the 'third ear' as it has been called) to answers and spontaneous offerings. This, of course, is your *interview*.

Before we look at particular approaches to assessment from which the professional can choose in his or her endeavour to help a family there is an important general consideration: the perspective, 'style' or model of help to be adopted. (The term *perspective* would be most apt, but I will stay with the commonly used word, *model*). Cliff Cunningham and Hilton Davis, authors of a book on children with special needs, have a useful device for working out where you stand with regard to your role vis-à-vis your client: on the one hand, the *expert model* and on the other, the *consumer model*. (Somewhere in-between is the so-called *transplant model*).

In the expert model the professionals view themselves as very much in charge because of their monopoly (or near-monopoly) of expertise, responsibility and therefore decision-making. The client is relatively passive as a recipient of advice, 'prescriptions' (about health or how to behave), or possibly therapy of one kind or another. At the other extreme clients (say parents) are viewed very much as consumers of the professionals' services, with the right to select what *they* believe is most appropriate to their needs. Decision-making is ultimately in the parents' control; professionals act as consultants and 'teachers' (or 'instructors'). Negotiation and discussion play a large part in the professional relationships.

In the transplant (or what might also be called the partnership) model professionals perceive themselves as having expertise but sharing it and (to some extent) imparting it to parents and other non- or para-professionals so that they *mediate* (i.e. facilitate) much of the training/therapy of the child.

Not all models suit all problems; it is a case of horses for courses. What is important is that a worker should know what his or her assumptions are. The authors referred to previously help you to uncover your orientation with these questions:

? Have I met the family?

? Do I consider the child in the context of his/her family?

? Do I have regular, two-way communication with the family?

? Do I respect and value the child as a person?

? Do I respect and value the family?

? Do I feel the family has strengths to help the child?

? Have I identified the parents' abilities and resources?

? Do I always act as honestly as possible?

? Do I give them choices about what to do?

? Do I listen to them?

? Have I identified their aims?

? Do I negotiate with them?

? Do I adjust according to the joint conclusions?

? Do I assume they have some responsibility for what I do for their child?

? Do I assume I have to earn their respect?

? Do I make the assumption that we might disagree about what is important?

? Do I believe they can change?

? Have I tried to identify the parents' perceptions of their child?

[A high proportion of YES responses suggests the generalized use of a consumer model; many NO responses indicates an expert model.]

The model you adopt will be determined not only by the agency you work in, the clients that seek help at that agency, but also *your* view of human nature — the way you *construe* problems and the solutions to these difficulties.

Problem parenting

I referred earlier to the difficulty for the worker of deciding when a problem can truly be considered to be serious. When should we begin to worry because behaviour – be it a child's or adult's – goes beyond the bounds and can be said to be abnormal? In other words, when is a problem really a problem?

There is no simple answer to this question. One would be hard pressed to find *absolute distinctions* between the characteristics of (say) parents who come to be diagnosed or assessed as problematic by psychiatrists or social workers and those of other unselected parents. The judgement of what is *ab*normal (that is, a deviation away from a norm or standard) is essentially a social one. Certain adults fail to meet particular expectations on the part of society of what constitutes appropriate parental behaviour. Unfortunately terms like 'normal' and 'abnormal' are commonly applied to parents (unfairly, more often to mothers than fathers) as if they are mutually exclusive categories. The point is that the attributes and actions which society judges in its evaluation of good and bad, normal and abnormal parenting, are ones that in some degree or other are manifested by most adults (see Figure 1a).

This figure demonstrates how a wide range of parental behaviours can be reduced to two major dimensions which can be described as Love— Hostility and Autonomy—Control. Thus we have parental transactions which are warm and loving at one extreme and rejecting and hostile at the other, and then again activities that are restrictive and controlling versus ones that are permissive and promoting autonomy. According to this model an antagonistic parent is one who combines hostility and restrictiveness, while a protective parent is one who is both loving and restrictive, and so on.

You can also see how the long-term consequences of these parental behaviours (trends only!) – illustrated in Figure 1b – guide us to a view of the kind of parenting which entails risks.

Signs of abnormal parenting involve *exaggerations*, *deficiencies* or *harmful combinations* of behaviour common to most, if not all, parents. Thus we would be concerned about overprotective and underprotective behaviour by a mother or father, and we would be concerned by a punitive parent who displays a combination of hostility and poor self-control.

Thus the differences are mainly quantitative; differences *not* in kind but in degree. The same (as we shall see) can be said of children's problems.

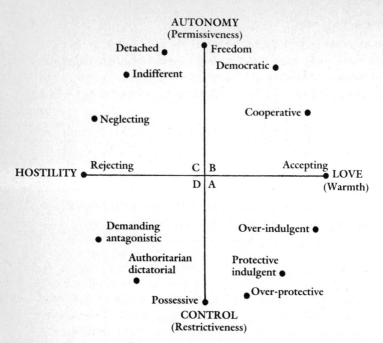

Figure 1a. The range of parental behaviour-types within two major dimensions: autonomy–control/hostility–warmth. (*From E.S. Schaefer, 1959.*)

	Restrictiveness	Permissiveness
Warmth	**A** { Submissive, dependent, polite, neat, obedient Minimal aggression Maximum rule enforcement (boys) Dependent, not friendly, not creative Maximal compliance	**B** { Active, socially outgoing, creative, successfully aggressive Minimal rule enforcement (boys) Facilitates adult role taking Minimal self-aggression (boys) Independent, friendly, creative, low projective hostility
Hostility	**D** { 'Neurotic' problems More quarrelling and shyness with peers Socially withdrawn Low in adult role taking Maximal self-aggression (boys)	**C** { Delinquency Noncompliance Maximal aggression

Figure 1b. Details of children's behaviour as influenced by the two major parental dimensions: restrictive parenting and permissive parenting. (*Adapted from W.C. Becker, 1964*)

Problematic children

Parents' enjoyment of their children is likely to diminish rapidly and give way to anxious concern, and perhaps anger and resentment, when they show signs of abnormal or deviant behaviour and emotion. Parents and teachers begin to worry about youngsters when their actions persist in being:

- **not understandable**, that is when their moods, attitudes or behaviours defy good sense and lack reason or meaning;
- **unpredictable**, such that there is a Jekyll-and-Hyde-like quality of changeability, disconcerting switches in mood, friendliness and cooperation;
- **rebellious** and uncontrollable in the sense that adults are unable to impose their authority and/or their youngsters seem unwilling or unable to control their own behaviour.

Few parents (or teachers) have not observed undesirable forms of behaviour in a particular child or adolescent, at one time or another, and they tend to be resigned about such manifestations. 'Well, that's what you'd expect, isn't it, of a toddler (or teenager)'. It is when such actions are *frequent* and *intense* that real concern is felt; in other words, it is a matter of degree.

At what point is it inapppropriate to be philosophical about your client's difficulties? When should your mental 'alarm bells' begin to ring; when do you cease saying to clients "Ah well, she'll grow out of it'?

At the most general level you might ask yourself:

? What are the consequences – benign or unfavourable – of the child's actions?

? Does the child's style of life prevent her from leading a contented life in which she is able to enjoy social relationships, and play and work (learn) effectively?

? Does the child's behaviour, in terms of his development towards maturity, represent a retrogressive trend – as when he resorts to thumb-sucking and temper tantrums as a way of deflecting mother's attention from the 'rival' baby sister?

By the way, you could substitute *parent* for *child* in most of these questions to assess the seriousness of their problems. Every stage of development is marked by certain life-tasks – physical, psychological and social skills and challenges which have to be mastered by the child, the adolescent and eventually, the adult. Some of the more important of these tasks can be indicated in chart form (see Table 1).

Table 1. Life tasks

Life stage	Life tasks – it is important to:
Infancy (birth–2)	• feel attached to one or more people • know that people and objects still exist even when they can't be seen • develop ideas through handling objects • develop movement skills
Early Childhood (2–4)	• begin to develop self-control • begin to develop language • explore and pretend in play • develop further movement skills
Middle Childhood (5–7)	• develop ideas about being male/female • begin to think about right and wrong • develop ideas of numbers etc. through practical experiences • play co-operatively
Late Childhood (8–12)	• develop co-operative skills • be a member of a team • begin to think about yourself • develop academic, artistic, craft and sporting skills
Early Adolescence (13–17)	• become used to a mature body • learn to use abstract ideas • gain support from same age friends • try out sexual activities
Late Adolescence (18–22)	• become independent and competent • make first decisions about work • set own behaviour limits • make close, intimate relationships • freely choose own values
Early Adulthood (23–30)	• develop patterns of family living • begin to be a parent • develop work plans • actively choose lifestyle • give to local community
Pre-Middle Age (30–35)	• look anew at what's worth spending time on • be sensitive to the 'looking anew' done by people important to you • be the parent of an older child
Early Middle Age (36–50)	• review commitments in mid-life • cope with children leaving home

	• develop relationships with partner • take an active part in community life
Late Middle Age (51–65)	• develop community involvement • complete or wind down working life • acknowledge the prospect of death
Old Age (65–death)	• negotiate increasing dependence on others • evaluate one's own life • deal with the deaths of close friends and relatives • come to terms with one's own death

Look at Table 1 and make some notes about the life tasks which most concern your clients at the moment. Ask them about their present priorities and preoccupations. The topic of family life maps (page 36) will examine how one individual's life tasks, and those of other members of the family, are interconnected.

The newborn infant (to take one example) needs to develop a sense of trust and later, a growing autonomy. A lasting sense of trust, security, confidence or optimism (as opposed to distrust, insecurity, inadequacy or pessimism) is thought to be based upon affection, a degree of continuity of care-giving and the reasonably prompt satisfaction of the infant's needs. Some parents may be too immature or preoccupied by personal problems to do this. The major hazards to the development of a perception of a benign, trustworthy and predictable world in which children initiate independence-seeking and perceive their own actions as having meaningful consequences, are neglect, abuse and indifference. Extreme inconsistency and other conditions – social and physical – interfere with the child's sense of personal adequacy or hinder the acquisition of skills. Such influences are likely to produce a child who behaves in a troublesome manner. Incidentally, physically-handicapped children are massively over-represented in the population of youngsters with behaviour problems. If such children can be helped to become more competent, then they may have less recourse to problem behaviour.

PARENT-TO-CHILD; CHILD-TO-PARENT INFLUENCE: TWO-WAY TRAFFIC

In many ways children's behaviour can have as much effect on their parents' actions as their behaviour has on them. So when parents meet certain extremely difficult, temperamental or inborn factors – a powerful individuality in their offspring – from a very tender age, they can be overwhelmed for a time, and change the direction and manner in which they intended to bring up their child. These individual characteristics may show themselves in moodiness (in particular, discontent), over-activity, defiance, over-sensitivity, unpredictability, biological irregularity, and unadaptability – that is, a noisy unwillingness to adapt to changes in routine. The impact may be greater on adoptive parents because they may ascribe the difficult behaviour to deprivation experiences, rejection of themselves by the adopted child, or even 'bad blood'.

What *is* important is that you assess the way clients *construe* situations and *attribute* meaning to what is happening to them.

The Case of Avril Hayes

This is what one mother told us about her child at the Leicester University 'Centre for Behavioural Work with Families' (echoed by many others we have worked with). [Names have been changed, and aspects of the case disguised.]

> **❝** *From the first day that I saw my daughter Avril, I realized that she was more lively than her sister Stella and wouldn't be content to be in a room by herself. She would scream and I went through endless months wondering if I was feeding her incorrectly, whether she had a pain or was unhappy, but finally came to the conclusion that she just wanted company . . . but on her own terms. I wasn't allowed to make a fuss of her but she didn't want to be alone. Meanwhile, other problems were emerging. She would never sleep during the day like other babies, and eventually wouldn't sleep much at night either; and when I went to cuddle her she would scream, bite or kick and this showed itself particularly at bathtime and changing time. Guilt was my first emotional feeling towards my baby. Pure unadulterated guilt. Guilt because no one really wanted her; guilt because I had foisted a child upon my family (I was the only one who welcomed the pregnancy) who was proving to be every parent's nightmare. Protectiveness came very quickly after guilt. I would protect her against the world if necessary. But love was hardly noticeable except in my fierce protective instinct. How can you love a baby who alternately screams and cries for 18 hours out of every 24, who won't feed without an all-out battle, who shows no response when you pick her up, cuddle her, talk to her, play with her, or just try to love her? Avril caused violent quarrels between my husband and myself (things unknown previously) and arguments between relatives on how to deal with her. I did so try to show my love for her, but she just didn't appear to want it.* **❞**

By the time Mrs Hayes came to us at the Centre she had lost all confidence in herself (a loss of what psychologists call self-efficacy). She was thoroughly depressed and demoralized and doubted whether anyone could help her. (We return to Avril and her family later on.)

Perceived self-efficacy

An eminent theorist, Albert Bandura, is of the opinion that human behaviour is subject to two major categories of influence: efficacy expectations and outcome expectations, represented in schematic form in Figure 2.

Figure 2. Perceived self-efficacy

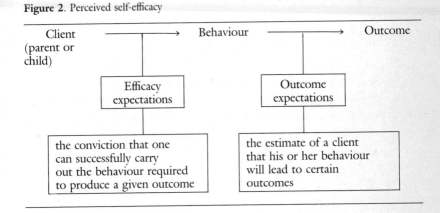

These are the constituent parts of this crucial notion of *perceived self-efficacy*. They are distinguished because (say) a mother may believe that a particular course of action (for example, a behavioural programme) will produce certain outcomes – an improvement in her child's behaviour. However, she may have serious misgivings as to whether she has the wherewithal (for example, patience and consistency) to bring about such a desirable outcome. All psychological procedures designed to bring about change, whatever their type, are thought (by some psychologists) to depend on beliefs about the level of skill required to bring about an outcome and the likely end result of a course of action. *Efficacy expectations* are thought to be the most important component. The main effect on *outcome expectations* is through the strengthening of efficacy expectations ('I *am* able to do it!'). Successful helping thus depends – in this view – on the degree to which the interventions create or strengthen the client's expectations of personal efficacy. It appears that verbal persuasion has only relatively weak and short-lived effects on such expectations. *Performance accomplishments*, on the other hand, are very potent: hence the success of techniques like behaviour rehearsal and modelling (where clients practise skills having had them demonstrated to them).

Fortunately most parents, with little or no training – and parenting is in large part a skill – rear their children (with the help of other socializing agents) into socially-acceptable and broadly rule-norm-abiding adults. Despite variations in family pattern and style of parenting, all societies seems to be successful, in the main, in transforming helpless, self-centred infants into more or less self-supporting, responsible members of their particular form of community (the process called socialization). Indeed, there is a basic 'preparedness' on the part of most infants to be trained – that is, an in-built bias toward all things social.

Summary and comment

This chapter has been concerned with the individual and his or her relationships; also with what goes wrong with them. We have seen that abnormalities of parenting and childhood behaviour are (in the main) matters of degree. Problems represent, most often, exaggerations, deficiencies or handicapping combinations of behaviours, emotions or attitudes common to all people. You are very likely to have to deal with, or refer elsewhere, the following categories of problem:

1. *Excessive behaviours* which require reduction or elimination (e.g. dangerous actions, self-injurious behaviour, aggression, phobic avoidance, etc.)

2. *Appropriate behaviours* which occur in the *wrong context*: for example cooperation with delinquent enterprises; honesty which hurts – Q: 'How do I look?' A: 'Awful'; talkativeness in the wrong part of the class lesson. These problems require training in discrimination – when to do what.

3. *Deficits* which need to be made good, for example, incontinence, s/elective mutism (selective or non-talkativeness), poor self-control, etc.).

Applying similar criteria to pinpoint deviant parental behaviour, we have physical abuse or overprotectiveness as examples of *excessive* behaviour; the continual provision of help when help is no longer required by the child as an exemplar of *inappropriate* behaviour; and unresponsive parenting as typical of the *deficit* type of problem.

We judge the seriousness of problems in terms of their disabling and/or distressing consequences – for the individual, and for others. Parents will often come to you with their self-confidence, their morale and self-esteem in tatters. Give them back their dignity by the manner in which you talk to them, treat them as 'experts' with regard to aspects of their own children, and involve them – where appropriate – as partners in the helping endeavour. In boosting perceived self-efficacy deeds speak louder than words. You will be looking (as we move on) for practical ways in which your clients can resolve their difficulties.

Chapter 2

A Step-by-Step Approach to Assessment

Children are usually a source of great pleasure and endless wonder to their parents. These joys are sometimes tempered by the concern and heavy sense of responsibility that also accompany parenthood: the pleasure may be transformed into anxiety and the wonder into puzzlement when the child begins to behave in a peculiar or erratic manner. Youngsters who have *not*, at some stage of their development, been the cause of quite serious worry to their mothers and fathers are unique.

Families, like individuals, also have their ups and downs, and go through stages – some more difficult than others. Family life can be the source of tensions and problems for its individual members in their various roles: as parents, grandparents, step-parents, substitute parents, children and teenagers.

As befits a book in a series entitled *Psychology in Action*, this one concerns itself with the psychological problems that arise within families, and particularly between parents and children. The research literature on parent – child relationships is pervaded by a belief (and one with a long ancestry) that optimal care and training of children during the impressionable years of life will 'inoculate' them against present and future problems. When one considers the intimate, protracted and highly influential nature of parents' relationships with their children, it seems self-evident that the quality of such relationships must have a vital bearing on the development of the child's personality and general adaptation.

It is worth noting that although society delegates its most crucial functions to the family, there is little formal education or training offered to would-be parents; even the informal learning and experience once offered to older children caring for younger siblings in large families, or the help from the experienced members of the extended family and from relatives living nearby, may not be available to the relatively small and isolated nuclear family (mother, father, children).

THE FAMILY AS A SYSTEM

People who work with families tend to refer to them as 'systems' because of a certain somewhat tenous analogy with a model based on systems theory (see Further Reading). The individual family members are seen as the elements or sub-units within the system. Whatever happens to one or more of its elements – say, mental illness in the mother or father, the death of a sibling, or serious marital disharmony – can affect the entire system. The heightened emotional intimacy and interdependence of the members of our small, intimate contemporary families, is thought to place a great burden on parents, most particularly the mother, and also the children. Parents are the crucial and therefore (potentially) the weak link in the chain of rearing and training children – a process called socialization. Taking care of young children is likely to be more stressful for some parents than others, especially in unfavourable circumstances (poverty or poor housing for instance). The identification and specification of 'pathological' parenting should, in theory, lead to the remediation and better still, prevention of problems; or, rather, this is the hope. Indeed, a popular aphorism of the 1950s (and the ideology underlying it persists today) stated that 'there are no problem children, only problem parents'. We shall see that this is a gross over-simplification.

Reviews of the literature repeatedly point to the conclusion that there is little evidence of a connection between specific parenting practices and later characteristics of the child. Available evidence suggests that what is important in childrearing is the general social climate in the home – the attitudes and feelings of the parents – which form a background to the application of specific methods and interactions of childrearing. For example, the mother does best who does, with a sense of confidence, what she and the community to which she belongs believe is right for the child. Feeding and toileting and the like are important elements of the child's daily activitties; but it is the social interactions they mediate – the manner in which parents undertake these tasks – that give them significance. It is how the young child is looked after that is crucial; and it is the social and psychological context of the care which matters, rather than its chronology and mechanics.

The implication of all this is that a good deal of the worker's attention is focused on the here-and-now – current events – rather than the past. This is not to say that you should neglect the client's (or his/her family's) history. The important thing is to get the balance right, a matter I shall return to. Another implication concerns the manner and form in which you get to talk to all the members of the family. There may be disagreements about the formal arrangements and theories about how best to achieve change, but there is likely to be a consensus that all members should be interviewed.

THE INTERVIEW

The interview is an essential method for gaining access to parents' and children's problems. It sounds deceptively simple and straightforward to say, 'I am going to interview the Smith family to find out what lies behind the referral by their G.P.'. But you need to be clear about the answers to several questions before you (in essence) *intrude* on the privacy of a home and its family.

? Do I have the right (and the family's permission) to conduct this and subsequent interviews? This can be a significant problem for social workers who frequently have to wear *two* hats called 'care' and 'control', and whose intervention may be unwelcome.

? What do I wish to find out (what are my objectives) in this interview?

? Who do I need to speak to in order to fulfil my objectives? (All the family members; parents only; the child alone; his/her brothers and sisters?)

? Do I invite them to meet me as a full family group? Do I speak to the mother first? both parents together? should the child be present initially?

? How do I begin the interview?

? How do I best express some quite complex and potentially threatening ideas?

? How do I reassure them about confidentiality?

? What is the best way of eliciting reliable and relevant information? How do I deal with their tendency to digress or to set an agenda which avoids key issues?

? Indeed, what *is* relevant (salient) information?

? How do I terminate the interview, without leaving clients feeling 'up in the air' or threatened?

These are psychological questions, as they have a bearing on psychological issues such as the development of rapport with clients, using communication, summarizing and memory skills, obtaining accurate and relevant (meaningful) information; maintaining a good working relationship; conducting one's business in a professional (which also means ethical) manner; and so on.

Communication. Young children tend to be talkative but are limited in their ability to reflect insightfully about their experiences; adolescents are usually introspective (reflective) but have a way of becoming monosyllabic when asked personal questions. This poses a problem for the would-be interviewer.

Children are not always very good at expressing their fears, frustrations or uncertainties. They cannot always tell their parents, let alone a comparative stranger, how they feel, but they have a language that adults can learn to translate – the language of behaviour and fantasy. What they do (in a direct sense in everyday life) and say (indirectly through play or story-telling) can be most revealing.

Projective techniques. The advantage of using projective techniques (which include play, puppets, dramatic creations, completing stories or sentences) for assessment, is that they involve relatively *unstructured* tasks that permit an almost unlimited variety of responses. The client has to fall back on his or her own resources rather than stereotyped, socially desirable answers. The techniques (as psychometric instruments) have their critics, but are invaluable if used cautiously as aids to communicating with children. The caution refers to interpreting the protocols – the made-up stories about pictured events, or the posted 'letters' (containing statements about feelings and attitudes) to various members of the family. It is thought that children *identify* with the central characters in their stories, *project* their own feelings (especially unacceptable or difficult-to-acknowledge impulses or attitudes) onto the fantasy figures, and *attribute* various motives and ideas that are essentially their own, into the play or other creative situations and plots.

Where the child is too loyal, too frightened or ashamed, or too inarticulate to speak about feelings (or painful events in the family) it may be possible to express these things in the evolving story (*you* can make up the basic structure, leaving spaces for the child to fill in) about a boy or girl of similar age. Thus you begin 'Once upon a time there was a boy/girl. What did he/she most like doing?'. . . . 'What did he/she not like doing?'. . . . (You gradually introduce, among neutral themes, topics such as secrets, fears, worries, preoccupations, family tensions, parental behaviours, and so on.)

Sentence completions are useful:

'I like to .... ,
'What I most dislike .... ,
'My best friend .... ,
'I wish.. ,
'My dad... ,
'My mum .... ,
'If only .... ,
'In my home the nicest thing is .... ,
'The worst thing is.. ,

With stories told as a response to pictures you need (as always) to be cautious about your interpretation. There is a tendency for us to project our own 'psyches' into our interpretations or to superimpose our 'theories' onto the projective protocols.

Nevertheless, play, drama (with puppets or miniatures) or stories are undoubtedly an invaluable adjunct to work with children. You would do well to have a store of miniatures, anatomically correct dolls, drawing materials and pictures available.

BEGINNING YOUR ASSESSMENT

We have looked at various conceptual issues and methods which set the stage for the actual assessment. In Flow Chart 1, I describe in summary form, ten steps you might take in seeking answers to the *what* and *why* questions.

Flow chart 1

INITIAL SCREENING	PHASE I	
	step 1.	Explain how you intend to work. Foster a good working relationship.
	step 2.	Obtain a general statement of the problem/s.
	step 3.	Specify the problem/s more precisely.
	step 4.	Elicit the desired outcome/s.
	step 5.	Construct a problem profile.
	step 6.	Introduce the idea of behaviour sequences by looking at your client/s typical day/s.

	step 7.	Establish problem priorities.
FURTHER ASSESSMENT		**PHASE II**
	step 8.	Work out a family life map.
	step 9.	Make an estimate of your client's assets.
	step 10.	Ask your adult clients about their goals (e.g. for their children). Ask the child about his or her wishes and requirements.

PHASE III

Collect more detailed 'baseline' data. Give clients homework tasks, e.g. keeping diaries, frequency charts, etc.

PHASE I

(One or possibly two interviews)

Step 1.

Foster a good working (therapeutic) relationship.

(*a*) Explain who you are and (briefly) how you expect to work.
(*b*) Establish a warm, friendly but 'businesslike' relationship, i.e. work systematically.

Step 2.

Provide the client/s with an opportunity to state the problem *as they see it*. (*These questions can be adapted and directed towards the child.*)

(*a*) Begin with an open-ended question. 'Tell me in your own words what is causing you concern . . . Do take your time'.
(*b*) Summarize at intervals that are not intrusive to clients. 'May we pause for a moment to see if I have understood correctly what you have said? I want to be sure that I get things right. As I understand it you are concerned about. . . .' Allow sufficient time for the clients to express themselves. Supplementary questions (probes) can be useful at this stage. 'What is going well in the situation you are concerned about at present with regard to _____ (say the child)?'; 'How does _____ contribute to family life?'; 'Has anyone else expressed concern about _____?'; 'Is there anyone – a gran, teacher, friend, or whoever – who does not see this worrying side to _____, because he/she is different when in their presence?'

Step 3.   **Begin to specify the problem(s) more precisely.**

(*a*) Ask for *examples* – preferably recent ones – which will illustrate the problem situation(s). 'Tell me, in detail, what happens so that I can see it in my mind's eye.' 'What leads up to the (say) confrontation? Who says what . . . to whom, who does what . . . to whom, with what consequences?' 'How does an episode usually end up?' (The use of role-play when your client has confidence in you can be very revealing about problematic transactions – see page 168.)

(*b*) Find out *when, how often,* with what *intensity,* and in what particular circumstances (what people, places, situations) the problems occur.

(*c*) Discover the details surrounding the *onset* of the problem(s). 'How long has this been happening?'; 'Are there any particular circumstances – life events – that may have been of significance because they occurred at the time that the problems made their appearance?'

(*d*) 'How have you tried to deal with the problems up to now. . . . With what result?'

(*e*) 'Who helps you cope with the problems?' 'Does anyone hinder you, as you see it?'

(*f*) 'You probably have some ideas – perhaps a theory – as to why this is happening. Would you like to try it out on me?'

Step 4.   **Find out about desired outcomes.**

'I am going to ask some questions to help us clarify what you and I should work towards. If, as is likely, other members of the family are involved, we should need to consult them.'

Step 5.   **Draw up a problem profile.**

Take account of the complaints and desired outcomes of all the members of the family.

Let us take time off for the moment to look again at Avril and her family. They were referred to our Centre for (specifically) *Avril's* problem. But it wasn't that simple.

Avril, aged four, demanded an inordinate amount of individual attention, monopolizing her mother's time wherever she was and whatever she was doing. She clung to her and followed her everywhere, even to the toilet, refusing to let her out of her sight, even for a few moments. Avril would not play with other children, including her sister — who had no real problems. By the time she was referred to us, her behaviour problems (including aggression, self-centredness of an extreme kind and other antisocial actions) were rampant and having serious implications for herself and her family. The problems were real enough, but there were other issues which required attention (see Table 2).

A glance at this problem profile tells us why those who call themselves systems theorists are agreed in focusing not on the individual but on the system of relationships in which they interact. We are not describing family therapy in minute detail in this book, but there is some overlap between home-based behavioural psychotherapy work (my personal approach) and family therapy. After all, the latter is not so much a school of therapy as a basic redefinition of the therapeutic task itself. A systems approach places the emphasis on the individual as a member of various social systems of which the most important is usually (especially for children), but not always, the family. Therapists attempt to conceptualize the problem in a more horizontal (rather than vertical-historical) manner, viewing the client as part of (say) a family group – the relationship of the members, each with the other, having a bearing on his or her present predicament. Whereas the older treatment model tended to identify the 'nominated patient' as the focus of attention (for example, the child referred to the child guidance clinic), diagnostic thinking has since been considerably influenced by what are called interactional frames of reference (explicit in systems thinking). The family as a system should always be considered in terms of its *interaction* with other community systems such as the neighbourhood, school and social and health service agencies.

The value of this 'open-ended' approach is (a) it does not assume that the family *is* 'the problem'; nor (b) does it jump to the conclusion that the child *has* 'the problem'. Rather it helps you to tease out, by careful and systematic assessment, the many possible 'targets' (as they are called) for a professional's intervention. Salvador Minuchin, the eminent family therapist, gives the example of the treatment of anorexic patients and their families: taking the child into hospital, encouraging her to eat with a behavioural programme; initiating family 'lunch' sessions; provid-

Table 2. Problem profile (The Hayes family)

Problem as defined	Who complains	Who manifests the problem/to whom?
Disobedience	Mother and Father	Avril/Mother (mainly) Avril/Father
Demanding	Mother	Avril/Mother
Aggression	Mother/Sister	Avril/Mother Avril/Sister
Rudeness	Father	Avril/Father
Not playing his part/'opting out'	Mother	Father/Mother
Depression	Father	Mother
Infantilizing	Avril	Parents/Avril
Rejection/ favouritism	Sister	Parents/Avril

Examples of problem	Settings	Desired outcome
Mother asks Avril to go up to bed. Avril ignores; if mother insists she says 'No'.	Bedtime; supermarket visiting	Avril should comply more readily
Avril demands attention or some task of mother, nags at her until she complies; tantrums if mother refuses her command, or does not 'obey' immediately.	Home, supermarket (especially when mother is busy)	Ask nicely, wait patiently; be more reasonable
Avril pinches, pulls hair, hits. Is also rude. When mother is driving car/attending to others (when sister teases).	In the car/home/almost anywhere when thwarted	Develop self-control, tolerance of frustration
Makes contemptuous remarks about/to father (e.g. 'You're fat'; 'You're stupid').	Home	Learn to be polite and respectful
Father opts out of confronting Avril; rushes off to work in the morning apologizing for leaving her to manage Avril's tempers. Obviously pleased to be 'escaping'.	Home. Tells mother she is best at dealing with Avril	Father to play his proper parental role
His wife is always weepy, miserable and lethargic. She doesn't enjoy life (or sex) anymore.	Everywhere	Be her old cheery, affectionate self
'They treat me like a baby'.	Home/playgroup	Treat me like my sister
'They spoil Avril'; 'She gets away with things I get punished for.'	Everywhere	Treat us the same

ing individual therapy for the child; and marital work for the parents. These interventions are, nevertheless, only separate moves in the direction of changing patterns of behaviour in the family system which he sees as maintaining the problem manifested by the child.

Group processes

Increased understanding of the effects of group influences on individual behaviour has also modified views of what should be taken into account in assessment, and it has become necessary to consider whether behaviour on the part of an individual is to be seen primarily in individual terms or is more readily explicable in terms of group processes. In a residential context, group processes assume particular significance and may themselves, rather than the individual, constitute the unit of attention.

It is a small wonder when we look at the history of Avril that we had a complex case on our hands: a depressed mother, an unhappy wilful child, a discontented sister, a frustrated and confused father, and a generally miserable, tense family life.

Avril, from early in life, had been a difficult and hyperactive child. From the day of her birth Avril would cry day and night. The nights were particularly difficult. Mrs Hayes spent most of them nursing her to allow the rest of the family to have some sleep. There were also serious feeding problems. The parents were worried that Avril would starve herself, so forced feeding was necessary for several months. It could take up to three hours to feed the baby. Indeed, she was an unusual child in other ways. She was difficult to amuse, taking only the most fleeting interest in toys. She seldom smiled. Her moods were volatile. When she didn't appear to be depressed and withdrawn she was often screaming for attention. Her mother and father found it impossible to enjoy their youngest child as she was so difficult to rear – she hated any change in routine and was predictable only in her unpredictability. Mrs Hayes felt guilty for having the child when she had been advised not to and any nasty remarks in that direction, from anyone, would turn her to the fierce protection of Avril, even though she might secretly agree with the criticisms. Finally, because of the marital tension and lack of husband's support when dealing with Avril's behaviour, Mrs Hayes reached a low point of depression, involving physical and nervous exhaustion; all this further minimized consistent and effective handling of her child.

Thinking in 'ABC' terms

We shall return to Avril later on. Even she had her good points! And this brings us to the next step in the assessment.

Step 6. **Teach your clients to think in terms of behavioural sequences.**

This will provide us with an understanding of *some* of the significant influences which *trigger* and *maintain* unhappy interactions within the family. Provide the client with materials to collect information in set homework tasks (see page 28).

Antecedent events .... What happens? What events precede, lead
↓   up to, set the stage for
Behaviour/interaction ....   the problematic behaviours/interactions
↓   being complained of; and
Consequence...................... what happens after the event? What social
                                   (or other) outcomes flow from the
                                   problematic interaction?

This is the basic learning equation; the ABC analysis. Sometimes called a *functional analysis*, it provides a helpful description of the key elements of an interpersonal situation and their interrelationships.

The records in Figures 3a, b and c elicit information about the behaviour of the child (say) and on the antecedent and consequent behaviours by members of the family. You might collect the information by means of (a) a handout such as that illustrated below by Avril's chart which, incidentally, incorporates a parallel measure (b) of the mother's reactions, or (c) a simple diary record with the kind of headings illustrated there.

CHART: Avril's

OBSERVER: Mother

DATE: 4/7

WEEK: 2

CODE:

BEHAVIOUR: <u>Defiance</u> = defined by situations when Avril
refuses to obey (despite warning) a
request/command: (i) to do something
                      (ii) not to do something   Ⓓ

      <u>Tantrum</u> = Avril screams/kicks/shouts   Ⓣ

ANTECEDENT EVENTS (BEFORE)	BEHAVIOUR	CONSEQUENT EVENTS (AFTER)
Avril asked for a chocolate at the checkout counter; I said 'No'. She grabbed one. I put it back. She snatched it. I put it back.	Ⓓ	Avril ran away and climbed on a display counter (see below). She only came down when a shop assistant offered her a chocolate.
I told her off when we got home.	Ⓣ	I went to the bathroom with a magazine. The noise subsided.

Figure 3(a). Handout ABC Chart

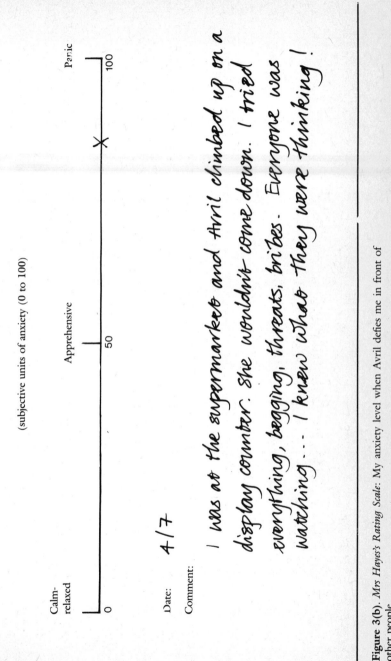

(subjective units of anxiety (0 to 100))

Calm-relaxed   Apprehensive   Panic

0   50   100

Date: 4/7

Comment:

I was at the supermarket and Avril climbed up on a display counter. She wouldn't come down. I tried everything, begging, threats, bribes. Everyone was watching... I knew what they were thinking!

Figure 3(b). *Mrs Hayes's Rating Scale:* My anxiety level when Avril defies me in front of other people

Time	Antecedent: What happens beforehand?	Client Behaviour	Consequences: What happens next?
9 p.m.	Mother asks Avril to put her toys away.	Avril takes no notice.	Mother tidies them up.
9.30pm	Father tells Avril to go to bed.	Avril says 'I don't want to, just give me a little while more.'	There is a debate. 1. Father tells her it is late (she ignores). 2. Mother pleads. Avril argues. There is a heated exchange. 1. Mother scolds. 2. Father shouts. Avril is given 10 more minutes.

Figure 3(c). ABC Diary

You will have to ask, observe, and possibly role play, over a series of interviews and home visits in order to know which events tend to follow which, in what circumstances.

You might ask parents to describe a 'typical day' in the life of the family: who does what, when, how . . . to whom or with whom . . . with what consequences. (Chapter 5 contains an example of a questionnaire/rating scale dealing with family functioning and family difficulties.) The typical day tends to highlight particular times and situations in which there is family friction.

Step 7.	**Establish problem priorities**.
	Those workers with mandatory obligations will doubtless have their own guidelines on priorities. But do ask clients what their greatest worry is; what their top priorities are for bringing about change.
	Yours and their hierarchy of tasks might be influenced by the following considerations with regard to the problem (s):
	• their annoyance value
	• their actual/potential dangerousness
	• their interference with the life of the family or its individual members
	• their accessibility to change (improvement) and an intervention
	• their frequency, intensity and magnitude
	• their disabling implications
	• the 'costs' of change in terms of resources (time, money, etc.) and other people's wellbeing
	• the ethical acceptability of the desired outcome
	• the availability of the necessary skills resources on your part or the part of your agency–to provide help.

Summary and comment

In this chapter we have asked the vital 'what' question which is the beginning point of any assessment of a family and its problems. The first 7 steps of this process were set out. This phase of your investigation should take two or three interviews/observation sessions. The need to be *specific* and *precise* was emphasized.

Start where the client *is*. Without necessarily accepting his or her (or their) assumptions, allow them the opportunity to describe the problem (initially) in their own terms. The client may see the difficulties as being the child's alone. Don't challenge this view immediately. Wait until you have your data, then gently extend the agenda to include parental and other factors.

Working with families requires a particular perspective – the so-called *systems* approach – which takes account of the interdependence of family members and the fact that what happens to one person 'is likely to affect the others. This focus on systems requires an understanding of group processes as well as individual influences for the assessment of child and family problems.

Chapter 3

Taking Account of the Family

By this stage you should have enough information to know whether the problems are sufficiently salient and serious for you to continue the assessment. There is a somewhat static feel to the assessment guidelines as they have been presented so far. But it is important always to bear in mind that movement (change, transition) is quintessential to the development of children, and, indeed, adults; the same can be said of family-life. Both individuals and families have their life-cycles and life- (or developmental-) tasks to accomplish.

The birth of a first child to a couple makes parents of them and transforms their partnership into a family. While their children are growing up and changing, parents too are facing shifts in *their* own personal development, from youthful maturity to early middle-age. We cannot consider children or adolescents and their problems without considering the manner in which they interact with their parents, who are not without their own preoccupations and anxieties. Let us take a typical example; parents are thirty years and upwards when their first child reaches puberty. Insensitive offspring would call this middle-age . . . or worse. Indeed, there are parents whose children reach their 'teens' when they are in their forties or fifties. And it is the prime of life for the fortunate ones. But what do the teenagers make of them – be they in their thirties, forties or fifties? For some their parents' generation seems to have lost its zest for living, to be staid and boringly settled and 'old-fashioned'. settled and 'old-fashioned'.

The point of all this is that a 'family life map' built up with the help of your client/s can illuminate interesting connections. It may indicate why confrontations occur between members of the family who face different life tasks (see Chapter 1) and life events (see below) or how the decision by one, to make a change in his or her life-style – or an unexpected life-event – can affect the entire family. The family plan illustrated on page 36 pinpoints the relationship between the life tasks and life events of the various members of the family.

LIFE-EVENT INFORMATION

Let us now look at other life-events faced by clients – information well worth recording as part of your data collection – which impinge at *present* (or which had an influence in the *past*) on your clients, with potentially disruptive effects.

Death of a spouse
Divorce
Marital separation
Detention in jail or other institution
Death of a close family member
Major personal injury or illness
Marriage
Marital reconciliation
Retirement from work
Major change in the health or behaviour of a family member
Pregnancy
Sexual difficulties
Gaining a new family member (e.g. through birth, adoption)
Major change in responsibilities at work (e.g. promotion, demotion, lateral transfer)
Son or daughter leaving home (e.g. marriage, attending college, etc.)
In-law troubles
Outstanding personal achievement
Wife beginning or ceasing to work outside the home
Beginning or ceasing formal schooling
Major change in living conditions
Trouble with the boss
Major change in working hours or conditions
Change in residence
Changing to a new school
Major change in usual type and/or amount of recreation
Major change in church activities (e.g. a lot more or a lot less than usual)
Major change in social activities

Step 8.	**Work out a family life map.**
	Your client's family map might look something like Figure 4.

Parents sometimes create their own problems by trying to live through their children, relying mainly on vicarious satisfactions. In this context, it is commonly asserted that middle age is a more difficult phase of life for women than men. The changes in her life are in many ways more obvious. The children are becoming less dependent, if not totally independent, of her; and until this period of her life her maternal interests may have been uppermost in her life. Although her concern continues, her direct role as a mother is coming to an end. But we must not exaggerate the 'empty nest' phenomenon. Among middle-aged people whose youngest child is about to leave high school most women do mention the approaching departure of the youngest child as a forthcoming change, but do *not* consciously believe that it will be a difficult time for them. Most men ignore the imminent event in their conversations with researchers, their attention being already directed to their own retirement in the future.

Marriages are likely to be undergoing greater *strain* at this juncture than at any time since the initial impact of the intimacy of living together when the (future) parents set up home. This is *not* to say the relationship is necessarily poor or terminal; but there may be special marital stresses. It is no joke coping with turbulent youngsters if a person is not getting full support from his or her partner. Difficulties in the marriage may become more exposed, more abrasive, if offspring are rebelling, getting into serious trouble or playing one parent off against the other.

This age group has been referred to as the 'middle generation' because their own parents are usually alive, and they are likely to feel obligations to the younger generation *and* the older one. Some parents feel trapped by the needs of ageing parents and demanding teenagers and wonder where those chances of 'doing their own thing' have vanished.

THE FAMILY AS A DYNAMIC ORGANIZATION

The family is a dynamic institution, that is to say susceptible to change in several ways. The family is more than the sum of its parts, more than the static aggregate of the individual personalities who make up its membership. It has, in a sense, a life of its own. The members interact in many

TIM: 22 months	ANNE: age 10 years	PETER: age 14	MOTHER: age 38	FATHER: age 45	GRANNY: age 66
LIFE TASKS	*LIFE TASKS*	*LIFE TASKS*	*LIFE TASKS*	*LIFE TASKS*	*LIFE TASKS*
• develop motor skills	• cope with academic demands at school (underachieving)	• adjust to physical changes of puberty	• review her life and commitments	• review commitments in mid-life	• deal with increasing dependence on others
• develop self-control	• developing her sense of self	• and to sexual awareness	• adjust to loss of youth and (in her perception) 'looks'	• develop new phase in relationship with wife	• come to terms with old age/death
• elaborate vocabulary	• learn to be part of a team	• cope with the opposite sex (shyness)	• cope with an adolescent as a patient and caring parent	• face physical changes – some limitations on athletic/sexual activity	• cope with loss of peers
• explore his world – make 'discoveries'		• deepen friendships (intimacy)			
LIFE EVENTS	*LIFE EVENTS*	*LIFE EVENTS*	*LIFE EVENTS*	*LIFE EVENTS*	*LIFE EVENTS*
• parents insist on obedience now	• afraid to go to school (cannot manage maths)	• worried about his skin (acne) and size of his penis	• coping with late child – an active toddler	• threat of redundancy	• poor health
• adjust to temporary separations when mother works	• bullied by a girl in her class	• has a girlfriend – his first	• has taken part-time job to relieve feeling trapped	• high blood pressure	• gave up home when bereaved (may have made a mistake!)
• not the centre of attention and 'uncritical' deference	• jealous of attention Tim gets (calls him a spoiled brat)	• upset by his parents' quarrels	• feels guilty	• worried about drifting apart from his wife	• enjoys the little one, but
	• worried about father's health	• complains that his mother is always watching him	• bouts of depression	• had a brief affair	• feels 'claustrophobic' with all the activity/squabbles
			• no longer enjoys sex	• feels unattractive	
TODDLERHOOD	PREPUBESCENCE	ADOLESCENCE	← MIDLIFE →		RETIREMENT

Figure 4. A family life map: Transitional stages of life

subtle ways which give a particular 'feel' or atmosphere to a family; they have different and *changing* roles which in turn change the 'personality' of the family as time goes by; they have their successes and failures which reflect on the family; alliances form, dissolve and reform. The family thus has its own life-cycle from 'infancy' to 'old age' with associated changes in its size, 'shape', and function. It also has its pool of skills. The all-important transmission of culture cannot be inflexible as would be a genetic code determining our physical equipment. But nor can it be left to chance. The welfare of the individual and the continuity of the culture depend upon there being a satisfactory means of indoctrinating the new generation into society's mores, attitudes and skills and to ensure that they, in turn, will satisfactorily transmit the culture. The family plays a major role in indoctrinating and training the child for life.

THEORIES OF FAMILY LIFE

Given the pervasiveness and importance of family life, it is incomprehensible why the family has been so neglected (relatively speaking) by theoreticians and scientists, and in particular, by psychologists. Arlene Vetere and Anthony Gale, authors of *Ecological Studies of Family Life* (see Further Reading), provide a valuable review of the major theories of family functioning and a significant contribution to the methodology of studying this complex and exceedingly private 'organism'.

Some of the concepts you will need to be familiar with include:

- *Cohesion*, which reflects the transactions – the emotional attachments of members – and their individual autonomy. It is at its highest in *enmeshed* (closely interrelated, mutually involved) families and at its lowest in *disengaged* (unattached) families.

- *Boundaries*, which delineate the components belonging to the system and those belonging to the environment; they are defined by *rules* which specify individual's roles, what subsystem he or she belongs to, and the appropriate behaviours which such membership entails. Boundaries can be *clear* (easily recognised and acceptable rules), *diffuse* (ambiguous and chaotic because rules are unstable or absent), or *rigid* (inflexible, unadaptable).

- *Adaptability*, which indicates that a family can modify its roles and relationships in response to influences for change.

- *Homeostasis*, which is a term that describes the 'steady state' of the 'organism' (for our purposes the family) – indicating that the various subsystems are in balance and the whole system is in harmony with the environment. To achieve and maintain homeostasis in the face of change and stress, a system (it is hypothesized) must be

- *Open*, which means that family members have a high level of exchange with the outside community, as compared with systems which are

- *Closed*, which have very little exchange with the community outside its boundaries.

- *Feedback* processes are believed to characterize social systems and reflect the ability of (say) the family to 'recognize' its own output as input at some later stage. For example, the family that is functioning well is capable of monitoring its progress toward family goals and correcting (modifying) its actions to bring itself back on track, if necessary.

Let us now look at a problem area where family 'cohesion' is often minimal, and 'boundaries' marked by either extreme 'rigidity' or excessive 'diffuseness'.

FAMILY VIOLENCE

The cosy image of the family as a nurturant organization and a haven of safety is shattered more often than we care to think, when it erupts with violence. The point has been made by experienced workers that people are more likely to be killed, physically assaulted, hit, beaten up or slapped in their own homes by other family members than anywhere else, or by anyone else in our society. Three groups of people are particularly vulnerable: children, wives and the elderly. It is not good enough to categorize (and 'explain away') the perpetrators of such awful deeds as degenerates, drunks, psychopaths or mental cases, as has been done in the past. It might be comforting but it is too simple.

The evidence suggests that many diverse factors – social and psychological – contribute to family violence. We consider these in Chapter 4. Various forms of physical abuse were mentioned in the quotation above, but we must not forget the possibility of psychological (or emotional) types of abuse.

Emotional abuse includes:

(i)   verbal or emotional assault (including threats of sexual or physical assaults),

(ii) close confinement (for example, locking a child in a dark cupboard),

(iii) other forms such as withholding food, warm clothing/coverings.

Emotional neglect includes:

(i) inadequate nurturance leading to physical, mental or emotional problems (e.g. the problem of a child's failure to thrive despite the absence of physical causes),

(ii) encouraging or permitting serious maladaptive (problematic) behaviour,

(iii) other forms of neglect such as refusing to allow a child to have a recommended and necessary treatment.

Other family problems (often referred to in the literature as 'family dysfunctions') which professionals are likely to be called upon to deal with include the following:

- *Chaotic* family organization; little or no organization which makes the management of change or coping with stress extremely difficult.
- Overly *rigid* organization which inhibits change when change is necessary or leads to a stereotyped and therefore inappropriate reaction to events.
- Too great a *distance* between members of the family leading potentially to emotional isolation and physical deprivation.
- Excessive *closeness* between members of the family leading potentially to overidentification and loss of individuality.
- An inability to work through *conflicts*, solve problems or make decisions.
- An inability on the part of parents to form a *coalition* and to work together, with detrimental effects on the marriage and/or the children.
- An *alliance* across the generations disrupting family life as when a grandparent interferes with the mother's child-rearing plans and actions.
- Poor *communication* between members.
- A failure to respond appropriately to each other's *feelings*.

Some of the ways in which a child may contribute (wittingly or unwittingly) to a family's inability to cope with conflict, have been described by psychiatrists and family therapists:

- *parent–child coalition*, where one parent attacks the other, using one of the children as an ally
- *triangulation*, where both parents attempt to induce a child to take *their* side
- *go-between*, where a child is used to transmit messages and feelings

- *whipping-boy*, where one parent, instead of making a direct attack on the other, uses their child as a scapegoat
- *child as weapon*, where one parent attacks the other using the child as a weapon
- *sibling transfer*, where the children agree to divert the parents from arguing
- *pacification*, where one child acts as a peacemaker
- *detour through illness*, where – children learn – that disagreements between parents may be reduced when they are ill.

Changing unwanted behaviours, or developing skills of interacting and relating, where skills are faulty or absent, usually requires the participation (and the willingness to change) of parents and, sometimes, the entire family. To this end one might say that every family makes use of its combined store of skills so that members can usefully share and learn from each other. Broadly speaking these skills fall into seven categories: relationship; social; communication; problem-solving; coping; study and work skills.

Parenting skills include several of these categories (see Chapter 9); deficits in parental abilities can lead to problems in the offspring – your analysis is by this time beginning to move toward a formulation of why things are going wrong for this family. The *what* question merges into a *why* question, the answers to which are the subject of the next step.

Step 9.   **Make an assessment of your client's skills (incentives, resources).**

Parenting is a complex series of skills, part commonsense, part intuition and part empathy (the ability to see things from another's point of view).

Parents *can* be trained in many of the necessary skills – child care and behaviour management – and the latter is a major theme of this book; what is not so easy (sometimes impossible, but *not* in all cases as we shall see) is to encourage those attachments and feelings that come so readily to most parents and children, but which are absent or distorted in some.

Ask your client (if a parent) to go through the skills listed in Table 3 with you. He or she may be pleasantly surprised at how many they can claim. Unless your clients know that they possess certain skills they may not be able to make the most constructive use of them. It is important not to demoralize clients with this exercise; not all of them are pertinent for the particular individual. There may have been little or no opportunity to develop some of them.

Table 3. A list of parenting skills

Me and my child	Me and significant others
Skills I need to relate effectively to him/her	Skills I need to relate effectively to others (e.g. my partner, teachers, friends) involved with my child
• how to communicate clearly	• how to be reasonably objective about others
• how to 'listen' carefully so as to understand	• how not to be possessive
• how to develop my relationship	• how to be assertive (without being intrusive or bossy)
• how to give help and care and protection without 'going over the top'	• how to influence crucial people and systems (e.g. school)
• how to teach and discipline	• how to work in groups (e.g. parents' groups, pressure groups)
• how to show and receive affection	• how to express my feelings clearly and constructively
• how to manage/resolve conflict	• how to inspire confidence and strength in others
• how to give and receive feedback	• how to see my child's friends from his/her point of view
• how to maintain a balance between extremes (e.g. loving without being possessive)	• how to resist/cope with jealousy
• how to negotiate sensible compromises	
• how to set limits – reasonable ones, and stick to them	

(*Adapted from B. Hopson and M. Scully 1980*)

Now do something rather similar for the child or teenager. Tease out positives in the child's situation: what is going well in the situation you are concerned about at present with regard to — (the child or teenager)? How does — contribute to your family life? What are his/her good points? You might draw up a balance sheet for — ; attributes perceived by parents as on the *credit* or *debit* side. You may find it useful to ask the youngster to carry out the same exercise with regard to himself/herself.

CREDIT	DEBIT
Sally has a nice sense of humour.	She's moody and unpredictable.
She is clever.	She has to argue over every little thing.
Etc.	She tells lies.
	Etc.

Step 10(a). **Ask your clients (parents) what their goals (ambitions, plans) are for their child.**

In the case of children, *change* and *development* must have some point – a destination and thus a direction. Only parents and children can decide on their goals (which take account of their aspirations) although your counsel, based on professional knowledge and experience, should play a part.

(b)	**Ask your clients (parents) what their goals are for themselves (in other words, their self-orientated goals).**

We have been discussing goals which involve children and the interactions between parents and children. But what of goals involving adults in their own right, where (say) you may have to counsel them? A mother may wish to increase her self-confidence and banish her recurrent bouts of depression. A father may ask for help in controlling his temper and reducing his irritability. A teenage brother or sister may desire to play a greater part in their family's decision-making (see page 79).

We have now reached PHASE III of the Flow Chart on page 21; it is good practice to have a pre-intervention record of the extensiveness of the client's problems based upon a week or two of observations and self-reports. This – the so-called *baseline* – allows you to evaluate any changes that occur before and after intervention. Baseline data provide the standard against which to measure the effect of your intervention.

Baseline Data Collection (further 1 or 2 interviews, preferably including home visit(s).)
From this point – the baseline – you collect information about the extent and precise circumstances of the problematic interactions.

You show your client(s) how to observe behaviour so that, in a sense, you can observe things through their eyes during the time you cannot be 'on the spot'.

Until now the main source of information has been the interview – a systematic approach to obtaining information about the problem, its nature, frequency, antecedents, consequences, etc. It may have been conducted at the office or in the client's home. Next the baseline data collected by interview are checked, supplemented, and quantified by:

- direct observation of the client in natural settings, for example, home, school, youth club;
- direct observation in other settings, for example, office, reception centre, etc.;
- self-recordings by the client (diaries, activity charts, self-ratings) in his/her day-to-day life or special situations;
- use of questionnaires, rating scales, etc., completed by the client or others; use of audio or video cassette recordings.

Summary and comment

We have carried forward the analysis of the dynamic interactions within the family in this chapter. By the end of Phase II of the assessment you should be in a position to decide whether the problems are sufficiently serious to continue on to the collection of baseline data. If not, you need to advise parents why you do not regard a further assessment or intervention as necessary. Perhaps the child's 'problems' are normal for his/her age and situation. Perhaps parents have exaggerated because of their personal anxieties or ignorance of child development. Of course, you cannot simply dismiss parents with a philosophical 'Don't worry' statement. They may require information about child behaviour and development, or some relatively brief advice on how to manage the child's *not unusual* (but worrying) fears or tantrums or bed-wetting. Knowledge of age-appropriate behaviour is obviously vital for the professional (see Further Reading).

We have seen that many of the problems affecting parents and their children are the problems of the family, *as a family*, and need to be construed as such. Problems within the family with which you are likely to deal are those involving relationships (e.g. sibling rivalry and jealousy, parental overprotection, marital discord); lack of knowledge (e.g. ignorance of what to expect of children at different ages); diasagreements over the sharing of finite resources (such as money, time, attention); conflict (over policies such as rules, discipline, routines). Helping parents to resolve conflicts with adolescents is a valuable contribution to happier family life, as is the reduction of aggravation brought about by planning of 'around the clock' rules and routines for the toddler – with regard to dressing, meals, visiting, shopping and going to bed.

Among the most serious problems you might be called on to deal with is violence within the family. Physical and emotional abuse are described, together with a range of family 'dysfunctions'.

Chapter 4

The 'WHY' Question

Some parents (and, indeed, professionals) dwell on the past when they look for the why's and wherefore's of their offspring's difficulties. It is important to maintain a balance between past and present when trying to find reasons or causes for current behaviour. The past cannot be changed, although you might 'liberate' someone from the past by resolving or changing present unhealthy attitudes which are *rooted* there. In any event, it is only in rare instances that current problems can be traced to specific past experiences with any degree of confidence.

Yet when things go badly wrong, our society gets an irresistible urge to find something or someone to blame. And when they go wrong with children, or the relationships between parents and their children, the finger is almost always pointed at the mother. The literature on childhood psychological problems is full of over-protective, dominating or rejecting mothers.

But is it really all so one-sided? What are fathers doing during these early years of their children's lives? The cynic might think that fathers were remote figures, because it is mothers who generally bring the children to the office or clinic, and are interviewed.

More surprising is the relatively neglected role of the child in all these unhappy events. Is it just a one-way process, with awful or stupid things being done to a passive infant? Certainly by encouraging some activities and discouraging others, parents influence their offspring's behaviour and personality. But in all sorts of subtle ways, their behaviour is also shaped by the child. In the crucial business of growing up, there is a two-way traffic in the relationship between parents and child. The distinguished theorist on childhood, Erik Erikson, wrote: 'A family brings up a baby by being brought up by him'.

Most current theories about the problem of, for example, child abuse place the sole emphasis on parental and, in particular, maternal psychopathology and environmental factors. The role the child can unwittingly play in his or her tragic predicament is usually overlooked. Yet research suggests that there are children who, from birth, show characteristics which make them not only difficult to rear, but also difficult to love.

It is clear from broadly-based surveys, that among all the allegedly harmful factors blamed in the clinical literature for this or that problem (be they adverse parental characteristics, family conflicts, etc.) it is possible to identify significant numbers of children who developed without serious problems, despite being subjected to these influences. Those practitioners who are behaviourally-orientated will lose little sleep over the doubts and uncertainties about the precursors of psychological problems – the tenuousness of the link between conditions (home and school circumstances) far removed in time from present manifestations of troublesome behaviour. This is because human actions – whether simple or elaborate, normal or abnormal – are brought about by *many* influences rather than a single factor. And whatever the influence of personality traits, attitudes and ideas, shaped over years of learning and development, the young person's day-to-day actions are powerfully controlled by *current events*, such as opportunities and temptations and the favourable outcomes (reinforcements) these actions give rise to. (We return to this idea shortly.)

Such observations give rise to a critical issue concerning the way you work: the theoretical perspective you adopt, or (as it is called) the particular 'model' of human behaviour that informs your practice. In order to help parents and their children effectively, you need to be clear about your underlying assumptions, as to how and why such individuals behave in the way they do. In what way (you may be eclectic and use several models) do *you* make sense of your clients and predict (i.e. anticipate) how they are likely to respond to your intervention?

FORMULATION OF CAUSES

You will soon detect the predominant model underlying our *formulation* of the causes of Avril's and her parents' difficulties – based upon the evidence we have chosen to seek. We had looked for patterns of antecedent and consequent stimuli which might be precipitating and maintaining the problem behaviour. We also examined other situations in which the child's behaviour differed from that in the 'problematic' situations (for example, evidence of prosocial behaviour and the settings in which it took place).

The case of Avril was thought to be one largely (but this was by no means the whole story) of faulty training and learning. Briefly, Mrs Hayes (for complex reasons that reach back to Avril's conception and birth) had become trapped in a pattern of behaviour in which she unwittingly 'encouraged' the very behaviours she wished to eliminate in the child's repertoire. Avril's demands, with few exceptions for being waited on, attention, etc., were acceded to following her display of tantrums and disruptive behaviours. The invariable outcome in the case of defiant actions was to increase the interaction between Avril and her mother. The resulting attention was reinforcing these non-compliant actions. It was quite straightforward to identify favourable consequences: to take but one example, she was being allowed to veto activities she did not like. Conversely, in all examples of misbehaviour, there were no really negative or unfavourable consequence (penalties) which might serve to diminish them.

With regard to the cues for the performance of problem behaviours, the most significant of these were the presence and actions of Mrs Hayes. The currency of her commands and threats had been debased; Avril did not trust her words. She had learnt that her wishes (for her mother's undivided attention, and 'obedience' to her commands) were likely to be met if she persisted long enough or escalated her coercive behaviours.

Essentially she had learned that certain antisocial behaviours were guaranteed to produce 'payoffs'. This lesson, applied in the school situation, could have aversive consequences for her and reduce her ability to learn. It was our opinion that they had affected her social development adversely – her manner was babyish and off-putting. From the point of view of other members of the family, Avril's egocentric, monopolistic and immature behaviour was undoubtedly undermining their well-being. Her sister was beginning to imitate some of her behaviours. As her parents saw things, they had endeavoured to provide 'the best' for Avril, and yet they were faced with a situation in which they no longer enjoyed their child. They increasingly quarrelled over how to deal with the situation. These considerations, among others, contributed to the decision that an intervention was required.

She was certainly receiving a large amount of attention (physical proximity, verbal exchange), but much of it took a negative form. It was precisely because of the endless round of disputations between parents and child that Avril was precluded from much of the usual range of symbolic rewards or social reinforcers which belong to happy and meaningful family communications. Avril, as a volatile, demanding child, had made constant 'assaults' on Mrs Hayes' self-doubts.

This is how her mother described the situation.

❝*As time went by, Avril has developed into a despot. She shows a general aggression, a degree of wilfulness, and various other unacceptable behaviours. She whines, clings like a limpet, is insecure, and worst of all for me, incessantly disobedient.... The situation over the years has deteriorated, compounded by an increasing tiredness on my part. This gradually deepened into general depression for which my doctor prescribed drugs. They didn't help; in fact feeling slightly drunk and rudderless made coping even more difficult. I was tearful, tense, often unreasonably angry, erratic and emotional, and then silent and withdrawn in turns. The tension in the house was painful. All the time her behaviour has got worse. We were trapped in a vicious circle. Life was so miserable for me at this time that when I think back I can still feel the emptiness inside, the feeling of isolation, the constant fear that I would totally lose control and hurt her. I was really desperate. It was an effort to go out, even to the shops. I looked awful, felt awful. Sometimes the loathing for Avril spilled over and I would find myself wanting to tell her, 'Go away out of my life, I hate you. You've ruined my life'. Sometimes I would start then have to bite back the words, remembering that I did love her. Afterwards I would feel consumed with guilt that I could even think these things. And overall was this dreadful sense of failure. Failure as a mother and failure as a wife, even failure as a woman. I have never been so close to a total breakdown.***❞**

As Mrs Hayes appeared to bear the brunt of most of Avril's misbehaviour, it might be concluded that her father was able to exercise control over her. This was not so; in fact, Mr Hayes' small part in this analysis of the problem situation reflects his minimizing of the contact he had with Avril – much to his wife's annoyance.

Having attempted to identify the conditions controlling the problem behaviour, the next task was to try to explain their origins. The importance of this is not so much to help the client achieve insight (although awareness may facilitate change) but rather to discover to what extent the original 'causal' factors continue to influence the current controlling conditions. Avril's developmental history was analysed in order to seek any possible contribution to the problem by somatic or other factors. Physical conditions might produce problem behaviour directly or might contribute to it indirectly through the reaction of children and/or their parents to any disability.

You may remember that Avril, from early in life, had been a difficult and overactive child, and that from the day of her birth she would cry day and night. The nights were particularly difficult. Mrs Hayes spent most of them nursing her. Being of such a commanding temperament, Avril learned from early on the strategy of how to gain attention from her mother and the rest of the family. The parents always intervened when she was crying, shouting, screaming; when she was frustrated, disobedient and aggressive, they often obeyed her commands for the sake of peace, to save time, or to avoid embarrassment. A variety of situations and settings became cues for verbal disputes and other forms of coercion (supermarkets, friends' homes, car drives). Here the parents were constrained even more than usual in responding to her oppositional behaviour. Here is a summary:

Avril appeared to be a child who displayed a range of 'surplus' behaviours almost from birth; these have been shown to be closely linked with the development of maladaptive behaviours at a later age. In addition, her mother's ability to cope had been considerably reduced in a number of ways. First Mrs Hayes had been handicapped by her fatigue and depression and in particular by the fiercely protective (defensive) attitude she had toward this 'unwanted' child who had turned out to be so difficult. This (together with a philosophy of child-rearing which was a reaction to her parents' methods) had considerably limited her choice of disciplinary procedures.

Clearly, from the number of times the word 'learning' appears in the formulation, I am drawing heavily on theories from the Social Learning Model.

Social learning model

It is hypothesized that a major proportion of a child's behaviour is learned, maintained, and regulated by its effects upon the natural environment and the feedback it receives with regard to these consequences. Behaviour does not occur in a vacuum; nor is it a passive process. It is a result of a complex transaction between the individual, with his or her inborn strengths and weaknesses, acting and reacting with an environment which sometimes encourages and sometimes discourages certain actions.

An important feature of the social learning model is the acknowledgement of the *active* role of cognitive variables (complex interpretive, thinking processes) in the way we learn. The part played by *understanding* in learning is significant. Not all learning (e.g. to walk, to ride a bike) involves understanding, but much learning involves knowing rather than simply doing. Stimuli have meaning to the learner, who acquires knowledge of the situation which can be used in adapting to it. The emphasis, therefore, is on *awareness* in learning.

Many problems in adults as well as children, are the consequences of failures or distortions of learning. The laws of learning which apply to the acquisition and changing of normal socially-approved behaviour are assumed to be relevant to the understanding of self-defeating and/or socially-disapproved (problem) actions. More specifically the behaviour problems of childhood are (in large part) due to the child's learning inappropriate responses; they are also the consequence of the child's failure to learn the appropriate behaviour.

With all forms of learning – the very processes which help the child adapt to life can, under certain circumstances, contribute to maladaptation. An immature child who learns by imitating an adult (observational learning) will not necessarily comprehend when it is undesirable (deviant) behaviour that is being modelled. Parents – Mrs Hayes is a good example – do not always realize they are 'reinforcing' unwanted behaviour by attending to it (instrumental or operant conditioning). If the consequences of a behaviour are rewarding (that is, favourable) to a child, that behaviour is likely to increase in strength. For example, it may become more frequent. Put another way: if Pat does something, and as a result of his action something pleasant happens to him, then he is more likely to do the same thing in similar circumstances in the future. When psychologists refer to this pleasant outcome as the positive reinforcement of behaviour, they have in mind several kinds of reinforcers: tangible rewards (e.g. sweets, treats, pocket money); social rewards (e.g. attention, a smile, a pat on the back, a word of encouragement); and self-reinforcers (e.g. the ones that come from within and which are non-tangible: self-praise, self-approval, a sense of pleasure).

Behaving in a manner that avoids an unpleasant outcome leads to the reinforcement of behaviour, thus making it more likely to recur in similar circumstances. If a young girl, say, does something her parents do not like, such as losing her temper too easily, they may increase her ability to think first and hold her temper, by penalizing her consistently for failing to do so; in this way they are providing what is called negative reinforcement. She avoids punishment by appropriate actions. They may not have to apply the penalty if she believes their threat because of their record of keeping their word. *Consistency* and *persistence* are watchwords in early learning, especially with certain volatile (hyperactive) children.

The reason why we look at the 'A' term (antecedents to problem behaviour/confrontations) in the 'ABC' sequence referred to on pages 27 and 28, is that it seems that the antecedents of a behaviour, its cues or triggers, are very important, and if you think about and watch the settings of your client's behaviour, it may be that the child behaves in a non-compliant way, or has a tantrum on some occasions but not on others; that is, some situations seem to act as cues to behave in a particular way (see Figure 5).

People tend to tailor their behaviour to the particular places and the different persons, in, and with whom, they find themselves; and in the case of children, this chameleon capacity often leads to misunderstandings between home and school – each blaming the other when (more often than not) they are difficult in the one setting but not the other.

The so-called operant conditioning rule is of great significance in social development (socialization). Fortunately, as we have seen already, there *is* a basic 'preparedness' on the part of most infants to be trained – that is a bias toward all things social. The baby *responds* to the mother's friendly (baby talk) overtures in a sociable manner that produces in her (in her turn) a happy and sociable reaction. The baby also initiates social encounters with vocalizations or smiles directed to the mother which cause her in turn to smile back and to talk, tickle or touch. In this way she elicits further responses from the baby. A chain of mutually rewarding interactions is thus initiated on many occasions. Parents and child learn about each other in the course of these interactions.

Learning to be skilful and social. And learning is the key to our understanding of the process of social training (socialization). Parents (and teachers) teach children skills and guide them towards prosocial actions and (when they can) away from antisocial activities. There seems to be a fair amount of latitude in learning conditions for those children with intact central nervous sytems, healthy bodies and relatively unvolcanic temperaments. They acquire an understanding of, and willingness to abide by, society's conventions, despite parental inconsistency, contradictory demands, ('double-binds') and ambiguous rules. For them, parental inexperience or poor judgment seem no more than a minor hindrance in the business of growing up.

The welfare of the individual and the continuity of the culture depend upon society's having a satisfactory means of indoctrinating the new generation into its mores, attitudes and skills and to ensure that they, in turn, will satisfactorily transmit the culture. The family plays a major role in indoctrinating and training the child for life. All parents are informal learning theorists and all are in the business of changing behaviour.

They use various techniques to teach, influence and change the child in their care. Among those used are material and psychological rewards, praise and encouragement, giving or withholding approval, and other psychological punishments such as reproof or disapproval. At its simplest level the rule-of-thumb is as follows:

Acceptable behaviour	+ Reinforcement	= More acceptable behaviour
Acceptable behaviour	+ No reinforcement	= Less acceptable behaviour
Unacceptable behaviour	+ Reinforcement	= More unacceptable behaviour
Unacceptable behaviour	+ No reinforcement	= Less unacceptable behaviour

Of course parents also give direct instructions, set an example (i.e. model desired actions) and provide explanations of rules (i.e. inductive methods). When the family fails in providing appropriate and consistent socialization experiences the child seems to be particularly vulnerable to the development of antisocial conduct and delinquent disorders (see Chapter 6). Typically the children with persistent antisocial problems come from families where there is discord and quarrelling; where affection is lacking; where discipline is inconsistent, ineffective and either extremely severe or lax.

Relationships. Many relationships can be understood (in part) in terms of social learning principles. Adults initiate and prolong relationships of intimacy – close friendships, courtship, marriage, cohabitation – as long as those relationships are reasonably satisfactory with regard to what are called their 'rewards' and 'costs'. It may seem crass to think of human relationships in terms of what are reminiscent of economic exchanges and bargains. Nevertheless, there is evidence in marital interaction (to take but one example) that a *social exchange* model not only helps us to assess what is going wrong with a partnership, but also to do something about it.

In this model marital discord is thought of as a function of prevailing rates of reinforcement (satisfaction) and punishment (dissatisfaction). Individuals, it is assumed, try to maximize satisfactions (the positives – rewards – arising from the partnership) while minimizing the dissatisfaction (the negatives generated by the marriage).

I shall return to the use of notions of *behaviour exchange* to bring about behaviour change in adults and young people, in Chapter 11.

Medical Model

The medical model provides explanations of human problems in terms of disease or other physical processes. Such explanations have been ques-

1. *Antecedent Events*

   Peter is asked to do something or to stop doing it. Or he is asked to answer a question about the work, or about his lateness.

   2. *Behaviour*

   (i) Non-compliance. He takes no notice; if Miss Smith insists, he resorts to

   (ii) Verbal abuse. He makes rude comments, criticises, occasionally swears and shouts.

   3. *Consequences*

   Miss Smith shouts at him, scolds him or discusses what he has done with him.

   Sends him out of the classroom.

   All classroom work comes to a stop; all the pupils watch the confrontation.

   The original cause of the confrontation is forgotten.

Persons: He's rude and disobedient mainly with Miss Smith; occasionally to other teachers; never with Mrs Simpson or Mr Jackson.

Places: Classroom only, never in the playground.

Times: Mondays in particular – usually at the beginning of teaching periods.

Situations: Mainly when asked to do something or when challenged over being late or without his equipment. Particularly when questioned about, or criticised for, his work.

Figure 5. Lay-out for a preliminary analysis of a problematic classroom situation. (*From Herbert, 1987, with permission.*)

tioned by social workers and clinical psychologists. But a critical exercise which rightly rejects 'pathology' explanations of actions and feelings (where inappropriate) has been taken to an extreme and is often neglected in cases where it is essential to consider the contributory influence of physical factors (for example, in cases of bedwetting and soiling). The tendency to 'throw the baby out with the bath water' is sadly a common one in the helping professions, where fads and fashions of working come and go.

Physical (medical) explanations may encompass, for example, infections (in so far as they affect bladder incontinence) and physical disabilities (in so far as they affect learning, and thus achievement and self-esteem). The concept of brain-damage is a popular explanatory notion for hyperactive, conduct-disordered patterns of behaviour. And it is a good example of the misuse of a medical explanation. Being tautologies (re-namings) in most instances, they tell us very little about the child and only too often are therapeutically pessimistic. For example, parents and teachers are sometimes told that a particular child's difficulties at home and at school are 'a result of brain damage', suffered perhaps as early as at birth. This is no more helpful than for a general practitioner to tell a mother her child is 'physically ill' when she takes him along for a diagnosis of a bodily malaise. Certainly no programme of rehabilitation – remedial teaching or treatment – could be planned on the basis of such a vague diagnosis as 'brain damage'. What is needed, in describing children, is not a meaningless label but precise information about their specific physical and intellectual problems, and also about any emotional and social difficulties which have a bearing on their ability to learn.

Psychometric Model

This model places a person high or low or somewhere in between on what is called an intelligence quotient (IQ). The average is 100. Avril's IQ is extremely high – a score equalled or bettered by only one or two per cent of children of her age. (This, by the way came as a shock to her parents who had now to reconstrue their 'somehow subnormal' child.)

One of the drawbacks of the psychometric model (like the previous one) is the tendency to classify individuals in terms of what they *cannot* do or what they haven't got, which is important as far as it goes but (in the minds of some people) can be used in a rather negative fashion – becoming a recipe for pessimistic inaction.

Personal Construct Model

Personal Construct Theory has a particular bearing on practice theories. Even the most proudly atheoretical social worker has attitudes. These attitudes (or theories) have, *inter alia*, a knowledge function which gives meaning to the world we live in; they provide a frame of reference with which people can make interpretations of life and they are an economical way of putting together a variety of facts and creating a model for action. The fact is that all individuals are concerned to anticipate (or predict) what happens to them and around them. If you are able to make sense of your world you can then make the necessary adaptations to changing circumstances. To this end each and every individual *constructs* in his or her thought processes a model of events. This model is like a figurative set of 'goggles' through which the individual *construes* life: its events and inhabitants. On the basis of this construing or interpreting he or she is able to take appropriate or (with faulty constructs) inappropriate actions.

The inventor of this model, George Kelly, uses the metaphor 'man the scientist' to illustrate his contention that individuals are constantly trying to understand and predict (i.e. anticipate) events. The term 'personal construct system' illustrates an important dimension of his theory. The term 'personal' underlines the fact that every individual lives in a unique world. People may resemble one another in their construing processes, but essentially, no one is a carbon copy of another. Every person lives in a world that is unique to him or her because it is idiosyncratically interpreted and experienced. For example, the way thought-disordered schizophrenic people see their world depends on the way they have arranged their hierarchy of constructs and the importance they attach to them.

Thus, Kelly provides one answer to the age-old question of why two people react very differently to the same situation; the two people are *not* in the same situation, it only looks the same from the perspective of a third observer. The situation may be very dissimilar from the point of view of each individual's construing system. Each may be reacting meaningfully in terms of his/her own situation as he or she interprets it.

A 'construct' is the basic unit of this theory and the term is differentiated from the term 'concept' in order to stress that it is a hypothesis rather than a category. A construct is also a discrimination of a bipolar kind. Thus, 'good' is not just a category of events, but specifically contrasts events which are 'good' with those that are 'bad', and others which are neither 'good' nor 'bad'. Constructs have a limited range of convenience; thus good – bad is applied to people but not to birds. A mother might construe her child as bad. One might find that the construct 'bad' is linked or associated in her mind most particularly with the dishonest pole of the honest – dishonest construct. The associations between constructs (construct-systems) are complex, often unconscious; some are shared, others are idiosyncratic.

Parents evolve a construct system to make sense of the world of children and family-life. The constructs used by parents (some developed in the bosom of their family of origin, others elaborated with more recent experiences of actual parenting) give meanings to their offspring's behaviour and facilitate mutually satisfactory interactions. Sadly some construct systems lead (or mislead) parents into confrontations with their babies. If the crying of a very young baby is construed as *wilful naughtiness* and smacking is construed as an *appropriate training method* or *punishment* for dealing with naughtiness, a fraught and potentially dangerous situation might arise.

The child, too, actively seeks to make sense of his or her world. It is an important part of your assessment to tease out how the child views those parts of the world that are salient to your quest for understanding. There are techniques (repertory grids) for eliciting child and adult construct systems. (I return to these shortly).

There are also active, role-play methods for helping clients to test out the way they perceive (and self-defeatingly misconstrue) their world. They are useful for those who have low self-esteem, feel persecuted and socially isolated (see the case of Avril's mother, page 130). These are the steps you take:

▶ The person is encouraged to explore (by trying out) patterns of behaviour contrasted to his/her own. This is based on a carefully scripted role – a sketch worked out with clients and derived from a compromise between what they are 'actually' like, and what they would like to be like.

▶ They are invited to practise these patterns in everyday life.

▶ From practice they gain some experience of how the environment can differ in appearance and 'feel', and how it reacts, when they behave in a different manner.

▶ Practice generates new and more effective skills, supplemented by novel experience from the feedback they have received.

▶ The expectation is that by receiving new and helpful forms of feedback from the environment they will change the self-defeating attitudes that control their behaviour.

There have been several developments in the measurement of personal constructs by means of *repertory grid techniques*, as they are called. In its original form the client was asked to name (say) twenty people he or she knew, according to different role titles. Thus we might get 'father', 'wife', 'person you admire', 'teacher you disliked', and so on. These are called *elements*. Constructs were then *elicited* by selecting three of the elements at a time, and asking the client: 'In what important way are two – any two – of the people alike and thereby different from the third?'. The repetition of this exercise produced constructs which gave some insight into the way the person construed his or her interpersonal environment.

The role titles were written along the top of a grid (from left to right) and the elicited constructs down the side (ranged from top to bottom). Kelly illustrates the recording of constructs (see completed example, Figure 6) in the following manner:

▶ When a decision has been made whether two of the three people indicated by circles (17, 18 & 19 in the grid) in the first row are 'alike in some important way that distinguishes them from the third person', the client puts an X in the two circles corresponding to the two people who are alike but nothing in the third circle.

▶ Next she/he is asked to write a word or short descriptive phrase under 'emergent pole' (the 'construct'), indicating in what way the two are alike.

▶ The opposite of the characteristic is then written down under 'implicit pole' (or 'contrast').

▶ Next she/he places a 'V' (tick) under every other person who has this important characteristic.

▶ The second row is now considered – this time marking circles of a different triad (circle 14, 15 and 16 in Kelly's illustrative grid). Other people in line 2 who have this characteristic are given a 'V' also.

▶ The rest of the grid is completed in this way.

Kelly's analysis proceeds as follows:

☐ He first looks at the grid without any statistical analysis to see something of what the person is telling one directly.

☐ Next it is possible to obtain matching scores between any pair of rows. Take a piece of paper and place it beneath the first row of ticks and blanks and mark each tick or cross on your piece of

CONSTRUCTS

SORT NO.	EMERGENT POLE	IMPLICIT POLE
1	Don't believe in God	Very religious
2	Same sort of education	Completely different ed.
3	Not athletic	Athletic
4	Both girls	A boy
5	Parents	Ideas different
6	Understand me better	Don't understand at all
7	Teach the right thing	Teach the wrong thing
8	Achieved a lot	Hasn't achieved a lot
9	Higher education	No education
10	Don't like other people	Like other people
11	More religious	Not religious
12	Believe in higher ed.	Not believing in too much ed.
13	More sociable	Not sociable
14	Both girls	Not girls
15	Both girls	Not girls
16	Both have high morals	Low morals
17	Think alike	Think differently
18	Same age	Different ages
19	Believe the same about me	Believe differently about me
20	Both friends	Not friends
21	More understanding	Less understanding
22	Both appreciate music	Don't understand music

Row elements (SORT NO.):

FAMILY: 1 self, 2 mother, 3 father, 4 brother, 5 sister

INTIMATES: 6 spouse, 7 ex-flame, 8 pal, 9 ex-pal

VALENCES: 10 rejecting person, 11 pitied person, 12 threatening person, 13 attractive person

AUTHORITIES: 14 accepted teacher, 15 rejected teacher, 16 boss

VALUES: 17 successful person, 18 happy person, 19 ethical person

Figure 6. An example of a completed Role Construct Repertory Test (*from Kelly, 1955*).

paper. Now move your paper one row down. You can count up the number of times blanks and ticks/crosses correspond in rows 1 and 2 (or any other row).

☐ The probability of actual matching scores (or lack of them) can be calculated statistically to see how significantly the constructs relate one to another. (Chance matching in this case would be half the possible total – nineteen.)

☐ The same method can be used for the columns to find out how the person sees the people in his/her life compared with one another.

☐ A matrix of matching scores would show (for example) which construct is most highly matched with all other constructs, and which element is most highly matched with all other elements.

Few individuals require more than twenty to thirty rows to express their repertory of constructs. One might ask the client to construe important *experiences* (e.g. your wedding; first serious quarrel with your partner; your first major disappointments with your child, etc.); *situations* (e.g. caring for children; being a housewife, doing housework) and so on. In other words you are not limited to persons. This and subsequent forms of repertory technique are designed so that statistical tests can be applied to the set of comparisons every individual has made. It is assumed that the *psychological* relationships between any two constructs, for a given person, are reflected in the statistical association between them when they are used as judgmental categories.

Problems in the statistical analysis of the matrix have given rise to procedures in which grids are analysed by asking people to *rank order* their elements (e.g. nicest to nastiest, most loving to least loving, etc.) or rating them on seven-point scales. *Exercise.* Try out on yourself an exercise in eliciting constructs.

1. Elicit constructs using members of your family as elements: mother; father; husband/wife; myself; child 1; child 2; . . .; grandparents; aunts; uncles; etc. Tease out the way you construe family relationships and family members by putting the name of each person on a card, taking three at a time and going through the formula: 'In what important way are (say) my father and my husband alike and thereby different from Uncle Joe?', etc., etc.

2. Elicit constructs using your *clients* as elements. This could be interesting! What are the important ways in which you construe the people you help?

3.   Elicit constructs using the people *who help you* as elements, e.g. GP, friend, mum, neighbour, etc. Add in, as elements, the persons who you feel are hostile or unhelpful in your life.

Psychodynamic Model

Psychoanalysis is one of the most controversial systems introduced to professional social work practice. Many psychologists, psychiatrists and social workers are now questioning the place of psychoanalysis in these helping professions. There is no questioning of the status of Sigmund Freud – the founder of psychoanalysis – himself. In the social and cultural climate of our time, Freud's thinking has been more pervasive than that of almost any other researcher; many of his discoveries are today's 'clichés'.

From psychoanalysis comes an accent on the one-to-one (dyadic) helping situation, on long-term intensive casework and a choice of methods involving the development of insight. What have come to be called psychoanalytically or (more popularly) psychodynamically-based theories represent a significant ideological strand in social work.

Many social workers describe their orientation as being 'psycho-dynamic'. The term encompasses theories of personality and therapies which assume the existence of unconscious mental processes, which concern themselves with the elucidation of motives, and which assume the significance of transference relationships (i.e. the transfer on to the therapist of attitudes and feelings attaching to significant others). It is the *verstehende* (understanding) aspect of psychoanalytically-based theories rather than the application of analytic treatment techniques which has contributed to social work practice.

It is sometimes argued that the interpretive-insight approach pro-motes excessive self-absorption and diverts attention from groups and structures as causes and remedies for psychosocial problems. Still, a psychodynamic perspective on psychosocial issues might be essential in social work because it is one of many ways by which meanings in exceedingly complex situations can be grasped.

A good example of this is the psychodynamic theory of ego defence mechanisms. The construct ego (or self) is seen by contemporary psychodynamic theorists as the central integrating aspect of the person, and any threat to its valuation and function is a vital threat to the very being of the individual. As a result a variety of 'devices' are gradually accumulated by the self so as to soften anxieties and failures and protect the integrity of the ego by increasing the feeling of personal worth. There is evidence that all of us learn to use strategies such as these. It is when we use them inappropriately or to excess, with too great intensity or too inflexibly, that they become maladaptive (and are called neurotic). The trouble is that they involve a certain amount of self-deception and distortion of reality and may prevent, by a sort of short-circuiting, the realistic and painstaking solution of problems.

To a very great extent we are unaware (unconscious) of our use of these strategies. One of the purposes of adopting particular strategies is to reduce tension. The minimizing of immediate discomfort reinforces their use. An individual makes choices and carries out actions which will reduce and, if possible, avoid anxiety, pain or any other distress.

Let us look at some of our psychological strategies:

Emotional insulation (isolation, dissociation). In all these defensive strategies the individual reduces the tensions of need and anxiety by withdrawing into a shell of numbness and passivity, also by lowering expectations, by remaining emotionally uninvolved and detached. Apathy and defeated resignation may be the extreme reactions to stress and frustration of long duration. Cynicism is often adopted by adolescents (among others) as a means of protecting themselves from the pain of seeing idealistic hopes disillusioned.

Displacement. Displacement is a defensive strategy which involves a shift of emotion or of an intended action from the person toward whom it was originally intended on to another person or object. An example could be a child who is a nuisance because she pinches, bites and scratches her playmates at school and harrasses the teacher in a variety of ingenious ways. Investigation might reveal that the fault lies only in part, in the playground situation at school, but also has its roots in the home situation.

Projection. When feelings arising from within ourselves are unjustifiably attributed to others, such behaviour is called projection. It helps us to avoid conflict over our own barely conscious or acknowledged feelings and impulses by finding scapegoats and ascribing these obnoxious, intolerable and therefore unacceptable ideas to them. By disowning these tendencies we protect ourselves from anxiety. Thus the individual who feels hateful jealousy and hostility to his wife may deny these feelings to himself but complain bitterly that his wife is unpleasant to him and rejects him.

Rationalization. Rationalization is a technique which helps us to justify what we do and to accept the disappointments arising from unattainable goals. The 'ego' uses rationalization to modify otherwise unacceptable impulses, needs, feelings and motives into one's which are consciously tolerable and acceptable. Rationalization helps to reduce 'cognitive dissonance'. In simple terms this means that when there is a discrepancy between behaviours and thoughts (cognitions), psychological distress is caused. This distress will persist until the behaviours and cognitions are made harmonious again.

Take the case of the professional who takes great pride in his or her skill with family problems, but is making no progress. The sense of failure and ineffectiveness is rationalized away by describing the family as 'chaotic' and the members as 'immature' and therefore unsuitable for treatment. By this rationalization the gap between the estimation of oneself and one's performance disappears. Thought and behaviour are made congruent. This tactic makes the repugnant more acceptable and the incompatible compatible.

Common rationalizations are called 'sour grapes' and 'sweet lemons' attitudes. In the former we justify failure to obtain something that is desirable on the grounds that it was not really worthwhile after all. In the 'sweet lemons' attitude we mollify ourselves for an undesirable outcome by saying that it was for our own good.

Fantasy. Fantasy is one of the favourite tactics of children. In order to cope with stressful circumstances we not only deny unpleasant reality but we create the sort of world of fantasy we would like to inhabit. Incidentally, fantasy also provides children with the opportunity to rehearse in imagination the solutions to their problems without entailing the risks of the real situation. Fantasy can be productive in such cases. Non-productive fantasy is the too persistent indulgence in a wish-fulfilling kind of mental activity. It compensates for lack of achievement. 'Walter Mitty' fantasies allow a person to be the conquering hero he or she would like to be. People may also explain away their failures and inadequacies by what are called 'suffering hero' fantasies – seeing themselves as misunderstood, 'put-upon', but nobly courageous victims. In this way the individual retains his or her self-esteem. Fantasy solutions gloss over unpleasant reality. Children who day-dream a lot are frequently trying to compensate for or escape from unacceptable environmental realities.

Reaction formation. Reaction formation is a method of defence whereby individuals suppress their desires and then adopt conscious attitudes and behaviour patterns which are quite opposed to the unconscious wishes. Reaction formation is extreme and intolerant in its manifestations.

Those who devote all their time to the obsessive condemnation of sexual licence in others may well be having trouble in coping with their own sexual inclinations. In children a 'dont care' independent attitude may well mask a craving for nurturance and a need for dependency.

Escapism (denial of reality). Clients may evade disagreeable facts of life by refusing to see them. Escapism is the name given to one of the methods for denying unpleasant circumstances. They may simply withdraw from competitive situations if they feel at a disadvantage and may fail. They may tend to be indecisive and procrastinate in times of stress, putting off the actions that have to be faced realistically.

The defensive strategies (or 'mechanisms' as the psychoanalysts call them) are not without some experimental confirmation. The mention of psychoanalytic or psychodynamic theory is a reminder to us that its tenets are not wholly antagonistic to behavioural theory, although many would claim that they are. The psychodynamic approach to problem development stresses the 'understanding' and historical element more than does the behavioural approach, with its emphasis on explanations of behaviour in the here-and-now. Nevertheless, the specification of reinforcers, the 'C' term in the ABC analysis (see page 50) is one in which some theorists would see a potentially useful borrowing from Freudian ideas.

Human beings old enough to have acquired even a rudimentary self-image demonstrate a need to perceive themselves in at least a moderately favourable light. A reasonable agreement between the self-concept ('myself as I am') and the concept of the ideal self ('myself as I would like to be') is one of the most important conditions for personal happiness and for satisfaction in life. Marked discrepancies arouse anxiety and can be indicative of psychological problems.

You might ask the client to write an account (or talk it out) on the theme 'Myself as I am', and another entitled 'Myself as I would like to be'. Compare them and discuss the points of mismatch with the client. It could be a help in setting realistic and meaningful goals.

There are sometimes heated debates about the status (and, indeed, viability) of psychoanalysis. There is wide disagreement among distinguished thinkers as to whether it is a science, a myth, a theory, a therapy or a premature synthesis.

Some theorists argue that it is perfectly possible for psychoanalytic investigations to be termed scientific (unless the word science is understood in a very rigid and narrow sense). Freud himself regarded psychoanalysis as a science.

An eminent psychoanalyst, Charles Rycroft, believes that the controversy between psychoanalysts and critics like Hans Eysenck is not a meaningful one. Freud's work was really semantic, but (owing to his scientific training and allegiance) he formulated his findings in the inappropriate conceptual framework of the physical sciences. As Rycroft puts it:

> If pyschoanalysis is recognised as a semantic theory not a causal one, its theory can start where its practice does – in the consulting room, where a patient who is suffering from something in himself which he does not understand confronts an analyst with some kind of knowledge of the unconscious – i.e. who knows something of the way in which repudiated wishes, thoughts, feelings and memories can translate themselves into symptoms, fantasies and dreams, and who knows as it were, the grammar and syntax of such translations and is therefore in a position to interpret them again into the communal language of consciousness. It seems to me that it makes better sense to say that the analyst makes excursions into historical research in order to understand something which is interfering with his present communications with the patient (in the same way as a translator might turn to history to elucidate an obscure text) than to say that he makes contact with the patient in order to gain access to biographical data (page 331).

The writings of psychonalysts can (if evaluated carefully and critically) open 'mental doors' for social workers to dimensions of experience which are not readily accessible to ordinary common sense. It is assumed that this insight will give them greater control over their behaviour. Many of our motives are unconscious and it is impossible to come to terms with an 'invisible enemy'. The therapist tries to make the invisible visible, the unconscious conscious, so that reality can be grappled with.

It would be safe to say that all insight therapies are 'talking' therapies. The patient or client does a lot of talking about his or her personal life, early history, personal relationships, work, ambitions, fears and worries. The psychotherapist, to a greater or lesser extent, also talks – offering interpretations of the patient's conflicts and problems, reassurance and sometimes advice in order to direct the person's thoughts and actions into potentially fruitful channels. If the child is very young, conventional psychotherapy is inappropriate. Children are not always able to put their anxieties into words. They are not always interested in exploring their past life. They are too close to the episodes that are thought by psychoanalysts to be crucial in the development of neuroses, to enjoy talking about them. They will not always free-associate. The main problem is that the motivation to participate in analysis is missing because children are often brought for therapy against their will.

Play as communication. Play makes use of children's familiar and natural mode of expression – play with dolls, miniatures, puppets, paint, water and sand – in a special playroom. This provides a background for the therapist to discuss their problems with them.

Theories of the importance of play in childhood go a long way back. The first person to advocate studying the play of children in order to understand and educate them was Jean Jacques Rousseau. There have been several theories put forward to explain the meaning and utility of play in childhood; they generally emphasize its function as a means of preparation for the future, as a natural process of learning and as a means of release from tensions and of excess physical energies. In many ways play, for children, is life itself. They use it in order to develop their personality and their ability to get on with other children.

Sigmund Freud's daughter, Anna Freud, used children's play in a manner analogous to the use of dreams with adults. Play was analysed so as to uncover unconscious conflicts. This involved the interpretation of the symbolic meanings, the unconscious motivations underlying drawings, paintings, games and other forms of imaginative play. She transposed classical psychoanalytic theory into a system of child analysis.

There have been several offshoots of psychoanalytical play therapy and also systems of play therapy which are not in this mould at all. The active forms of play therapy have much in common with the desensitization techniques used in behaviour therapy. Other forms of play therapy – relationship therapy and non-directive therapy – have evolved and continue to be used. I return to this topic in Chapter 9.

Family Process Model

The family process perspective, exemplified by the model of intervention known as family therapy, shifts the focus for understanding problems (and dealing with them) from the individual's behaviour to his/her relationships with the family. In this view many problems have their source in family behaviour patterns that are faulty or self-defeating ('dysfunctional') in different ways (see page 39).

Family therapy and family-orientated behavioural work are commonly (but certainly not exclusively) used when children present problems. Like other psychological therapies these approaches are made up of several variations on a theme – the theme here being that the family is more than the sum of its parts, and vital to work with in its own right. Some of the many techniques focus specifically on the presenting problems, dealing with *current events*, while others grapple with the question of how the *family history* has influenced the family unit.

Empirical Research Model

A typical approach to the understanding of family problems is the accumulation of data on the basis of studies – clinical and experimental research – of particular topics. A matter of particular concern to us is family violence. This illustrates the value of the empirical research model, especially where no theoretical model fits neatly.

The various forms of family violence – physical, sexual and emotional abuse – perpetrated on children, spouses or the elderly, have been the subject of much research but remain poorly understood and certainly cannot be fitted into any simple theoretical model. Certain characteristics of *those who abuse* (individuals) seem to apply to all types of family violence. The research literature points to similarities in the following areas:

- poor or low self-esteem
- a sense of incompetence (low self-efficacy)
- social isolation
- a sense of being unsupported/helpless
- depressed
- lack of warmth and empathy
- poor impulse/self-control
- aggressive
- experiencing marital difficulties
- misperceiving the victim
- likelihood of having been a victim of abuse in childhood.

These findings represent factors which are associated (correlated) with family violence. Appendix 5 contains a table describing common *family* attributes based upon empirical research. It is important to remember that a correlation does not necessarily imply causation. A correlation is sometimes found between criminality, alcoholism, drug abuse and low intelligence and the various forms of family violence. Obviously there are many people who drink heavily or have criminal records but never abuse children, wives or grandparents. Causation is a difficult concept; some factors may set the stage (predispose) a person toward abusive behaviours (say, the childhood experience of being abused oneself), while others trigger (precipitate) particular incidents of assault.

Many causal agents ('multifactorial causation') operate in this, like so many other, areas of family dysfunction. The majority of child abusers are under 20 to 30 years of age; most wife abusers are between 20 and 30; while most abusers of the elderly are between 40 and 50 and above.

Both sexes are implicated in family violence. Unemployment, low income and extramarital problems are stresses which can contribute to family violence. (Immaturity and early marriage play a part in child abuse.)

Those who are abused (all categories) tend to have one or more of the following attributes:

- a poor relationship with the abuser
- a relationship of dependency
- physically weaker than the abuser
- emotional and social isolation
- ill-health/handicap.

In some families all forms of violence take place; in others it is one category. In some homes violence is accepted as the 'norm'. Abusing families are particularly distinguished from non-abusing families by their lack of affectionate relationships, and by the abuse of power by the strong over 'the weak', for example, children, the frail elderly and others who are susceptible to being scapegoated for frustrations experienced by the abuser.

Affectionate relationships within a family act as a buffer against stress; they generate supportive action for those who are distressed. Individual coping skills, self-confidence and personal strengths also mitigate the influence of stress and make violence less rather than more likely as a response to frustration and misery.

The influence of all these psychosocial factors and the potency – for good or ill – of family relationships make it imperative that you observe all the family *together* as well as *individually*, and that you tease out their perceptions of each other. Look carefully at

- their attitudes
- their perceptions
- their expectations
- their actions
- their feelings towards each other.

Check on their knowledge of child development (and of ageing processes/old age). *Detailed* and *rigorous* observation and monitoring are vital where high-risk families are brought to your notice (see Appendix 3).

Summary and comment

We have looked briefly at a few (but perhaps the more important) of the models used by members of the helping professions in the quest for an understanding of their clients' difficulties. The assumptions, attitudes or constructs held by practititoners also have implications for their choice of intervention. For example, a common assumption underlying many therapeutic endeavours entails a cathartic or hydraulic view of emotion. This assumption is based on the belief that antisocial, unpleasant and atavistic feelings can be channelled away through a figurative 'overflow pipe' leaving behind the loving, cooperative, prosocial human being that exists underneath. The way in which the cathartic purging is administered varies widely, but the principle remains the same. Such an assumption can lead to quite opposite therapeutic advice or procedures in psychotherapy and behaviour modification respectively, especially with regard to aggression.

At present aggressive children, whatever the reasons for their problem, may be subjected either to therapeutic regimes which encourage them to 'act out' their hostile behaviour (as in the 'regression therapy' used in some residential establishments and the permissive atmosphere encouraged in some intermediate treatment schemes), or to models (and programmes) which seek to inhibit such expressions and to encourage alternative prosocial actions. Adherents to the former theory view the latter course of action as 'symptomatic treatment' – tinkering with surface phenomena. They would expect the 'real' or 'underlying' causes to break out elsewhere (a phenomenon called symptom substitution) as a result of such superficial attempts at battening down emotional 'safety hatches'.

But the latter (social learning) group would see this as a self-deluding argument and would accuse the proponents of 'acting out' theory of sustaining, by reinforcement, the very behaviour they claim to want to remove, and of simply relabelling such problematic behaviour with some technical term of doubtful validity – and then calling this the cause. There is very little (if any) evidence of an empirical nature for symptom substitution. In any event, the answer to such fears is to conduct a comprehensive and rigorous assessment and an ongoing (plus follow-up) evaluation of outcomes for the treated client.

Part 2

Development and Change

The essence of life is development – hopefully, a forward momentum toward greater maturity and fulfilment – and this presupposes change. These aspects of life apply not only to individuals, but also to the families within which they reside. Life is all about change – expected and unexpected, welcome and dreaded.

Change is often painful and not infrequently resisted. This tension between adapting to new circumstances (transformation) and resisting change which is a feature of the individual's attempts to maintain some equilibrium in his or her life (homeostasis), is also characteristic of family systems. General Systems Theory highlights the significance of the concept of system *adaptability*. Within the family different members may be involved in adapting to very different life circumstances. While (say) a girl is moving toward womanhood and experiencing some of the unwelcome 'side-effects' of puberty and adolescence, her gran (who lives in the same house) is adjusting, not to development, but to the *dissolution* of some of her strength, vigour and independence. Both are in a stage of transition and each strives in her own way to come to terms with new realities.

In the following chapters we examine some of the salient features of childhood and adolescence, as well as those involved in the adult role of parenting in its various manifestations (e.g. adoption, fostering, single parenting).

Chapter 5

Childhood and Adolescence

All sorts of terms or euphemisms have been used to refer to the troublesome but common behaviours (and the more serious psychological difficulties) displayed by children and adolescents. There is the popular expression 'maladjusted', and others such as 'abnormal', 'nervous', 'highly strung', 'emotionally-disturbed', 'difficult', to mention but a few. They include a large and mixed bag of problems ranging from depression, anxiety, inhibition and shyness to non-compliance, destructiveness, stealing and aggression. In essence, these problems represent *exaggerations*, *deficits* (deficiencies) or *disabling combinations* of feelings, attitudes and behaviours common – at one time or the other – to most young people. Aggression, shyness, and a combination of low self-esteem and poor concentration are examples of each category.

There is a distinction between those difficulties which primarily lead to emotional disturbance or distress for the young people themselves (e.g. anxiety, shyness, depression, feelings of inferiority and timidity) and those which involve mainly the kinds of antisocial behaviour (e.g. disruptiveness, aggression, lying, stealing and disobedience) which disrupt the well-being of others, notably those in frequent contact with the young person.

Terms like 'normal' and 'abnormal' are commonly applied to children as if they are mutually exclusive concepts like hard and soft; the label 'abnormal' attached to particular children seems to suggest that they are deviant in some absolute and generalized sense – members of a different species. This is misleading; every child is unique and the most that can be said of any child is that certain of his or her actions or attributes are more or less abnormal – a deviation from a *norm* or social standard.

ASSESSMENT

It is obviously very useful to know about the social norms and the norms of development when making an assessment. You might incorporate into the assessment steps (set out in Chapter 2), some of the material included in the following pages because of their direct relevance to children's behaviour problems. Thus you might ask the parent(s) to rate the child's difficulties (Table 4) and the situations in which they occur (Table 5).

Table 4. A child behaviour rating scale (for parents)

How much difficulty do you have with your child's behaviour on the following items? Circle the number that best sums up your opinion: 1 = never; 2 = sometimes; 3 = often. Indicate whether it represents a problem to you.

BEHAVIOUR	Never	Sometimes	Often	Do you see it as a problem?
Aggressiveness	1	2	3	Yes/No
Whining	1	2	3	Yes/No
Temper tantrums	1	2	3	Yes/No
Lying	1	2	3	Yes/No
Jealousy	1	2	3	Yes/No
Attention-demanding	1	2	3	Yes/No
Disobedience	1	2	3	Yes/No
Bedwetting	1	2	3	Yes/No
Daytime wetting	1	2	3	Yes/No
Shyness	1	2	3	Yes/No
Speech difficulties	1	2	3	Yes/No
Fears	1	2	3	Yes/No
School refusal	1	2	3	Yes/No
Soiling	1	2	3	Yes/No
Overactivity	1	2	3	Yes/No
Reading difficulty	1	2	3	Yes/No
Boredom	1	2	3	Yes/No
Apathy	1	2	3	Yes/No
Mood changes	1	2	3	Yes/No
Irritability	1	2	3	Yes/No
Wandering	1	2	3	Yes/No
Tics	1	2	3	Yes/No
Oversensitivity	1	2	3	Yes/No
Quarrelling	1	2	3	Yes/No
Poor/faddy eating	1	2	3	Yes/No
Timidity	1	2	3	Yes/No

Table 5. A situational rating scale (for parents)

Do you have difficulty with your child at the following places or in the following circumstances? Circle the number that best sums up your opinion.

PLACE/CIRCUMSTANCE	Never	Sometimes	Often	Do you see it as a worrying problem?
Visiting friends	1	2	3	Yes/No
Shopping (e.g. supermarket)	1	2	3	Yes/No
Going on a bus	1	2	3	Yes/No
People visiting your home	1	2	3	Yes/No
Taking the child to school	1	2	3	Yes/No
or nursery	1	2	3	Yes/No
Leaving the child at playgroup	1	2	3	Yes/No
Getting the child dressed	1	2	3	Yes/No
Mealtimes	1	2	3	Yes/No
Getting the child to bed	1	2	3	Yes/No
Getting the child to stay in bed	1	2	3	Yes/No
Quarrelling with brothers/	1	2	3	Yes/No
sisters/	1	2	3	Yes/No
friends	1	2	3	Yes/No
Getting the child to go to parties (friends' homes)	1	2	3	Yes/No
Getting the child to speak to people	1	2	3	Yes/No
Taking children's toys	1	2	3	Yes/No
Getting the child to share toys	1	2	3	Yes/No
Getting the child to be polite	1	2	3	Yes/No

In the case of concern about *relationships* (be they child–child, say, jealousy; or adult–child, say, hostility/rejection; or child–adult, say, clinging) draw up a balance sheet of the positives (benefits) in the relationship and the negatives (costs); there is an example on page 42. At the most general level (as we saw in Chapter 1) you need to ask of the client: 'What are the consequences – in the short-and longer-term – of his or her *behaviours* (*style of child management*, in the case of parents)?'

There are supplementary questions (applicable to parents as well as child) to ask. Affirmative answers to several questions like these might well be of significance:

? Does the client get excessively miserable, embarrassed, shy, hostile, anxious or morbidly guilty?
? Does he/she give vent to anger too easily?
? Is his/her tolerance of frustration low?

? Is he/she inflexible in the face of failure?
? Does he/she find it difficult to cope with novel or difficult situations?
? Does he/she experience difficulty in establishing affectionate, lasting relationships with adults and peers?
? Does he/she fail to learn from experience (e.g. from disciplinary situations)?
? Does he/she find it impossible to get on with most teachers or other adults in authority?

Your answers to these questions could be important 'diagnostically' (i.e. for indicating seriousness) because problem behaviours have unfavourable consequences for the youngster and/or those in contact with him or her. Generally speaking, there is an association between intense and prolonged feelings of unhappiness and psychological disorder; there is a loss of a sense of well-being.

Typical problems of childhood

A feature of much problem behaviour in childhood is its transitoriness. So mercurial are some of the changes of behaviour in response to the rapid growth and the successive challenges of childhood, that it is difficult to pinpoint the beginning of serious problems. Among the problems which decline in frequency with age are elimination (toilet training) problems, speech problems, fears, and thumb sucking. Problems such as insufficient appetite and lying reach a peak early and then subside. Many problems show high frequencies round about or just before school-starting age, then decline in prevalence, and later rise again at puberty. Among these are restless sleep, disturbing dreams, physical timidity, irritability, attention-demanding, over-dependence, sombreness, jealousy and, in boys, food-finickiness. Only one 'problem' increases systematically with age – nail-biting. This habit reaches a peak and begins to subside only near the end of adolescence. Among the problems which show little or no relationship to age is oversensitiveness.

We know as a result of longitudinal studies (investigations that follow up children over many years) that for the most part, children who suffer from 'emotional' problems such as fears, phobias, shyness and inhibitions, become reasonably 'well adjusted' adults; they are almost as likely to grow up 'normal' as children drawn at random from the general population. In a sense these difficulties are the emotional equivalent of 'growing pains'. But that is not to deny that they sometimes persist and reach levels of intensity which cause all-round suffering.

There is another category of difficulties which declines at a rather later stage, and at a slower rate, than most others, for example, over-activity, destructiveness and tempers. In fact, one-third of boys still have temper explosions at 13. In their *severe* forms these and other types of aggressive, antisocial behaviours constitute a constellation of problems referred to as 'conduct disorders'. They involve physical and verbal aggressiveness, disruptiveness, irresponsibility, non-compliance and poor personal relationships; delinquent activities, early drug and alcohol use and substance abuse may also feature as part of the syndrome. This behaviour pattern is notable for the fundamental inability or unwilling-ness on the part of the youth to adhere to the rules and codes of conduct prescribed by society at its various levels: family, school, and indeed the community at large. The problem may become particularly trouble-some (disruption in the classroom) and/or serious (delinquency) during adolescence. I deal with it in the next chapter.

It is a useful assessment skill to be able to identify the periods when children are most vulnerable to emotional problems, so as to mobilize resources to help them (and their parents) through a difficult patch. The term 'crisis intervention' has been used to describe the expert assistance needed at certain times in people's lives when they not only experience a heightened desire for help, but are more susceptible than ususal to the influence of others. Children also experience such periods of crisis when, for example, they go to hospital, endure parental illness, separa-tion or death, cope with the birth of a sibling, or learn to live with a handicapped sister.

Developmental tasks

A developmental task arises at a certain period in the life of an individual, successful achievement of which leads to happiness and success with later tasks, while failure leads to unhappiness in the individual, disap-proval by society, and difficulty with other tasks. The tasks might be ones such as learning to talk or to control elimination; or they may involve the development of self-control over aggressive and sexual inclinations, acquiring moral attitudes and social skills, adjusting to school life and mastering academic competencies, becoming self-directed and self-confident. Some are vital psychosocial tasks.

Erik Erikson, has put forward ideas about the interplay of 'ego' and 'alter' which is so critical in personality development – namely, the achievement of a balance between the poles of recognizing and accom-modating the needs of others as opposed to imposing self-centred demands on other people. An extreme lack of balance in reciprocity between self and others (in either direction) gives rise to unsatisfactory social relationships. Children demand parental support and they try to limit the restraints parents put upon their pleasures. The balance, therefore, is about a compromise between sometimes incompatible mutual demands.

Erikson's scheme of child development – and its tasks – is given below.

Table 6. Developmental Tasks

Age period	Characteristic to be achieved	Major hazard to achievement
Birth to 1 year	Sense of trust or security.	Neglect, abuse or deprivation of consistent and appropriate love in infancy; harsh or early weaning.
1 to 4 years	Sense of autonomy – child viewing self as an individual in his/her own right, apart from parents although dependent on them.	Conditions which interfere with the child's achieving a feeling of adequacy or the learning of skills such as talking.
4 to 5 years	Sense of initiative – period of vigorous reality testing, imagination, and imitation of adult behaviour.	Overly strict discipline, internalization of rigid ethical attitudes which interfere with the child's spontaneity and reality testing.
6 to 11 years	Sense of duty and accomplishment – laying aside of fantasy and play; undertaking real tasks, developing academic and social competencies.	Excessive competition, personal limitations, or other conditions which lead to experiences of failure, resulting in feeling of inferiority and poor work habits.
12 to 15 years	Sense of identity – clarification in adolescence of who one is, and what one's role is.	Failure of society to provide clearly defined roles and standards; formation of cliques which provide clear but not always desirable roles and standards.
15 to adulthood	Sense of intimacy – ability to establish close personal relationships with members of both sexes.	Cultural and personal factors which lead to psychological isolation or to formal rather than warm personal relations.

(*Adapted from E. Erikson, 1965*)

From birth to about four years of age the child needs to develop a sense of trust and, later, a growing autonomy. The major hazards to the development of a perception of a trustworthy and predictable world, in which children initiate their independence-seeking, are social and physical conditions which interfere with their sense of personal adequacy and/or which hinder their acquisition of skills.

Even very young babies exhibit a need to be competent, to master or deal effectively with their own environment. Psychologists consider it to be related to such motives as mastery, curiosity and achievement. The psychologist Martin Seligman, has this to say:

> The infant begins a dance with his environment that will last throughout childhood. I believe it is the outcome of this dance that determines his helplessness or mastery. When he makes some response, it can either produce a change in the environment or be independent of what changes occur. At some primitive level, the infant calculates the correlation between response and outcome. If the correlation is zero, helplessness develops. If the correlation is highly positive or highly negative, this means the response is working, and the infant learns either to perform that response more frequently or to refrain from performing it, depending on whether the correlated outcome is good or bad. But over and above this, he learns that responding works, that in general there is synchrony between responses and outcomes. When there is asynchrony and he is helpless, he stops performing the response, and further, he learns that in general responding doesn't matter. Such learning has the same consequences that helplessness has in adults: lack of response initiation, negative cognitive set, and anxiety and depression. But this may be more disastrous for the infant since it is foundational.

During the next stage, from approximately four to five years, comes a sense of initiative, a period of vigorous reality testing, imitation of adult patterns of behaviour and imaginative play. Overly strict discipline, interference, overprotection and the like can disrupt the successful achievement of these attributes, making for poor spontaneity and uncertain testing and appreciation of realities.

A sense of duty and accomplishment is the next developmental task – from six to 11 years – when the child puts aside much of the fantasy and play-life and undertakes real tasks at school and develops academic and social skills. Excessive demands or competition and personal limitations which lead to persistent failure can make a crisis of this important stage – resulting in feelings of inferiority and poor work habits.

From 12 to 15 years, children consolidate their sense of identity, clarifying who they are and what their role in life is to be. Society may make for difficulties for the early adolescent by failing to provide clearly defined or valued roles and standards for the young person.

In later adolescence, from 15 to adulthood, a sense of intimacy is desirable – an ability to establish close personal relationships with members of both sexes. (The last two stages are described in more detail, in the section on adolescence.)

Failure to master previous developmental tasks are thought to hinder the individual in the next psychosocial endeavour.

Underachievement. Perhaps one of the most serious consequences of emotional and behavioural problems is its deleterious effect on children's learning in the classroom and hence their achievement. Even when highly intelligent, those pupils with psychological difficulties tend to have real difficulties in school performance. The greater the number of problems manifested by the child, the poorer, on the whole, is school performance.

Friendlessness. Many of the difficulties which children have to cope with are social ones – the problems of getting on with other youngsters of the same age, with teachers, with their own parents, and also with themselves. Young people (like the rest of us) need to like themselves, to rely on themselves and to know themselves. It was Aristotle who suggested that friendly relationships require a certain liking for oneself. Also needed is a degree of self-awareness and social sensitivity. The boy or girl's self-image plays a part in all of this; if it has been endlessly subverted by criticism or rejection they are likely to feel unworthy and inferior and display gauche and 'off-putting' behaviours which betray defensiveness and over-anxiety.

Children who are acceptable to their peers tend to:

- demonstrate sensitivity, responsiveness and generosity; they help others and give attention, approval and affection to their peers;
- be confident in their social contacts, active and friendly;
- see things from the other youngster's point of view;
- be good at resolving day-to-day (and difficult) dilemmas involving person-to-person relationships;
- make others feel accepted and involved, promoting and planning enjoyable group activities;
- demonstrate empathetic actions. Empathy involves the youngster's capacity to contol his or her behaviour by considering its effect on the experiences of others, particularly the potential victims of pro-scribed behaviour.

If you are concerned about your client's inability to make or keep friends, carry out a small exercise in 'accountancy'. Look at things from the other person's point of view. Is your client *mature* enough to sustain the reciprocity of friendship or is he/she being insensitive, too demanding, or disloyal? Is his or her company rewarding enough?

DEALING WITH UNWANTED BEHAVIOUR

If an intervention seems likely, encourage parents to think of positive outcomes as well as the reduction of *unwanted* behaviours. Suggest that they consider their priorities, thinking of their child's behaviour as falling into three colour codes: green, amber and red.

- *Green* is the 'go-ahead' code for the type of behaviour they want from their child, the actions which they facilitate by praise and encouragement, for example, sharing toys with another child or eating meals without a fuss. They should include those individual attributes of the child – aspects of his or her personality which make for their uniqueness.

- *Amber* is for 'caution' behaviour, which is not encouraged but is tolerated because the child is still learning and making mistakes; for example 'decorating' the bedroom's walls with finger paints or hurling toys across the room in a moment of fury. Any sort of stress like moving house, illness or some upset in the family, may mean a temporary step backwards in the child's behaviour.

- *Red* is definite *stop* (No! No!) behaviour which needs to be curbed as soon as possible. Obviously anything which could be dangerous for the child or for others has a red code: running into the road, touching the hot iron, attacking the baby.

Any limits set should be for the child's safety, well-being and development. Parents should be advised to keep them to essentials. It is crucial to ensure that children know exactly what they are and what is expected of them. Chapter 11 develops this theme of rules and routines.

ADOLESCENCE AND ITS DIFFICULTIES

To the layperson, adolescence refers to the period of transition between childhood and adulthood. It coincides roughly with the so-called 'teens', but the number of years devoted to adolescent development varies from culture to culture. If the physiological changes of puberty are most commonly taken as the onset of adolescence then it is sociological phenomena such as status, duties, privileges, the end of education, the right to marry and enjoy economic independence, which are most frequently taken as the termination of adolescence. During the past half-century or so, adolescence in Western societies has become a progressively longer span of years – indeed as long as ten years in duration. This reflects the mixed feelings we have about the decision as to *when*, in law or social custom, a young person is grown-up and responsible: old enough to drink in a pub, mature enough to manage a bank account, to indulge in sexual intercourse, to get married, to vote, or to be held responsible for a criminal act.

Puberty: the gateway to adolescence

The physical and physiological changes that take place at 12 (on average) in girls, and 14 in boys, are due to the action of hormones, and are quite dramatic; growth in virtually all parts of the body is sharply accelerated. During so-called transitional periods like adolescence, individuals are in the marginal position of having lost an established and accustomed status and of not yet having acquired the new status toward which the factors impelling developmental change are driving them.

Self-discovery

The major task of the adolescent stage – according to many contemporary psychologists – is the young person's need to shape, and consolidate, his or her own identity as a unique and mature person. The development of self-identity refers to the core of an individual's character or personality and is thought to be a vital precursor to true intimacy and depth in personal relationships. It begins with teenagers' intense concern for discovering their individual nature, and ends when they have established a coherent sense of self and personal identity. This task of *becoming* a unique person is usually completed between the ages of 18 and 22.

It is important to remember (and to remind parents) that adolescents are *individuals* and they are as different one from the other in their personal qualities as are children and adults. Their tendency to conform to teenage culture and fashion may present a superficial similarity which the media find convenient to headline, especially when there is a sensational incident involving young people. Social (and other) workers would do well to encourage parents and other adults to recognize and accept the new challenges, tasks and needs which preoccupy these sometimes puzzling (and worrying) young adults who are emerging from childhood.

Individual and Gender Differences

Girls' development is roughly two years ahead of boys', and it tends to be so (on average) throughout the developmental timetable. There is usually no need for alarm if the child is somewhat early or late. Children vary quite markedly – the gap may be four years or more – in the age at which they become pubertal. For girls, the age at which the menstrual cycle makes its first appearance can differ by several years. One may find an early-developed girl at the age of 12 or 13 who is already physically a woman, with fully developed sexual characteristics and destined to grow very little more in height. At about the same age, and therefore in the same classroom and social group, may be a later-developing girl who is just about to begin her growth spurt and who is little more than a child in her physical characteristics. The same conspicuous differences might be seen in boys of 14 or 15. It is obviously simplistic to think about teenagers as a homogeneous group.

Puberty is not just a matter of changes in the size and shape of the body. Physiological developments in glandular secretion, particularly those affecting sexual function, occur. Up until puberty, males and females have similar quantities of *both* sex hormones in the bloodstream, with only a slightly greater proportion of the sex-relevant hormone. Thus boys have nearly as much oestrogen (the female sex hormone) as androgen. At puberty, however, there is a sharp increase in the secretion of the sex-related hormone. Hormonal changes bring, in their wake, increased sexual arousal; parents will also have to deal with their offsprings' increased (and, in part, hormone-driven) assertiveness.

As I have mentioned earlier, adolescent self-centredness has its basis in the immense physical changes taking place at puberty. It also has its roots in the discovery of identity, but there are sometimes disconcerting swings from out-and-out self-admiration (narcissism) to self-hatred and self-deprecation.

How young people perceive themselves depends very much on how others see them; but it depends most of all on how they *think* others see them – which could, of course, be different from the way in which they are actually perceived. And most particularly children accept into their self-image what they believe to be their parents' view of them: and these views can have consequences over the long-term for their behaviour. If your client believes that his or her parents' opinion is negative or critical (even if this is not really the case) they may exhibit insecurity and low self-esteem. If people believe things to be real, they are real in their consequences. This applies with force to the delicate area of a person's self-image.

The development of identity doesn't always proceed smoothly. But what evidence we have calls into question Erik Erikson's belief that adolescents usually suffer a crisis over their identity. Most teenagers actually have a positive (but not unrealistically-inflated) self-image: furthermore this view of themselves tends to be fairly stable over the years.

There is a growing altruism and idealism to be seen in many young people. These different facets are gradually integrated into the adolescent personality. Self-esteem is a vital element for healthy 'adjustment'. When there is a large gap between the teenager's self-concept ('myself as I am') and his or her idealized self ('myself as I would like to be') there are also likely to be anxiety and over-sensitiveness in close attendance.

A sheep in wolf's clothing. Parents worry about the imminence of adolescence and small wonder, given that adolescence has such a bad reputation – largely due to the 'jaundiced' writings of clinicians. But then clinicians tend only to see people who come to clinics. And people – adolescents in this case – who attend the clinics would not be there if they did not have problems. What is really required is a wide cross-section of adolescents drawn in large numbers from the general population. Does such a sample present problems of sufficient seriousness or in sufficient numbers to give adolescence a 'bad name'?

Adolescence, while certainly not immune from its share of pain for those growing up (and for those guiding the growing-up processes), is not usually the scourge of folklore. It is something of a sheep – albeit an unruly sheep – in wolf's clothing. For one thing the problems (and hurdles) of growing up do not all arrive at one and the same time.

The more serious psychological (or psychiatric) conditions are probably a little commoner during adolescence than during middle childhood, but the difference is not a very great one, and most adolescents do *not* manifest psychiatric disorders. Nevertheless, some 10 to 15 per cent of adolescents *do* experience significant psychological difficulties. The category, referred to by psychologists as 'emotional disorders', are manifested by about two and a half per cent of pre-adolescent children. Their prevalence increases somewhat by adolescence, and we find that boys and girls are about equally prone to them. For most children (as we saw in the previous chapter) these kinds of problems manifest themselves briefly and then become minimal or disappear completely.

This is all very well, but you might well wish to know whether there are any *typical* adolescent problems, typical in the sense that they reflect stresses and strains which differ from those emerging in childhood, or indeed, adult life. There certainly are serious psychiatric disorders such as schizophrenia and anorexia or bulimia nervosa whose onset is particularly associated with the teenage years.

We can witness in the transition from childhood to adulthood an upsurge of moodiness and feelings of misery. Adolescents are often tormented by ideas which are self-critical, worries about the future, and fears about such matters as attending school or becoming involved in social activities.

It is reassuring to realise that although the *rates* of unhappy feelings and self-depreciation reach a peak during adolescence, the *majority* of teenagers seem generally to be happy and confident and are not the victims of serious depression or of other emotional disturbance. In fact, adolescence does not quite live up to its reputation. This may help those of your clients who are bracing themselves with trepidation for their child's 'run-up' to the 'teens'.

Striving for independence

By the middle years of adolescence the striving for independence – more and more visible in any normal growing child – is no longer simply one aspect of a youngster's activities; it is, in a very real sense, an end in itself. It involves striving for psychological freedom from parents – freedom to be one's own person, to have one's own thoughts and feelings, to determine one's own values and to plan one's own future.

It is also about the more mundane freedoms, to find the clothes, companions and pastimes of one's own choice and to enjoy the privacy of one's own room and belongings. However, there are as many dangers in granting independence to young people (by promoting too much freedom too soon) as in strongly opposing all signs of it until late adolescence. There is, as seems usual in child development, a 'golden mean' – a need to avoid extremes.

Plus Factors. The reason why adolescent development is (relatively speaking) so unremarkable in the personal disturbance it causes is that there are many strength-giving continuities in this development. The adolescent builds on what has gone before; coping skills developed when younger are not necessarily redundant. Many of the changes of this stage of development represent pluses, not minuses. They take the form of increased capacities of various kinds. It is as well to remember these pluses when considering how much to advise parents to 'let go'. Cognitive skills in adolescence become more complete and more flexible as new powers of abstraction and logic make problem-solving easier than it was in childhood. Social skills increase in range and complexity.

Alienation

The public has been led to believe that 'distancing' of teenagers from their parents is almost inevitable, and they may be expecting not to be able to communicate with their children when they get older. Alienation is *not*, however, a typical pattern. Most adolescents are still attached to their homes in a positive way, and they continue to depend upon the emotional support, goodwill and approval of their parents. The family continues to be of critical importance; parental concern and supervision (as long as it is not oppressive, or too intrusive) is vital during a phase when youngsters are experimenting with life. It does appear that rebelliousness and alienation are more likely in teenagers who, in spite of considerable maturity, remain economically or in other ways, dependent on their parents. Students in higher education are one example.

A majority of adolescents share their parents' attitudes towards moral and political issues, and are prepared (by and large) to accept their parents' guidance on academic, career and personal matters.

Sexuality

Teenagers enjoy the full range of sexual activities earlier than the previous generation. The number of teenage pregnancies has certainly increased markedly, despite innovations in contraception. The incidence of venereal disease among young people has also gone up.

Although adolescents have become more accepting in their attitudes to premarital sex, this does not imply a massive rise in casual sexual relationships. Young people, and particularly girls, continue to emphasize the importance of love and stable emotional attachment in premarital sex, although intended marriage or an engagement is not so often seen as a prerequisite of such relationships. The emphasis on a stable relationship with one sexual partner at a time is referred to as 'serial monogamy'. Girls do, however, display more conservative attitudes to these issues than boys.

Most young people express a wish to get married and have children. Certainly, a committed relationship is generally thought to be essential for the rearing of children, and, although a majority would wish such a longstanding commitment to take the form of marriage, a substantial minority reject such a view.

Surveys suggest that the first experience of sexual intercourse is usually with someone who is already experienced; the first partner is often older and, in the case of the girls, is quite often an adult. Intercourse is usually with a friend and, more often than not, takes place in the parental home of the beginner or the partner.

Sexual Counselling. The adage 'prevention is better than cure' is certainly not platitudinous when alerting sexually active adolescents to the possibilities of unwanted pregnancy and the importance of genital hygiene and the risks of sexually transmitted diseases (see 'References' for texts on counselling on these subjects).

Problem Areas

Adolescence has its share of problems like any other stage of development but (as I've indicated) its reputation for emotional disturbance is worse than the reality. Many parents create problems for themselves and their offspring by *expecting* the worst. This is the notorious self-fulfilling prophecy. 'Anticipate the worst and by behaving in certain ways you make it happen!' But there are certain problems that do occur in a sizeable minority of adolescents.

Depression. The new responsibilities of young adulthood and the difficulties of sexual adjustment bring in their wake feelings of misery and inner turmoil. These lead on, in some adolescents, to more serious moods of depression — a sense of helplessness and powerlessness, of events being out of or beyond control. Some adolescents even entertain ideas about committing suicide; a small number actually do it.

The milder form of depression may show itself as a lack of physical energy and wellbeing. In its more severe manifestation, adolescents tend to be irritable and bad-tempered, and, when it is at its worst, they sleep poorly, lack an appetite, and are always dejected, apathetic and lifeless. Young people who are (for whatever reason) depressed, feel helpless, sad and useless and find it sometimes impossible to meet the challenges of life. They cease to strive and to use their full effectiveness in whatever sphere of activity they find themselves.

The checklist below will help you to detect signs of depression in your client:

☐ a demeanour of unhappiness and misery (more persistent and intense than 'the blues' which we all suffer from now and then)

☐ a marked change in eating and/or sleeping patterns

☐   a feeling of helplessness, hopelessness and self-dislike
☐   an inability to concentrate and apply oneself to anything
☐   everything (even talking and dressing) seems an effort
☐   irritating or aggressive behaviour
☐   a sudden change in standards of school work
☐   a constant search for distractions and new activities
☐   dangerous (but exciting/distracting?) risk-taking (e.g. with drugs/ alcohol; dangerous driving; delinquent actions).

Depression can be masked in adolescence and thus not easily detected. Another problem is that any item in the list above can occur normally in the adolescent without in any way indicating a depressive disorder. The questions below will help you to judge whether to seek professional psychiatric advice if the answers tend to be in the affirmative.

?   Are there several of the signs (listed above) present in the teenager?
?   Do they occur frequently?
?   Have they persisted for a long time?
?   Do they cause *extensive* suffering to him/her?
?   Do they stand in the way of his/her development towards maturity?
?   Do they get in the way of his/her relationships with (a) peers, (b) adults?
?   Do they cause distress in others?

Anorexia nervosa. A problem particularly associated with adolescent girls (it can also occur in pre-pubertal children) is anorexia nervosa. The anorexic girl deliberately restricts her food intake; indeed, she does not want to eat at all, because she believes she is fat and wishes to lose weight. The word 'anorexia' means loss of appetite. However, the absence of hunger or appetite is not a crucial feature of anorexia nervosa. Nevertheless, the teenager will characteristically act as if she has lost her appetite.

Anorexia nervosa is essentially about weight rather than eating. The really central feature of the disorder is a body weight which is abnormally low for the age, height and sex of the person. There is a further crucial feature: the individual's attitude to her weight. What makes life difficult for would-be helpers is that someone with anorexia nervosa will not always be truthful about her feelings. If she is, she will say that she is ashamed and very frightened of the thoughts of being heavier. She may suffer in various ways through being thin, but compared with putting on weight it is seen as the lesser evil.

What causes this problem? The truth is that anorexia nervosa remains a mystery. The anorexic who appears so thin and emaciated is quite likely to misperceive her appearance. What for her is slender or fat, what is normal weight for her height and age, or what is an attractive shape, is quite at odds with the judgement of most other people.

The acts of eating and fasting are loaded with meanings – personal, familial, cultural and religious. They also carry the connotations of control and self-mastery, of nurturant love, comfort, sociability, and, indeed, sexuality. The 'meaning' of the eating disorder for one anorexic teenager is likely to differ at certain points compared with another. Each must be individually assessed by professionals who are *trained* and *expert* in this potentially fatal psychological disorder. Parents need to be alerted to the signs in their teenager of incipient anorexia nervosa: a preoccupation, indeed obsession, with calorie counts, with having 'a say' (control) over her diet, loss of weight, cessation of periods, concern over appearance, moodiness, and so on. It would be advisable to seek psychiatric or clinical psychological advice early rather than late, if your mental 'alarm bells' begin sounding – in the light of what you are seeing and hearing.

Conduct Disorders. It is quite likely that these problems – described on page 74 – constitute the most frequent as well as the fastest growing problem area of childhood. If this 'informed guess' is correct then there are serious social implications; the children manifesting these problems in severe form cause themselves and those who are close to them the utmost misery. Antisocial activities tend to disrupt and hinder the acquisition of crucial life skills. Their presence in childhood is predictive of problems of adjustment in later adolescence and adulthood. Children with more extreme forms do not necessarily 'outgrow' their problem behaviours; the case histories of delinquents repeatedly indicate the onset of serious antisocial behaviour when they were very young.

Delinquent behaviour. A sizeable number of children with conduct problems become delinquent, as their rule-breaking becomes law-breaking. Delinquency is perhaps the most noteworthy of all activities as an adolescent manifestation. It reaches a peak at 15 years for boys and 14 years for girls. By their twenties most of the former offenders have gradually become broadly law-abiding members of the community. But sadly, the number of young people committing detected and adjudicated crimes in the United Kingdom and the United States has increased markedly. What was once an almost completely male preserve now includes substantial numbers of female offenders. The average age for the first court appearance of juveniles is lower, and there is a marked trend towards more violent offences.

The term 'juvenile delinquent' is merely an administrative term, not a clinical diagnosis. It has to be recognized that relatively minor delinquent activities (for example, petty thefts, vandalism) are surprisingly common in the teens. Such activities tend to be transitory. However, there is a small but hard core of adolescents who habitually break the law, thereby creating enormous social problems of punishment, prevention, and rehabilitation – none of which has been satisfactorily resolved.

Drug abuse. Drug abuse is relatively infrequent among children, but not as rare as it used to be; it becomes more common during the years of adolescence. Most young people who try drugs out of curiosity do not continue to use them regularly. Those who take drugs tend to do so infrequently and give them up altogether after a year or so.

The terms 'drug abuse' and 'drug misuse' refer to the observation that a particular form of drug-taking is a harmful (abuse) and/or socially unacceptable way of using that substance (misuse). 'Users' are likely to develop 'tolerance' for a drug, which means that their body has adapted to the repeated presence of the drug so that higher doses are required to maintain the same effect. The body may react with 'withdrawal effects' to the sudden absence of a drug to which it has adapted; they involve severe physical discomfort. When this occurs and leads to a compulsion to continue taking the drug so as to avoid these symptoms, we speak of 'physical dependence'. The more important and widespread problem of 'psychological dependence' refers to an irresistable psychological compulsion to repeat the stimulation, pleasure or comfort provided by the drug's effects.

The key factor in drug-taking is opportunity – the availability of drugs and people to tempt and 'prompt'. Users have generally been exposed to drugs by their peers or by people (not infrequently family members) whose values incline towards nonconformity or even deviance. Rebelliousness, low self-esteem, a poor sense of psychological wellbeing (including depression) and low academic aspirations are among the characteristics commonly found in adolescent drug users. The boredom and hopelessness of unemployment also play their part. Substance abuse (for example, glue-sniffing) presents a similar picture. High-risk drug-taking is defined as uncontrolled use, whether or not it is already demonstrably harmful. A person is also taking an unacceptable risk if he or she is a regular user, that is to say taking drugs at predictable intervals.

It is most important for professional people (and parents) to be on the lookout for signs that may lead them to suspect drug use. It isn't easy, because some of the signs are not uncommon in adolescence generally. There is often a gradual change in the adolescent's habits and a general lethargy. Other signs include: aggression; loss of interest in school work, sport, hobbies and friends; furtive behaviour and frequent lying; bouts of drowsiness or sleeplessness; unexplained disappearances of money and belongings from the home.

Heroin addicts usually stop bothering about their appearance, their speech may become halting, and they tend to drop old friends and take up with new ones. Users of heroin may receive unexplained messages or telephone calls, followed by an immediate and unexplained departure. Spots of blood may be noticed on their clothes, and (most important) needle marks on the back of the hand and the inside of the elbow. There may also be thickened brownish cords under the skin, which are veins, solidified as a result of the injections.

There is a tendency for the addict to be hostile to society, and therein lies part of the trouble when it comes to treatment and rehabilitation. A hospital too often epitomizes society in the mind of the addict. More informal methods are therefore required, and in most countries clinics run on 'non-institutional' lines within the community, and more casual in style, are being set up. Sadly such agencies and local drug advice centres are thin on the ground in the UK.

Most promising seem to be those communities which are run by ex-addicts. The addict who is desperate for drugs has an uncanny instinct for putting the most subtle and painful pressures on families and doctors alike, but these tactics are familiar to ex-addicts and therefore get nowhere with them.

SEXUAL ENCOUNTERS

Almost all children encounter rather explicit (if minor) sexual situations between the ages of six and twelve, and most children cope quite well. It is unlikely that occurrences such as the sight of an exhibitionist will unhinge the well-adjusted child, though they may be traumatic for the already neurotic child. Many minor confrontations that occur seem to pass children by, and leave them practically unscathed. This is where robust and healthy attitudes to sex are so important.

Not all children get to adulthood with only minor sexual experiences to assimilate. And this is really one of the most pressing problems facing parents of young (and older) children, and their social workers. How much might one traumatic sexual encounter at an early age affect a child's later personality development? If a seven-year-old girl is coaxed into some kind of sexual play by an older male relative, what effect will it have on her chances of establishing a happy physical relationship with her husband when she is grown up and married? If a twelve-year-old boy is seduced by a homosexual older boy or a grown man, is the boy likely to be deflected from normal heterosexual interests himself? There are no ready-made answers to such questions, and, as is the case in many matters dealing with human sexuality, there is very little solid evidence to produce.

Adult contacts

Heterosexual seductions/incidents. Many childhood sexual experiences of different kinds come about through sexual contact with adults. Alfred Kinsey in his innovative 1950's research into human sexuality, found that, among 4,441 women interviewed, 1,075 (or nearly one in four) recalled sexual contacts before adolescence with males at least 15 years of age, and at least five years older than themselves. In 609 cases in which the older males were identified, they were strangers in 52 per cent of incidents, friends or acquaintances in 32 per cent, uncles in nine per cent, fathers in four per cent, and brothers in three per cent. In more than half the cases, the 'contact' consisted of an exhibition of the male genitals to the child. In an additional nine per cent, the approaches were verbal only. In 32 per cent, there was fondling without genital contact, and in 27 per cent, there was either manipulation of the girl's genitals or manipulation of the man's genitals by the girl. Oral contacts with the male or female genitals were reported in about 20 cases (two per cent), and actual coitus (sexual intercourse) in about 30 cases (three per cent).

Little *physical* harm was ever reported from these contacts. By contrast, 80 per cent of the women reported having felt *emotional* distress or fear. A small proportion were seriously disturbed, but in most instances (according to Kinsey), the reported fright was of the order that children manifest when they see insects, spiders, or objects against which they have been adversely conditioned. It has been suggested that in cases like these it is wise to heed the old adage that 'one swallow does not make a summer'. This is a general principle which has some empirical support in the psychopathology of sexual development. A child whose prior development has been at least reasonably healthy is likely to withstand a 'traumatic' sexual experience without showing any visible scars from it in later life. All the good work put in by parents during a young child's life is not likely to be swept aside by one chance encounter with a sexual deviate. If, on the other hand, the parents have sensitized the child to negative attitudes and fears about sex, such a traumatic event may well serve to trigger off a real emotional problem.

Serious problems tend to arise when sexual contacts (initiated say, by a relative) continue over a long period of time, and the child is too frightened, guilty or emotionally involved to say anything to his/her parents. The Kinsey report offers some advice to parents:

> When children are constantly warned by parents and teachers against contact with adults, and when they receive no explanation of the exact nature of the forbidden contacts, they are ready to become hysterial as soon as any older person approaches, or stops and speaks to them on the street, or fondles them, or proposes to do something for them, even though the adult may have had no sexual objective in mind. Some of the more experienced students of juvenile problems have come to believe that the emotional reactions of the parents, police officers, and other adults who discover that the child has had such a contact, may disturb the child more seriously than the sexual contacts themselves. The current hysteria over sex offenders may very well have serious effects on the ability of many of these children to work out sexual adjustments some years later in their marriages. (p. 204)

These comments have a curiously (and depressingly) familiar ring to them today.

Homosexual seductions. Seductions, apparently, are not an important cause of homosexuality. Where seduction incidents do appear in homosexual case histories, they seem to be at the most, precipitants of already existing tendencies.

None of this is meant, of course, to make light of a very serious and worrying problem – the sexual abuse of children and teenagers.

SEXUAL ABUSE

Although this emotive subject – a problem directed *toward* rather than *of* young persons – appears in the adolescent section, it is also about acts perpetrated (as we have seen) on children, indeed very young children. The term sexual abuse includes the following acts:

- Rape
- Sexual Intercourse

- Buggery (anal penetration)
- Masturbation
- Digital (finger) penetration
- Fondling
- Exhibitionism or flashing
- Involvement in pornographic activity.

C. Henry Kempe, the American paediatrician who made extensive studies of the problem, defined sexual abuse as 'the involvement of developmentally immature children and adolescents in sexual activity they do not truly comprehend, to which they are unable to give informed consent, or that violates the social taboos of family roles'.

It is not within the scope of this book to deal adequately with such a disturbing and complex issue (see Further Reading). However, it is as well to be alert to possible warning 'signs'. *Do* seek experienced and expert help as many of these signs in children and adolescents are open to alternative explanations; and are thus vulnerable to *misinterpretation* as sexual abuse. Tables 7 and 8 present (respectively) some of the physical and behavioural warning signs (in young people) of possible sexual abuse.

Table 7. Physical warning signs of possible child sexual abuse

- Sleeplessness, nightmares and fear of the dark
- Bruises, scratches, bite marks
- Depression/suicide attempts
- Anorexia nervosa
- Eating disorders or change in eating habits
- Difficulty in walking or sitting
- Pregnancy – particularly with reluctance to name the father
- Recurring urinary tract problems
- Vaginal infections or genital/anal damage
- Venereal disease
- Bed wetting
- Vague pains and aches
- Itching or soreness

Table 8. Behavioural warning signs of possible child sexual abuse

- Lack of trust in adults
- Fear of a particular individual
- Withdrawal and introversion
- Running away from home
- Girl takes over the mothering role

Table 8 continued

- Sudden school problems, truanting and falling standards
- Low self-esteem and low expectations of others
- Stealing
- Drug, alcohol or solvent abuse
- Display of sexual knowledge beyond the child's years
- Sexual drawing
- Prostitution
- Vulnerability to sexual and emotional exploitation
- Revulsion towards sex
- Fear of school medical examinations

Summary and comment

I have attempted in this chapter to sketch in the broad developmental themes that are important for your understanding of childhood and adolescence. A framework of *normal* development is vital for your assessment of what is *not* normal, usual, 'healthy' or functional, in a potential client's behaviour. It is particularly difficult to pinpoint the onset of serious problems when childhood and adolescence are notable for the changes that take place, some of them very rapid indeed. So many signs of normal change look like 'symptoms' of emotional disturbance. So you need multiple criteria (working guidelines) for arriving at the decision that you are dealing with a problem with serious implications. Proceed cautiously (and consult acknowledged experts, colleagues or supervisors if necessary); this is a ferociously complex area fraught with value judgements, ethical issues, and technical difficulties. You will find a few of the typical problems illustrated in these pages but the topic is so vast that you should (if it is new to you) supplement your *knowledge base* from texts in the section on Further Reading, and your *experience* from workshops and supervised practice.

This advice is particularly pertinent to the fraught issues of physical, emotional and sexual abuse. The legal, moral, technical and social ramifications of these problems go far beyond the scope of this kind of book. What is critical to remember is that most children can cope with one-off or short-duration trauma *if* the aftermath is sensitively dealt with by adults (parents and/or the authorities). What is more damaging in the short- *and* longer-term is the abusive situation that goes on and on. As so many emotional, physical and sexual incidents of an abusive kind occur in the child's home, this is precisely what tends to happen.

Chapter 6

Responsiveness in Parents and Children

Family groupings have been traced back to the Pleistocene period, some 500,000 years. This durability, and universality, of the family suggests that as an organization it has significant survival value for the individual and the species. But longevity of this order does not mean that the family is unchanging. It has been, and is, susceptible to social, economic and historical forces. For example, the large extended family has given way in industrial societies to small nuclear units of parent(s) and offspring. There is an increasing number of single parent families and not infrequently these days, the sole parent could be a man. Then again, there are several variations in parental roles to take into account.

Birth parents give the child's life, physical appearance, intellectual potential and certain personality characteristics and special talents. The *legal parents* carry responsibility for the child's maintenance, safety and security, and make decisions about the child's residence and education. *Parenting parents* provide the day-to-day love, care, attention and discipline. For many children the three components of parenting are embodied in one set of parents.

In the case of foster children there will at least be a split between birth parents who are also legal parents and the foster parents undertaking part of the parenting function. In foster care there is quite commonly a three-way split, with birth parents, parenting (foster) parents, and the local authority as legal parent. Adoptive children are likely to have two sets of parents: the birth parents and the adoptive parents. The latter combines the legal and parenting roles.

The Egyptians, Romans, and Greeks all sanctioned adoption. In earlier periods adoption was utilized primarily to serve adult ends – particularly to acquire heirs in order to provide continuity for a family line. Views on adoption have changed markedly over the years. Today's philosophy is unmistakably child-centred. In essence the value of adoption in modern society is that it safeguards the child by providing a permanent family arrangement. Of course, adoptive parents – like biological parents setting out to rear an infant – are faced with the rather daunting task of transforming helpless, unsocial, and self-centred infants into more or less self-supporting and responsible members of the community.

PARENTAL RESPONSIVENESS

With the birth (or adoption) of the first child the tasks of the parents, the roles they occupy, their orientation toward the future, all change profoundly. This simple step into parenthood, so often taken by biological parents as an inadvertent 'slip up', provides a severe test for the parents. The inevitable changes in the partners will, in turn, alter their relationship and may place stress upon it until a new equilibrium can be established in their lives. In order to re-establish a degree of equanimity they rely on various coping 'mechanisms' (see page 61). There may be reverberations in all of this for the child.

In working with parents the professional (let us take the social worker as an example) will be particularly interested in assessing the parents' responsiveness to their child because so many of the parental functions are dependent to some degree on this attribute. The needs of children which are potentially at risk (if not responded to consistently) are of two kinds: *survival* functions such as the need for food, shelter and physical care, and *psychosocial* functions, including the child's requirements of love, security, attention, new experiences, acceptance, education, praise, recognition, and belongingness.

Infants and children – if they are to survive – must also acquire vast amounts of information about the environment they inhabit. The transmission by adults of information of various kinds from one generation to another, as we have seen, is called *socialization*. One of the main objectives of this training is the preparation of children for their future, one of the major themes of this chapter.

Problematic parenting

The definition of problematic parental behaviour is a difficult one because it *is* largely a relative judgement, and a social, subjective one at that. It is formulated largely in terms of its consequences for the offspring – his or her well-being. Social workers sometimes aid paediatricians and health visitors in cases where infants fail to thrive, in the absence of any organic (physical) illness. They have to explore the social and emotional context in which the child feeds.

The point is that maternal responsiveness is important in something as apparently basic as providing sustenance to a baby. Typically, feeding times must be adapted to the cycles of hunger and satisfaction expressed by the infant and responded to by the parent. During the feeding sessions mothers should preferably be calm, and sensitive enough to respond from moment-to-moment to changes in the baby's behaviour. For example, they commonly respond to pauses in the child's sucking at the breast by jiggling the baby. They will gaze back at the baby and talk to it. They will be alert to the child's changing needs for nourishment as it matures, by altering its diet.

Parental responsiveness is a complex and many-sided phenomenon, but there are at least three different elements which make for what one might assess to be *sensitive* responsiveness: the tendency to react *promptly*, *consistently* and *appropriately*, to their offspring. A social worker or health visitor would be concerned if parents continually failed to show these reactions in response to their child's hunger and pain, crying or other communications and actions.

The interactions between parents and children (particularly the early ones involving communication between mother or 'mother-figure' and baby) are of crucial significance in the child's development. Personal factors can interfere with these intricate processes. To take the extreme case: a mother suffering from depression may find it difficult to 'tune in' to the child in a sufficiently sensitive manner to be able to construct with him/her a mutually beneficial and stimulating sequence of interaction. Psychologists have observed infants under conditions in which their mothers simulated depression and found their behaviour to be markedly affected, with an increase in protest, wariness and generally negative behaviour. Infants, confronted by mothers who have been asked to adopt an immobile expression during the interactive session, look puzzled, become unhappy and avoid prolonged eye contact with the mother.

The same reactions of puzzlement and strong signs of unhappiness were evident when the mother's attention was experimentally switched from the infant to another adult by means of a change of lighting either side of a partially reflecting window. The mother's response to her child was then no longer contingent on his/her own behaviour; and though the infants were only eight weeks old they reacted with confusion, distress, inert dejection and withdrawal. Mismatching, through the adult's faulty timing, may well have drastic consequences if continuously experienced as part of the child's daily life.

Parent–child attachment (bonding)

The question of sensitive or insensitive responsiveness has been linked (in part) with the quality of the emotional 'bond' or 'attachment' that forms between the parent and baby. Obviously, the infant's survival depends upon a loving and long-term commitment by adult caregivers. Social workers and health-visitors are on the lookout – especially these days – for signs of rejection, neglect and abuse (see page 102).

When all goes well – and it usually does – a 'bond' is cemented between a mother (say) and her infant, a relationship implying unconditional love, self-sacrifice and caring attitudes which, for the mother's part, are quite likely to last a lifetime.

What is this doctrine of mother-to-infant bonding? Put briefly, it is suggested that in some mammalian species, including our own, mothers become bonded to their infants through close contact – skin-to-skin – during a short critical period, soon after birth. This is an awesome claim, considering that no other adult human behaviour, and a complex pattern of behaviour and attitude at that, is explained in such 'ethological' terms (i.e. the language of animal behaviour).

The close-contact, critical-period bonding theory is said to be justified on two grounds. One is rooted in studies of animal behaviour. The other has to do with observations of human mothers, comparing those who have had little or no contact, and those who have extended contact, with their newborn babies.

I have commented elsewhere (see Further Reading) how liberalizing ideas in the field of child care – for example, 'maternal deprivation' theory – can become oppressive when elevated into prescriptive dogmas. The eminently realistic and humane idea of allowing a mother and her new baby to get to know one another early on, by means of frequent and intimate social interaction, becomes intrusive and unrealistic when the permissive 'ought' of physical contact is transformed into an authoritarian 'must' – whatever the condition of the mother or her offspring. Mothers-to-be, often exhausted and hypersensitive to potential dangers, may be undermined by the fear that if they do not have contact with their babies soon after delivery they may not fall in love with them.

This is not the place to review the complex and detailed studies of bonding'; however there seems to be no reliable evidence that skin-to-skin contact is necessary for the development of mother-love, and, what is more significant, mother-to-infant attachment does not depend on such contact occurring during a sensitive period of short duration after the birth of the baby.

I am *not* putting forward the idea that early human contact and relationships are of no consequence. Far from it. All relationships have to have a beginning; close mother – infant contact is decidedly desirable whenever possible. Mothers tend to like it and lactation is facilitated. Where better to begin than at the very beginning, with the newborn child placed in its mother's arms? Mutual awareness and familiarity have an opportunity to develop. What we are talking about is foundational learning, learning how to relate to (and love) a stranger, a baby. It would seem that this learning comes quickly for some but for others more slowly. The range of individual differences is wide.

The period after birth, with its heightened emotional arousal and excited expectation and fulfilment of a new family member, may have tremendous significance for *all* members of the family. Remember that parental bonds and relationships have their own complex, many-sided developmental histories, stretching over many years. Among the factors which can influence the way a mother behaves and relates to her offspring are her age, her cultural and social background, her own experience of being parented, her personality, her previous experience with babies and her experiences during pregnancy and birth.

Insensitivity to cultural values in clinical and social work practice can lead to much individual suffering if methods used offend against cherished cultural and/or religious beliefs. For some ethnic groups bonding ideas, if applied insensitively by doctors and nurses, may have disturbing repercussions. In many Asian families, for instance, birth is a less personal event than in European families. An Indian baby is thought to be bonded to the family group rather than to the mother in particular. Unless hospital staff are sensitive to ethnic differences in behaviour and attitudes after birth, these parents could feel intense conflict over 'bonding procedures'.

Understandably the hard-pressed social worker cannot afford to be as complacent as the scientist in risking what the statisticians call 'Type II errors' – i.e. denying relationships which actually exist – because of a cautious attitude to evidence. After all, it has been suggested that separation of the mother and infant for several weeks immediately after birth may not only damage (irreversibly) the subsequent mother–child relationship, but additionally that such mothers are prone to child abuse. In fact, the evidence for such far-reaching claims is simply not available; these notions do not stand up to painstaking enquiry and investigation (see Further Reading).

It is reassuring to realise that there are variations in the way that maternal feelings arise and grow. Mothers generally expect to have positive maternal feelings towards their infants at the time of birth. Indeed, some mothers *do* report an instant love towards their newborn babies. Others report that they feel nothing. However, you can reassure mothers that they do not need to worry if they feel initially detached from their babies, as this appears to be a fairly common occurrence. Some 40 per cent of mothers of first-borns have been found to express an initial indifference to their infants, a state of mind which soon evaporates as they get to know their offspring.

When subjective and objective reports of the development of mother love are scrutinized, it becomes apparent that the growth of maternal attachment is usually a gradual process.

Allaying parents' fears. The practical advice to parents who have had an enforced separation – at whatever time – from their children is: do not spend time worrying needlessly. Adult bonding need not be impaired, in the case of those separations in the maternity hospital, unless you talk yourself into a crisis.

Where the separation occurs later in life, children may be upset for a short time, but they will soon recover if parents appear their usual selves and avoid fussing over them in nervous expectation of the worst. We know that a child's separation from its caregiver *does not inevitably* result in maladjustment. Far from it. Brief separations are fairly common for all children and seem to have little adverse effect. The key issue is to provide good and stable substitute care during the absence or absences.

Paternal bonding. Paternal love puts a large question mark over the bonding doctrine, for it implies that a father's love is of a lower order and quality than the mother's. Yet it is not always the female that cares for the baby. This is so even in some animal species: male marmosets, to take just one example, carry the infant at all times except when it is feeding.

Most human fathers develop a strong love for their offspring, even if they were nowhere near the delivery room when they were born. A study of first-time fathers suggests that they began developing a bond to their new-born by the first three days after the birth and often earlier. They tended to develop a feeling of preoccupation, absorption and interest ('engrossment'). There are no clear indications that the early contact by the father with the newborn facilitates this engrossment. Nevertheless the opportunity for father and infant to get to know one another early on would seem to be a good idea, especially as contemporary western society is witnessing a massive increase in the number of single-parent families, and in some it is the father who is the care-giver.

Fostering and adoption. If maternal bonding theory were correct, it would hardly be possible for foster or adoptive parents to form warm attachments to their charges, whom they may not have seen as babies at all. It could be said that it is possible to look after children satisfactorily without ever becoming attached to them, but how many adoptive or foster parents would say that they felt no bond with their child? Tragic 'tug of love' cases have occurred because foster parents have grown so fond of the children in their care that it becomes unbearably hurtful to hand them back to their biological parents.

Not only is there no 'blood bond' between adoptive mother and the child, but she has missed out vital weeks, months and sometimes years of exposure to the youngster. Not surprisingly there is nothing to suggest that adoptive parents are in any way inferior in their familial or parental roles than biological parents. A painstaking study of children who had been in care throughout their early years followed them up on leaving care. One group of children was adopted, another returned to their own families. It was found that the latter did less well than the adopted children, both in the initial stages of settling in and in their subsequent progress. The reason lay primarily in the attitudes of the two sets of parents: the adoptive group 'worked' harder at being parents, possibly for the very reason that the child was not their own, in a genetic sense.

The attitude of some people to adoption in this country in the 18th and early 19th century was very different from the one shared by most of us today. We gather from George Eliot's novel *Silas Marner* that on religious grounds it was believed that 'to adopt a child, because children of your own had been denied you, was to try and choose your lot in spite of Providence: the adopted child . . . would never turn out well, and would be a curse to those who had wilfully and rebelliously sought what it was clear that, for some high reason, they were better without'. Adoption was only permissible and likely to succeed if it came about by chance, not intent. George Eliot, in her usual insightful manner, made the point that the 'blood bond' is less important than the bonds forged by long-term tender care and affection. And she has been shown to be correct.

Researchers provide evidence that adoption is notable for its high 'success rate' both in absolute terms, and relative to other forms of substitute care. Like other parents, adopters will have their share of difficult children and will try to make sense of them. A commonly-held belief which can be very worrying to adoptive parents is the notion that infants who are deprived of maternal care and love (evident in the history of some of the older children who are adopted) are affected adversely in their ability to form bonds of affection and also in their ability to develop a repertoire of socially appropriate attitudes and behaviour.

An attitude of therapeutic pessimism was created in the minds of many social workers when considering problems in older children who were adopted, or the breakdown of fostering arrangements as a result of their belief in a link between their experience of early maternal separation/ deprivation and the development of an irreversible affectionless (psychopathic) personality. An intolerable burden of anxiety about the child's future was also placed on parents who adopt older youngsters. But what is the evidence for such misgivings? It all began with studies of babies and young children in Dickensian-like institutions. The plight of these infants was linked theoretically to what happens to animals separated from their mothers.

RESPONSIVENESS IN CHILDREN

Examples of chicks or ducklings following a person have been seen by many people in nature films. Although normally attached to their birth mother, such infants can become attached with ease to an 'adoptive' parent or (in the laboratory) to a moving inanimate object. Konrad Lorenz found that during a restricted period – just after hatching – goslings instinctively follow the first large moving thing they see. These young creatures not only tend to follow this moving object but they come to prefer it to all others, and after a time will follow no others.

This type of early learning is referred to as *imprinting*. The fascinating question that arises from studies of imprinting is whether human attachments, preferences, or other behaviours are acquired (and perhaps even 'fixed') during restricted periods of development on an imprinting-like basis. The most influential writings have been those of John Bowlby. His early opinion was that the child's strong attachment to its mother was necessary for normal, healthy development. Bowlby argued that the period in the infant's life when a major new relationship (e.g. to the mother) was being formed was a vital one for determining the nature of that relationship.

At that time he thought that deprivation of maternal affection, or protracted maternal separation, was liable to result in maladjustment which could show itself in a variety of ways, including delinquency. He was suggesting then that not only the presence of adverse influences (for example, a harsh rejecting mother) but the absence of crucial stimulation (the lack of a mother or mother-surrogate), disturbs – possibly irreversibly – the child's ability to make relationships with people. Fortunately more recent, painstaking reviews on the effects of maternal deprivation and other types of early experience indicate the more optimistic conclusion that early experience if distressing *can* be remedied, 'damage' can be reversed. Such early experience is no more than a link – albeit an important one – in the chain of development, influential but shaping behaviour less and less powerfully as age increases. What is probably crucial is that for some children some aspects of their early learning – those experiences of an adverse kind – are continually repeated and reinforced (one thinks here of sexual abuse) and it is in this way that long-term effects appear. We must not forget the likelihood that later problems and deviance may be the result of later adverse life experiences (e.g. exposure to delinquent peers) and not only early learning experiences.

John Bowlby's revised view, following an examination of such research findings, was that the child's separation from its care-giver did not inevitably result in the maladjustment of the child. This is not to deny the vital importance of the comforting presence of a loving parent or parent substitute – especially before the age of about five years – in facilitating the child's healthy psychological development (see Chapter 7).

The idea of a critical or sensitive period implies that parents are all-powerful, all-responsible. Such an ideology places a great responsibility on parents to 'get things right'! In fact, our knowledge about what parental practices are appropriate or beneficial must of necessity be tentative. That said, just what are the implications for children of differences in maternal and parental behaviour?

PARENTAL PATTERNS

There can be too much of a good thing, a point when mothering – in its excessive zeal – becomes smothering. And, of course, the same applies to fathering. There can also be too little parental input. Parental nurturance is undoubtedly a vital ingredient in the child's and adolescent's healthy development, but as with everything *moderation* is the watchword.

Parental over-protection

Over-protective parents frequently alternate between dominating their offspring and submitting to them. There are two types of parental over-protection. The dominating form of over-protection may lead to excessively dependent, passive and submissive behaviour on the part of the child. It is thought that if youngsters are discouraged from acting independently, exploring, and experimenting, they acquire timid, awkward, and generally apprehensive behaviours.

Parental dominance/restriction

Children whose parents are authoritarian (that is, who cling to a set of rules in which the adolescent has no voice) and who use physical punishment as a means of discipline, tend to have more dependent and, at the same time, rebellious adolescent offspring. Restrictive, authoritarian parents attempt to shape, control, and assess the behaviour and attitudes of the child according to a set standard of conduct, usually an absolute standard, often motivated by theological considerations. Obedience is valued as a virtue, and punitive, forceful measures are favoured in order to curb self-will at those points where the child's (and later on, the teenager's) actions or beliefs conflict with what parents think is correct conduct. They believe in *bullying* – as opposed to educating – their offspring into such values as respect for authority, respect for work, and respect for the preservation of traditional order. Verbal give and take is discouraged because the child should accept unquestioningly the parent's word for what is right.

The children of domineering parents often lack self-reliance and the ability to cope realistically with their problems; later they may fail or prove slow to accept adult responsibilities. They are apt to be submissive and obedient and to withdraw from situations they find difficult. They also tend to be the sort of boys and girls who make up (later) many of the adults who have never left home, psychologically, and in many cases, physically as well.

Parental rejection (physical and emotional abuse)

There is a group of parents whose concern for their children is minimal and whose attitudes are casual, laissez-faire, lax or even indifferent. For some, rejection means callous and indifferent neglect or positive hostility from the parents; but it may also be emotional and subtle. Children come to believe that they are worthless, that their very existence makes their parents unhappy. The term 'emotional abuse' has been added to the concept of 'physical abuse' and is defined in terms of the neglect of all or some of the basic needs of children. Let us first look at a list of the physical injuries that *may* indicate that a child has been the victim of non-accidental, abusive acts (see Table 9).

Table 9.   Physical injuries in child abuse

- Bruises, weals, lacerations and scars
- Burns and scalds
- Bone and joint injuries
- Brain and eye injuries
- Internal injuries

Emotional abuse is less tangible and even more difficult to diagnose or 'prove'. It is defined in terms of the neglect of all or some of the *basic needs* of children. There follows a list suggested by the distinguished paediatrician and analyst, Donald Winnicott.

- Physical care and protection.
- Affection and approval.
- Stimulation and teaching.
- Discipline and controls which are consistent and appropriate to the child's age and development.
- Opportunity and encouragement to acquire gradual autonomy, i.e. for the child to take gradual control over his or her own life.

Emotional abuse is 'signposted' by parental indifference. The child is ignored, there may be inadequate physical care, the child lacks stimulation, physical contact, security. The child is thus denied emotional warmth and love and is denied protection, support and discipline. Overall negative attitudes may lead to abusive threats, constant criticism and scapegoating. With older children this is sometimes accompanied by ridicule and denigrating all the child's efforts to please. Some apply the term emotional abuse also to severe overprotection.

The concept of emotional abuse is in danger of being over-inclusive and far too vague. It is therefore an advantage to have rather more tangible indicators to pinpoint the presence of emotional abuse. In particular there are four types of damaging parental behaviour.

Indicator 1 entails punishment of positive 'operant' behaviour such as smiling, mobility, manipulation.

Indicator 2 is behaviour which results in discouragement of parent–infant bonding. (for example. pushing children away everytime they seek proximity, comfort and affection.)

Indicator 3 involves the punishment of self-esteem as when parents endlessly criticize their child.

Indicator 4 is parental behaviour leading to the punishing of those

> inter-personal skills (for example friendliness) which are
> foundational for adequate social presence and performance
> in environments outside the family, such as schools, peer-
> groups, etc.

One might say that emotional abuse consists of behaviour that seriously
undermines the development of the child's competence.

A rejecting or abusive parent tends not only to ignore the offspring's
need for nurturance, but also to punish manifestations of that need. One
would expect, therefore, that more severe forms of rejection would lead
the youngster to suppress such behaviour. Parents who are sparing (in
the face of their offsprings' need for dependence) with their attention
and care, but do not actually punish dependent behaviour, are likely to
intensify their offspring's needs for attention and care. The more a
youngster is 'pushed away' (figuratively speaking) the more he or she
clings. A guide to the treatment of child abuse together with a case
vignette is provided in Appendix 4.

Parental permissiveness

Permissive parents attempt to behave in a non-punitive, accepting and
affirmative manner toward their offsprings' impulses, desires, and actions;
consult with them about policy decisions and give explanations for family
rules: such parents allow young people to regulate their own activities
as much as possible, avoid the excessive exercise of control, and do not
encourage them to obey absolute externally-defined standards.

PREVENTION

Can parents pre-empt the development of antisocial attitudes and behaviour? Life is too unpredictable and people too mysterious and complex in their make-up to justify our saying *yes* in an unqualified manner.
Many persons other than parents have an influence on children's personality and behaviour. But parents can encourage a strong 'immune
system' in their offspring – protection against some of the stresses and
snares of growing up. Such a system would depend, in part, upon:

- strong ties of affection and respect between themselves and their
  children
- firm social and moral demands being made on their offspring
- the consistent use of sanctions
- techniques of punishment that are psychological rather than physical

(for example, threats to withdraw approval)
- an intensive use of reasoning and explanations (these are referred to as inductive methods)
- responsibility given to children and adolescents.

I shall translate these generalizations (based upon many studies) into guidelines which you, in turn, can interpret to meet the particular values and circumstances of your clients.

Guideline 1: **Foster bonds of respect and affection**.
Such bonds tend to make all teaching endeavours that much easier; the more affection there is as a foundation for disciplinary tactics, the more notice the child will take of what he or she is being told.

Guideline 2: **Make firm social and moral demands (set limits).**
This means attempting to establish and convey a reasonably coherent idea of the aims and objectives that lie behind the training and supervision of young people. Children whose parents set firm limits for them, grow up with more self-esteem and confidence than those who are allowed to get away with behaving in any way they like. Supervision does not mean intrusive surveillance, but it does mean knowing where children and teenagers are, who their friends are, and so on. It is important to give the youngster a reasonable amount of freedom of choice within those limits.

Children who get their own way all the time interpret such laissez faire permissiveness as indifference. They feel nothing they do is important enough for their parents to bother about. So, you might advise clients if they have to cope with recrimination, invidious comparisons and abuse from their son or daughter, to take heart and take the long view. Being 'safe' and 'solid' will pay off in the longer term.

Guideline 3: **Prepare children for life by developing family routines**.
Most routines are useful short-cuts to living. For example, routines help a child to master and carry out automatically such daily tasks as feeding, washing, dressing, going to bed – thus helping him or her to achieve more with less effort.

Habit is taught by repetition of routine. A child feels secure if the main events of his or her day are as regular and familiar as the sunrise. If going to bed, eating and washing always happen in more or less the same way, the child accepts them with little or no fuss. The morning ritual of preparation is a potent 'push' factor in getting a child off to school. The bedtime ritual is a particularly powerful habit; a regular routine of supper, bath and then a story before bed makes the child's world seem well-ordered, safe and comfortable. It is not trivializing to set up these routines. Psychologists and social workers who visit chaotic homes – strangers to certainty, regularity and routine – know how disturbing this is to young children, and not helpful to older ones who enter the relatively orderly life demanded at school.

Guideline 4: **Teach children the family rules**.

Everyone needs some self-discipline (rules of conduct) in order to adjust his or her needs and desires to those of others*, and this is necessary (paradoxically) in order to be a free and happy person. Children *need* the affection and approval of people around; being self-centred and egotistical will not win this approval. Nowadays it is not rules for rules' sake.

The ultimate aim is to give children the ability to discipline themselves, to compromise between what they want and what society demands of them. Once they can do this, their dealings with other people will be easier.

Guideline 5: **Choose rules carefully.**

Parents are in trouble if they proliferate the don'ts – making demands for the sake of making demands, rules for the sake of making rules. Any limits set should be for the child's (or adolescent's) safety, well-being and mature, emotional and social development. It is crucial to ensure that children know exactly what the rules and constraints are, and what is expected of them. Rules are most effective when they are relatively uncomplicated, fair, understandable, and applied fairly and consistently so that the youngster knows what will happen if they are broken.

No one can advise parents about which rules to insist upon. Every family has different values, different interpretations of what is right and wrong. Their standards of behaviour will accord with those of their community or religion, as well as their own values, life-styles and personalities.

Guideline 6: **Be consistent**.

When teaching your child to distinguish between appropriate and inappropriate actions, it is important to be consistent. It is confusing if he or she is punished for their behaviour today and gets away with the same thing tomorrow, merely because your reasoning or mood has changed. Parents are indignant if asked whether they ever break a promise (say) to give their child a treat. Of course not! It would undermine the child's trust and devalue the currency of their words. Yet they may be quite prepared to make idle threats.

Guideline 7: **Be persistent**.

Parents often stand out against rebellious, non-compliant behaviour for some time, only to give in eventually. The child will soon infer that the meaning of their parents' word is ambiguous and that if he or she makes a nuisance, the parent will give way.

Guideline 8: **Give explanations/reasons**.
Parents might well say 'I wouldn't automatically obey a regulation myself unless I thought there was a good reason for it. So why not try to explain to children, and more particularly adolescents, why we have to have rules in a complicated world, and what would happen if everyone went their own way?' Children are more likely to internalize (take within their 'consciences') standards if they are justified in terms of their *intrinsic* value, rather than in terms of the punishments and odium that follow from their violation. They do need to know! When small, they cannot comprehend, unaided, the reasons for training. Later on, when in a position to understand explanations, they may be side-tracked; worse still, there may be no possible meaning to the demands made upon them, because what is being asked is unreasonable.

Guideline 9: **Tell children what they should do, not only what they can't do**.
Explain clearly to children what is required of them. Emphasize the positive, not only the negative. Catch the child out in good behaviour, not only naughty behaviour. By attending to positive actions parents make them more likely to occur.

Guideline 10: **Giving young people responsibility gives them the opportunity to practise, and to be responsible**.

Guideline 11: **Encourage parents to listen carefully to what their child says**.
When children are expected to be seen and not heard, their parents suppress undesirable behaviour without paying attention to the needs and 'messages' that lie behind it. Children's communications are often in code. This is done unwittingly as they wish (as all of us do) to be understood. So we, as professionals (or as parents) need to be empathic, looking at what they are saying with an ear tuned to the hidden messages. Those children who show off in front of strangers may really be communicating their uncertainty, even (paradoxically) their shyness.

For parents, and professional people who work with children, it is vital to be able to communicate understanding. Haim Ginott is concerned that the *two-way* nature of good communication between adults should also form the basis of conversations with children. A dialogue with a young child requires respect and skill. He advises parents to listen carefully to what children say. Messages should preserve the child's and its parents' self-respect; statements of understanding should precede statements of advice or instruction. Ginott says that in this way parents provide a mirror to their children's personality; they learn about their emotional likeness (as they get to know their physical likeness) by having their feelings reflected back to them.

The child who comes home saying 'I hate school' learns that it is not *everything* about school that she dislikes when her mother says 'It's been a bad day today, hasn't it; you have physical education on Monday – are you still feeling a bit embarrassed getting changed in front of the others?'. Or when Tom says, 'My teacher made me stay in today', parents would do well to resist the temptation to answer: 'Now what have you done?', or 'I suppose you deserved it', both of which would have inflamed his feelings. Instead, they might acknowledge them by saying: 'You must have felt awful . . . would you like to tell me what happened?'

Summary and comment

The themes of parental responsiveness, including parent – child attachment (bonding), and parental styles, are explored in this chapter. The effects of parenting variations (including aberrations such as physical and emotional abuse) are described, and I have included some *guidelines* for you to do preventive work with families – the sort of child-rearing advice which may facilitate prosocial behaviour and protect against antisocial behaviour in children.

There is a discussion of fostering and adoption and of some of the unnecessary fears that adoptive parents have about the latter. Fortunately, it is possible to allay many of the anxieties parents have about separations and substitute care when you have the research evidence at your finger tips.

Responsiveness in children is another theme dealt with. The concepts of imprinting and attachment are described, and there is some reassuring evidence that adverse early experiences do not, by any means, lead inevitably to psychological disturbance in maturity. Painstaking preventive work can be effective.

Chapter 7

Experiencing Loss and Change

Psychologists have shown an increasing interest in the themes of change, loss and gain which feature in any major period of transition during our lifetime. We looked at adolescence in Chapter 5 and the task that teenagers face in mastering massive changes in their lives. It is truly a stage of transition. They lose one identity, that of child, and don another, that of adult. Here is what it feels like according to one fifteen year old:

> **❝**Lately I've been in a daze, and I can't think straight. Maybe because some of my brain cells are dying and I'm just about sixteen. My whole world is changing. Before I used to have a regular routine and all I was concerned with was school. But now I'm thinking of my future.**❞**

The point about this, whether it is an adolescent change or some other life crisis – such as divorce, the breakup of a family or the constituting of a new one – is that new behaviours, different responses to changing circumstances, are required.

STAGES OF TRANSITION

This is where your understanding of typical reactions to major transitional events – the fairly predictable sequence of reactions – will help you to guide your clients in their efforts to cope with the difficult changes in their lives. Here are the stages which tend to occur following disruptive life experience.

Immobilization. The individual has a sense of being overwhelmed, being unable to make plans, to understand or to reason. A kind of paralysis sets in.

Minimization. The person may cope with this state of 'deep freeze' by minimizing the changes. The sorrow and pain caused by the girl's bereavement – the separation of her mother and father – are made light of. The youngster may try to trivialize the changes brought about by his new step-mother's entry into the home ('I don't know why everyone makes such a fuss over nothing'). Some persons will deny that a change has occurred.

Depression. This is a common experience for adolescents; menopausal women and the elderly; the physical changes of puberty, middle life and old age represent a dramatic transition. Don't be surprised if there is an upsurge in feelings of misery and inner turmoil for any of these groups. Misery gives way in some vulnerable individuals to more worrying feelings of depression (see page 84) – representing a statement of helplessness or powerlessness – of events being out of, or beyond, control. Some clients entertain ideas about committing suicide.

Letting go. This is the stage of accepting reality for what it is, of figuratively 'letting go' of the past, which means for the toddler the dependency of infancy, for the adolescent the safety of childhood, of total parental nurturance or childlike irresponsibility.

Testing. The 'letting go' provides a bridge to the testing phase, in which the individual may begin testing him or herself vis-à-vis the new circumstances – trying out new behaviours, skills and even (to the chagrin sometimes of family and friends) new life-styles. At this time there can be quite a lot of anger and irritability expressed.

Search for meaning. Following this stage of activity and self-testing, there is a more gradual movement towards a search for meaning and understanding of how things are different, and why this is so.

Internalization. Eventually these new meanings are internalized, taken into the 'psyche' and behavioural repertoire of the individual.

First aid

Transitions, it is important to remember, involve considerable stress. They are most distressing if they are unpredictable, involuntary, unfamiliar and of high intensity and magnitude – that is, if the rate and degree of changes are excessive. Professionals can help parents and parents (in their turn) can help their sons and daughters by warning them of the likely changes, or interpreting them, thus making them more predictable and manageable. Of course, being able to talk about personal and intimate matters to clients will depend upon a relationship of trust and good communication, in the case of parents fostered in earlier years, in the case of professionals, nurtured over several sessions.

CHILDHOOD BEREAVEMENT

Childhood security may be shattered temporarily by the death of a loved parent or relative. The trauma can be lessened for the child, by sensitive caring and explanations. The quality of the relationships – the continuity and reassurance of loving care – matters more than the disruption of bonds as such. Where ill effects do occur, they are more likely if the mother dies when the child is very young; the father's death is more likely to have adverse effects if it occurs when the child is older.

Children are remarkable in the way in which they seem to accept the sad facts of life and get on with living. A simple, straightforward explanation of the death (say) of a grandparent is usually sufficient, particularly if given in a calm manner.

Long-term problems are less associated with the decease of a parent (despite the finality of the break in an emotional attachment) than it is with divorce where attachments may still be retained.

PARENTAL BEREAVEMENT

There is a lack of a clear policy in many hospitals, for dealing with the kinds of problem that arise when babies die. This means that even when well-meaning personnel, knowledgeable in the bereavement literature, make suggestions about management – departures from usual practice – the lack of coordination can cause 'painful muddles'. Doctor Lovell investigated various aspects of the loss of a baby through late miscarriage, stillbirth and perinatal death by interviewing bereaved mothers. She concluded reluctantly that 'in many instances the pitiless attitudes prevalent in the Middle Ages have not altered nearly enough.' Stillborn babies are not normally buried in individual graves and the mother is not usually treated as a bereaved parent (i.e. as having been bonded in some sense), but as if the baby has not existed. If the baby is delivered before 28 weeks it can be treated, from the legal point of view, in the same way as gynaecological scraping and incinerated. It is not treated as a dead *person*.

The women in Lovell's sample often felt that having a dead baby was an act of deviancy; they were discharged with what seemed like indecent haste. Overall they had a sense of unreality, not knowing what became of the dead baby. Lovell acknowledges that there is an increasing awareness of the needs of mothers of stillborn babies. Thus, in some hospitals efforts are made to encourage the mother to see the dead baby and/or to arrange a funeral. There is a popular myth that miscarriages and stillbirths are lesser losses than early neonatal deaths. But women whose babies had lived, even for a very short time, found it easier to accept the loss because the infant's life, although fleeting, was at least public. This eased the bereavement; the baby was acknowledged as a person.

DIVORCE OR SEPARATION

If all divorces, all broken homes, led to serious psychological difficulties, society would indeed have an appalling problem on its hands. The divorce rate is so high. The highest risk or likelihood of a divorce (at present) occurs in the fourth year of marriage. In other words, it is very likely to be *young* children who are involved in the lead-up to, and aftermath of a divorce. Separation – the event that really hits children – is likely to precede divorce by several years.

It is often said that children hold themselves responsible for the break-up of their parents' marriage and feel very guilty about this. In fact such reactions do not seem to be very widespread; much more common is anger towards the parents for separating. Children of all ages frequently express the wish that their parents be reunited, and they blame either, or both, of them for the split.

Most children do not want their parents to separate and they may feel that their father and mother have not taken *their* interests into account. A marital separation may result in children's reappraising their own relationships with their parents and, indeed questioning the nature of all social relationships. For younger children in particular, there is the painful realization that social relationships do not last forever. Pre-school children usually appear to be very sad and frightened when their parents separate, and they become very clinging and demanding. Bedtime fears and a refusal to be left alone, even for a few minutes, are not uncommon. Children attending school or nursery may become very anxious about going there, and may protest strongly when left. Vivid fantasies about abandonment, death of parents, and suchlike, are encountered. Such children often express aggression towards other children.

Many childish reactions at such a time are expressions of the fear of the child's of being abandoned by one or both parents. Such fears are likely to be most acute if contact has been lost with a parent. If, however, relationships between parents and child can remain intact and supportive, these fears are usually short-lived.

With somewhat older children, grief and sadness remain a prominent feature but anger becomes more marked. This is usually directed at the parents, especially the one with whom the child is living – which more often than not means the mother. Regardless of the actual events leading to the breakdown, she is likely to be blamed by the child for everything that has happened. The absent father is quite likely to be idealized (again, regardless of realities) while the mother is held responsible for driving him away. Children, especially in the age group seven to eight, may express very strong yearnings for their father.

Pre-adolescent children tend to demonstrate less of their inner hurt and distress, which is not to say that it does not exist. Covering-up is common, and they seek distractions in play and other activities. It may be difficult to get through to such children; they are loath to talk about what they are feeling because of the pain it causes them. Underneath this apparent detachment is often anger; again, they may align themselves very strongly with one parent and even refuse to see the other.

Adolescents sometimes show overt depression; they appear to 'opt out' of family life and withdraw into other relationships outside the home. Worries about their own relationships, sex and marriage may surface.

These are the immediate reactions to parental separation. Usually they are seen in an acute form for a matter of months and then (hopefully) begin to subside. Unfortunately, the evidence concerning long-term consequences is very meagre and difficult to evaluate. Researchers have found that those people who experience a broken home in childhood have only a slightly higher risk of developing psychiatric problems compared with those from unbroken homes. For those from a comfortable economic background, there is no difference at all in the risk factor.

There is a close relationship between fatherlessness and poverty, and many of the unfavourable consequences of deprivation of a father, are primarily the consequences of financial difficulties. Many worries may deplete the last emotional resources of the mother left alone. Young children need special attention and care but she may have to seek employment. Finding substitute caregivers can be expensive. Housing, too, is a common and costly problem. Children from broken homes may fare better than youngsters from unhappy, unbroken homes. There is no room for complacency. Such relatively reassuring information is not repeated in the area of delinquency.

Delinquency is associated with the break-up of homes where there has been a great deal of parental disharmony; the association is not with the disruption of the home, as such. The loss of a parent through a marital separation is much more likely to cause long-term problems than a loss through death.

From the professional's point of view, if called in to work with a family, it is vital to appreciate how an atmosphere of strife and turmoil in the home, prior to separation, is one of the most corrosive influences. This quarrelling is something that children describe as very damaging – especially episodes of hostility between mother and father.

Of the factors that are significant to a benign outcome for children – after all the misery of a divorce – three are of the utmost significance:
– communication about separation
– continued good relationship with at least one parent
– satisfaction with custody and access arrangements.

Children who consider themselves most damaged are:

- those whose parents are not able talk to them about divorce (apart from blaming their ex-spouse);
- those who do not get on well with at least one parent after separation;
- those who are dissatisfied with custody and access arrangements, whatever these happen to be.

Most children would like two happily married parents, but most would prefer to live with a single parent rather than two unhappily married ones. It is a natural wish on the part of workers to keep parents and children together; but there are times when 'heroic' work to r aintain an intact family is counter to the best interests of all concerned.

Reconstituted families

Reconstituted families, in which one or both partners have been married before, and are combining two families into one, are a very common (and sometimes problem-engendering) phenomenon. In one out of every three marriages today, one or both parents have been married before. The difficulties of being a step-child are legendary; so are the problems of being a step-parent of such families. Research studies have confirmed these 'legends'. There is an increased risk of psychological problems in persons whose parents remarry, especially where it is the parent of the same sex as the child who finds a new spouse. These findings are statistically significant but reflect a slightly increased risk only.

There are, of course, many instances of step-parents who have brought great happiness and solace to the children in their new lives. The friction, jealousy and ambivalence which are a common feature of step-child/step-parent relationships can be overcome with empathetic handling – trying to see things from the child's point of view. For example, if the step-child lets herself go, and calls her step-father 'daddy' and shows him affection, might she not lose the love of her real father because of her disloyalty?

The step-parent herself (or himself) is not immune from conflict. To what extent should the step-mum try to be a 'mother' when X still has a mother? Should a step-father be permitted to discipline the child?

More devastating than the fear and jealousy aroused by remarriage, may be the fear of abandonment felt by a child whose parents allow a succession of romantic attachments to take priority over their relationship with their child.

The family plan (illustrated earlier) will assist you to compare the current life tasks and life events of the various members of the 're-shuffled pack' – the reconstituted family. Assess whether these individual needs and problems clash, thus adversely affecting the new family's ability to get on with life.

Single parent families

The number of such households is on the increase and the lone mothers and fathers tend to have a difficult time of it. The problems tend to be the same whether parents are on their own involuntarily or from choice, because of death, divorce, separation or through being unmarried.

You are likely to meet the assumption that children from one-parent families will have more problems than children from two-parent families, but there is little hard evidence to confirm this fear. Children from one-parent homes are no more likely to become delinquents, drop-outs, vandals or drug addicts than those from more 'conventional' families. Such problems are related to social and economic conditions and to adverse parental styles (attitudes and behaviours). It is not then a matter of being brought up by a single parent *per se* that puts children at a disadvantage, but (as we saw earlier) the *poverty* that is only too often associated with single status.

The worries that single parents may consult you about are the following:

Disciplinary problems. Can I manage a teenage boy alone?

Understanding. Father: 'I'm not sure I have the understanding and sensitivity of a woman for bringing up a girl.'

Interests. Mother: 'I can't really work up the enthusiasm and knowledge for fishing – his great love.'

Sex education. Father: 'How do I explain to her the facts and practical matters to do with her periods?'

Gender identity. Mother: 'Will he grow up effeminate without a father to identify with?'

None of these anticipated difficulties are of necessity real problems, or, if they are perceived by the parent as such, insuperable.

Support. The main need of a lone parent is support and then, good accurate information about children and their development in special circumstances. The *National Council for One Parent Families* and *Gingerbread* are two groups organized to help single parents.

The man or woman alone will need financial, practical and personal help. They need support over their feelings. Looking over your family life map can highlight the tasks and events which arouse the strongest emotional reactions in them. Review with your client their support system (see page 137). Problems arise when the parents cling to their children to make up for losing their partners, requiring them to grow up prematurely and creating a kind of emotional claustrophobia. Or they may try to support their children by overcompensating for what they are missing – waiting on them hand and foot, letting them do what they like.

Substitute care. Any working mother comes to see how inadequate the facilities for full-time day care are in most areas. As we saw in Chapter 6, the need to make reliable and stable arrangements for substitute care for young children while the single parent is at work can make all the difference between a reasonable standard of living for the family and a miserable penny-grabbing insecure existence. The choice is usually between childminders, day nurseries and cooperative grandparents.

If you are asked for advice about childminders bear the following points in mind:

- A reliable minder *can* provide stable and good quality care.
- She must be *registered* with the local Social Services Department.
- Choose someone who is only looking after two or three children,

thus providing a *family atmosphere* and a *personal relationship* with the child.

- The parent should *interview* the childminder and preferably *observe* her at work in her home-setting.
- He or she should check on the space available and the presence of toys, books, small chairs and a table for painting and drawing.

Day nurseries – sadly far too few – are provided by Social Services Departments of local authorities to meet the needs on social or health grounds of families with children under five years of age. They cater for unsupported mothers who have to work in order to keep the family going, and sometimes take a physically or mentally handicapped child. They also provide for children from deprived or disadvantaged homes (see note about Family Centres in Appendix I).

Summary and comment

Transition and change have been the theme of this chapter. An understanding of typical reactions to major transitional events should help you to guide your clients in their attempts to cope with difficult changes and trauma in their lives. The theme of change is the 'bread-and-butter' of many of the helping professions dealing, as they do, with bereavement and the effects of separation and divorce. These issues are discussed in some detail. The chapter endeavours to explode some of the myths surrounding substitute care, single-parenthood and reconstituted families. Some of the real difficulties of rearing children alone, of step-parenting and fostering are dealt with. There is a list of the worries that single parents may consult you about, and the chapter describes the kinds of support and the range of support systems that will be useful in their endeavours to cope with difficult situations that sometimes arise (for example, financial hardship). An understanding of transitional events and the characteristic reactions they generate should help you to support your client through a crisis.

Part 3

You as Helper

The most important instrument in your work with parents and children is yourself. It is essential, therefore, to spend some time preparing yourself before you start work. There are several questions you need to ask yourself.

? Why am I involved in this? You may be involved in work with parents and children for a variety of reasons. We have all been children and adolescents, and many of us are parents. So we have our own experiences and prejudices; and will be immersed in family matters at both the personal (subjective) and the professional levels. Whatever your reason for being involved, examine your personal motives and underlying assumptions (see page 6). The area of child care is value-laden; certain kinds of problem are particularly sensitive (indeed, threatening) to us. The issue of trying to help people change involves important personal, moral and ethical considerations.

? Do I have the right to intervene? Behaviour therapists (like others who set out to change people) are accused of *controlling* behaviour. Such allegations imply that clients exist in a vacuum of free will before entering an intervention. Behavioural workers (for example) talk, on the one hand, of liberating clients from some of the unwanted controlling forces in their lives, but assume, on the other hand, a freedom of choice when it comes to accepting an intervention. They tend to say, as do other therapists, that if a client requires help and requests it, then help should be provided.

The difficulty with this comforting principle is that people can be *coerced* in ways subtle and unsubtle, tangible and intangible, to 'seek' help. Some clients, for example children, are not in a position to ask for help or (to put it another way), clear enough about the issues (or powerful enough) to reject the offer of help. These matters should be thought through very carefully. Advocacy – speaking up for the child – will be an important part of your work. Indeed, advocacy on behalf of hard-pressed, demoralized mothers will be another.

? What is my support system? Working in a team provides an ideal support system. It is important to have people around you to back you up, share ideas, stimulate and challenge you. You may require supervision from an experienced practitioner if you are learning to use a specialized approach like family therapy or behaviour modification. If these caveats sound rather daunting then do remember the positives: your potential to help individuals and families in distress (we have many effective methods to choose from) and the support you can give to your colleagues. This support may be 'moral' – when a colleague feels that he or she has failed with a client; it may be 'technical' – a word of advice or a different and perhaps more objective perspective on the case.

Enthusiasm is an important 'therapeutic ingredient', enhancing (as long as it does not go 'over the top') the effectiveness of the intervention. You need to believe in what you are doing. Confidence is antitherapeutic only when it becomes dogmatic certainty or impedes the professional's willingness to evaluate his or her work and change tack when a strategy is not working.

Chapter 8

The Intervention: Preliminaries, Planning and Implementation

PRELIMINARIES

No one profession has all the skills with which to remedy the range of problems we have been looking at in Parts 1 and 2. Social workers are likely to be heavily engaged, often because of their statutory responsibilities. Members of primary care teams – GPs, nurses and health visitors – are also in the front line. At times several professionals may be engaged in a family's life and problems; so it may be good practice to identify a key worker who coordinates and monitors a complex situation which, otherwise, might become confused because everyone thinks someone else is doing x, y or z.

Cultural factors

Ethnocentricity in clinical and social work practice can lead to embarrassment, and worse if ideologies and methods are in conflict with deeply held cultural and/or religious beliefs. Let us take two examples, one from Asia, another from Africa, to illustrate how the bonding doctrine – an issue we dealt with in Chapter 7 – if applied insensitively by doctors and nurses, can have disturbing repercussions. We should note how, in some Asian communities, mothers are considered unclean for the first three days after birth and close physical contact with the baby is avoided. The infant is handled by a close relative of the mother or father, depending on local custom. Some immigrant parents could feel intense conflict over 'bonding procedures'. Then again women from certain parts of Ghana are said to 'lie between life and death' when in labour. The period of confinement is regarded as an anxious time because it is widely believed that a newborn baby may in fact be a spirit child and not a human child at all. If it is a spirit child, it will return to the spirits before a week is out:

121

thus for the first seven days (in some areas, three days for a boy, or four for a girl) mother and child are confined to the room in which the birth took place. If the child dies during that time it is assumed that it was a spirit child. The body is mutilated and buried in pot, to prevent its return in similar circumstances. *The parents are not allowed to mourn its loss* but should show signs of joy at being rid of such an unwelcome guest. It is possible to see the 'adaptive' element in such cultural beliefs; they may help parents to come to terms with death, especially in areas where there are high infant mortality rates. This is speculative; what *is* more certain is that when it comes to making decisions about arrangements for birth, possible bereavement, and early child care, the primary consideration should be the well-being of parents and child, and a sensitivity to their personal and cultural values.

What resources are available?

Parents and members of the community are important resources. Other sources of support are the:

- social worker
- health visitor
- district nurse
- general practitioner
- school counsellor/pastoral teacher
- head/deputy head teacher (or year head)
- educational or clinical psychologist
- teacher
- educational welfare officer
- psychiatrist
- child and family guidance (psychiatric clinic)
- probation officer
- youth/commnunity worker
- priest/vicar/minister
- citizens' advice bureau
- marriage guidance counsellor
- psychotherapist
- CRUSE (widowed parents)
- Gingerbread (single parents)
- police.

It is useful for workers to attend as many workshops and courses on family work as possible in order to learn and test new techniques and strategies. One advantage of working in a team is that members can pool and share their learning.

Communicating with clients

The language you will encounter in your work could range from adult speech through teenage slang, to baby talk. There is a great deal of power in language, and most parents and young people are not familiar with technical terminology. So don't put them at a disadvantage. At the same time guard against the embarrassingly artificial tone of voice and speech styles some people adopt with children (and the very elderly.).

Collect your own examples and metaphors which aid clients in obtaining a vivid idea or mental picture of an important concept.

Examples:

I tell my clients to imagine that their child has an L plate on his or her back to remind them to be patient and tolerant when the child makes a mistake or forgets a lesson. They are, after all *learners* about life.

I remind them of the time they learned to ride a bike and had first managed to gain balance. They continued to have a *wobble* and occasionally fell off. When we imagine a child has mastered a new skill (for example, not wetting his or her bed), there is still likely to be a failure or two – representing the 'wobble' at the top of the learning curve.

Reviewing goals

You would be wise to carry out a careful review of *goals* which have been negotiated and agreed with your clients.

As a reminder:

☐   Goals are the changes to be sought. The goal tells you how the 'target behaviour' (the focus of therapeutic attention) is to be changed: whether the aim is to increase, decrease, maintain, develop, or expand the target behaviours.

☐   Prior to designing a programme a goal should be translated into a set of behavioural objectives.

     A behavioural objective specifies:

(i)   the desired behaviour

(ii)   the situation in which it should occur

(iii)   the criteria for deiciding whether the behavioural goal has been reached.

Here is an example:

Target behaviour = teasing brother.

Goal = play with brother without teasing him.

Behavioural objective = play with brother without teasing him, in the absence of mother.

Monitoring change

Not all interventions lend themselves to the measurement of behaviour change *per se*. The goals – particularly if the intervention involves a counselling approach – may require an evaluation of a rather more subjective (self-report) kind. Carole Sutton and I (at the Centre for Behavioural Work with Families) have been attempting to develop methods which encompass the subtle complexities of clients' thoughts and feelings without sacrificing the requirement of rigorous monitoring of their progress.

At every session it is our practice to invite people to indicate on (for example) a –5 to +5 scale (see Figure 7) how they feel they are progressing towards the agreed goals. What we may perceive as 'progress' is not always felt to be so by the client. Sometimes our own feelings of pessimism are contradicted by the client's reporting a renewed feeling of confidence and of being able to cope.

Parental involvement. The extent to which parents (or others) will be involved in the specification of behavioural objectives, observing and

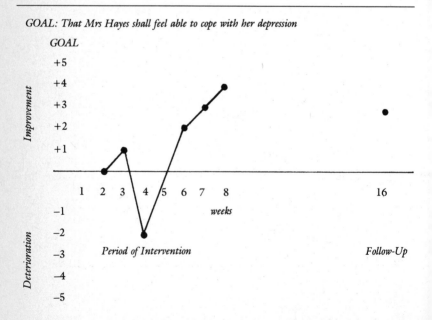

Figure 7. An example of goal-setting and evaluation by the client. (*From C. Sutton, 1987, with permission.*)

recording and implementing, an intervention plan will vary, according to the setting in which the difficulties most often present themselves, and with whom. A programme may involve work in the consulting room, classroom or institution, the parental home, or even on the neighbourhood street, and the use of specific techniques by a professional, a significant adult, or the child itself.

PLANNING THE INTERVENTION

The flow chart below is a general guide only to the intervention and some of the points of procedure you need to bear in mind.

Flow Chart 2: FROM PLANNING TO IMPLEMENTATION

PLANNING	PHASE 1
Step 1	Consider informal and/or direct solutions
Step 2	Accentuate the positive
Step 3	Consider the wishes of those around the client
Step 4a	Begin with problems where success is likely
Step 4b	Select relevant areas of change
Step 5	Choose your intervention
Step 6	Monitor your client's progress

IMPLEMENTATION	PHASE II
Step 7	Implement the intervention
Step 8	Review your intervention
Step 9	Gradually fade out the programme

FOLLOW-UP	PHASE III
Step 10	Conduct a follow-up exercise

PHASE I: PLANNING

Step 1: **Consider informal and/or direct solutions**.
Before going further with a formal intervention, consider whether informal and/or direct approaches are worth trying. These may include:

- ☐ medical or physical examinations – for example, a hearing defect may result in a child being viewed as disobedient and difficult;
- ☐ changing a child's bedtime routine may make him or her more likely to stay in bed and go to sleep;
- ☐ separating two children who disrupt classroom activities;
- ☐ giving children responsibility may encourage them to behave more responsibly;
- ☐ direct requests to change may be effective – for example, telling a child firmly that his teasing is causing upset to his sister and that he *must* stop.

Step 2: **Make the first priority for your clients the acquisition or strengthening of positive actions.**
It is generally easier to develop new behaviours/attitudes than to eliminate them.

Step 3: **Consider the wishes of those in the client's environment.**
This is particularly important if they are suffering as a result of the behaviour and have a potential part to play in a programme.

Step 4(a): **Begin with those problems that have a high probability of being successfully changed.**
With success, the incentive to take on more difficult or complex behaviours will be enhanced.

(b) **Select areas of change which are relevant to the individual.**
If changed, the client's new actions are likely to be encouraged and maintained.

Step 5: **Select your intervention approach (and specific methods).**
The choice is wide and confusing. Some of the options are listed in Chapters 9 to 12. Whatever method you use it is desirable to monitor your client's progress.

Step 6: **Monitor ('track') your client's progress (or lack of it).**
Choose a method of measuring or assessing the behaviour that reliably estimates the extent of the problem, which can be used conveniently, and which does not involve redundant information. Although there are various sophisticated procedures for assessing behaviour, for most programmes straightforward and simple methods are adequate.

The three main methods of assessing behaviour are by rating the difficulties (see Figure 3b), recording how often the behaviour occurs (known as frequency counting or event recording and illustrated in Table 10).

Table 10. Event recording of parent–child interactions (From Iwaniec, 1983, with permission.)

Visit No: _____   Recorder: _____   Name of Client: _____

Child's reactive and proactive behaviour	Often	Occasionally	Never
1. Playing freely			
2. Laughing, smiling			
3. Running			
4. Talking freely			
5. Comes for help			
6. Comes for comfort			
7. Cuddles up to mother/father			
8. Responds to affection			
9. Responds to attention			
10. At ease with parents near him/her			
11. Joins in the activity with other children			
12. Is frightened when approached or corrected by the parent			

Mother's/Father's reactive and proactive behaviour	Often	Occasionally	Never
1. Talking to the child			
2. Looking at the child			
3. Smiling at the child			
4. Eye contact (loving)			
5. Touching (gently)			
6. Holding (closely, lovingly)			
7. Playing			
8. Cuddling			
9. Kissing			
10. Sitting him/her on lap			
11. Handling him/her in a gentle way			
12. Giving requests (as opposed to harsh commands)			
13. Helping him/her if in difficulties			
14. Encouraging him/her to participate in play and other activities			
15. Being concerned about him/her			
16. Responding in a nurturant manner when he/she cries or when hurt			
17. Answering his/her questions			
18. Ignoring his/her presence			
19. Even-handed with the children			

PHASE II: IMPLEMENTATION

Step 7: **Implement the intervention**.

Begin your intervention. Keep a close watch on what happens in the early stages to ensure that the programme is being followed correctly and any unforeseen problems that arise are dealt with quickly. This may mean contact by visiting or phone with the parents every two or three days in the first week or so.

Data collection begun in the baseline period continues throughout the intervention period.

Step 8: **Review your intervention**.

In the light of the data collected relating to the target behaviour(s), or any other objective information, it may be necessary to modify or change the intervention in some way. In the case of behavioural work the programme is *flexible* and if the chosen target behaviour is not changing after a reasonable period of time (e.g. a fortnight – although there is no set time), review all aspects of the work.

One of the features of behavioural work is that it is 'an approach' rather than a technique. This means that if your intervention is not working, examine most carefully the behaviour of all participants and the programme, and change (if necessary) some features of the in-tervention. If you have the 'story' about the 'why's' and 'wherefores' of the case right (see Chapters 11 – 12) any difficulties are likely to be traced to the application of the approach rather than the approach *per se*.

Ask the following questions:

(i) Are there powerful competing reinforcers or interfering factors in the client's environment operating against the programme? Can these be modified?

(ii) Are the reinforcers well chosen and effective?

(iii) Is the parent working effectively and being reinforced for his or her participation?

(iv) Are the behavioural objectives realistic? Are they within the client's repertoire?

(v) Have you proceeded too quickly? Is it necessary to go back to an earlier stage in the intervention plan?

Step 9: **Phase out and terminate treatment**.

Do this with care: the durability of any improvements may depend upon it. The decision to terminate treatment should be made jointly with your client. The time for the programme to end depends upon the goals established at the beginning of treatment. Mind you, new (or elaborated) goals may emerge during the intervention.

Try to ensure natural, intermittent reinforcement in the child's different settings. A guideline is to teach only those behaviours which will continue to be rewarded after training, provided they are adaptive in the sense of contributing to the child's effectiveness and well-being, and that of the community.

PHASE III: FOLLOW-UP
Contact your client(s) to check on the maintenance over time ('temporal generalization') of the improvements they made.

Step 10: **Conduct a follow-up exercise**.
You may find the following questions useful in a semi-structured interview.

- When did the programme end? . . . . How long did it take? . . . .
- How would you describe the situation with X now?
- What were your original 'target' behaviours?
- Have any of these behaviours re-occurred? (frequency)
- How badly? (intensity)
- When, where and how often?
- How would you describe your relationship with X now?
- Do you still worry about X?
- Do you now feel more in 'control' than you did before?
- Do you spend more time playing and talking with X?
- Do you find it easier to praise X than you did before?
- Has the amount of physical contact between X and yourself changed more/less?
- Has your relationship with your other children changed?
- Have X's relationship with his/her brothers and sisters changed?
- Has X's father changed in his attitude to X?
- Has X's behaviour towards his/her father changed?
- Do you feel that your relationship with your husband has changed?
- Do you think the programme worked/failed?
- Who or what made it work/fail?
- How would you describe your relationship with the therapist?

AN ILLUSTRATION OF AN INTERVENTION

We left Avril's family on page 49; we decided to initiate an intervention. Her mother now takes up the story.

    CC From the beginning of the psychologist's visits my feelings were mixed! First of all there was a feeling of relief. Something was at last being done. Something concrete. I was going to be helped. For a short while I felt euphoric . . . but I was defensive as well because I knew that I must accept a certain responsibility for the way Avril was. I did not want to do that. I had had enough of failure. But I recognized I would have to face up to the truth if I went ahead with a management programme. It was quite a struggle at times and my pride took quite a battering. I was very pleased that all the work in the programme was going to take place in the home. It seemed natural and logical that it should. **""**

There were problems in initiating the programme as Avril's mother says:

""*At the beginning of Dr H's intervention, however, I was unable to cooperate effectively. I was desperately unhappy and depressed with no clear understanding of how I came to be so. Each day I moved through a suffocating fog of failure, frustration and guilt. Myself I saw as an unattractive and undesirable individual. I felt that my intellect had atrophied. My daily round of housework and child-rearing held no rewards, but left me bored and exhausted. Against this background a natural shyness had developed into a real fear of going out and talking to people. The fear of rejection was greater than the fact of loneliness. My home had become a prison. Because of these feelings Dr H. decided to work on two levels: with the family on Avril's management programme and with myself – a total lack of social and personal confidence with its resulting social isolation for the children as well as myself; the accumulating anger from failing to cope with her. The angry feelings gradually eased as Avril's programme progressed and I learned to express the resentment I felt when she misbehaved, but in a more controlled manner, by giving appropriate commands. We discussed my parent's way of bringing me up and how it had influenced my attitudes. The hardest problem to deal with was the self-doubt and isolation. Being depressed for several years and feeling inadequate had eroded my self-confidence and produced a profound dislike for myself. It was necessary to change that before I could look up and outwards.*

Dr H. asked me to role-play as a means of learning new ways of coping with my fears and suspicions of people. I started by writing a self-portrait. Dr H. took each point and changed it to some extent. Where I was serious, introverted, careful, I was to be rather more spontaneous and impulsive, even a little frivolous – without 'overdoing' it. I was to think and act like an attractive woman; in fact we created a different 'persona' and role to my usual ones, but not too far out to make the task impossible. We went over it in great detail like a script.

The next step was not easy. What I had to do was go out and live my role daily. It was certainly very difficult at first. I felt like a second-rate actor with severe stage-fright. But the remarkable thing was how it gradually became easier; and when the results were good I felt elated. I discovered casual conversations with local mothers, in the park or at the shops, soon unearthed common interests and I gradually developed new friendships with women in similar circumstances to myself, all with children for Avril and Stella to play with. For the first time since Avril's birth we were making regular visits outside the immediate family. Social skills are like any other, the more practice you get the better you become. As my confidence grew with each success so Avril also relaxed and she began to look forward to these visits eagerly.

Throughout this period, during which there were regularly held discussions about my own situation and problems, we also worked with Mrs — (a social worker) on Avril's problems. 》》

Selection of goals for treatment

Treatment objectives were negotiated between the therapists and the parents. The first goal was to increase adaptive behaviours in certain specified situations, as identified by the parents, with the main aim of creating opportunities for Avril to win positive reinforcement for socially apropriate behaviour. There were four specified situations, one of which was tidying up her toys. The second goal was to reduce the frequency of five target behaviours specified during assessment: (1) non-compliance, (2) aggression, (3) whining, (4) commanding, (5) tantrums. All were carefully defined.

It should be noted that the introduction of the positive side of the programme (rewards) was not a smooth one. There arose a series of disputations between mother or father and Avril about incentives (see page 50). It was evident that we had planned a reward system which contained several loopholes as far as a perceptive and resourceful entrepreneur like Avril was concerned. As so often happens in behavioural programmes, we had to think again. A detailed plan was worked out with regard to the behaviours that the parents wished to encourage. A more careful contract was designed, one which specified precisely how the parents were to respond. The parents and therapist spent much time going over precisely what both parents were going to say when they issued commands to her. What came through very forcibly was that both parents tended to indulge in an internal debate when action was required (for example, the removal of Avril from the room, the technique called 'time-out'). They would silently argue with themselves 'Should I?' or 'Shouldn't I?' before they gave Avril a command. They were often reluctant to carry through a threatened (i.e. promised) sanction, feeling 'sorry' for her or guilty afterwards. The author's ploy in cases like this is to ask the parents if they would break a promise to give

their child a treat. The inevitable denial and explanation of the importance that a child should trust one's words, invites a discussion about
breaking promises about punishment and the consequent debasement of
the currency of words (and trust).

Precise cues were suggested to the mother so that she might avoid
these agonizing dilemmas and so she could act at the right time in a
decisive manner. Authoritative commands, it was hoped, would nip
Avril's target behaviours in the bud and prevent their unpleasant repercussions. On the consequential side, it was suggested that when she tried
her delaying strategies, at the point of implementing time-out, she was
to be picked up, with no eye-contact and no verbal communication, and
placed in the hall (for three minutes), thus eliminating the attention she
was gaining from her diversions. The response to this detailed plan was
encouraging and the frequency of some of the target behaviours began
to diminish.

A critical point came at about the sixth week of the programme. Mrs
Hayes became very despondent about the programme, feeling that
Avril's target behaviour of aggression was not responding to her efforts.
But despite the protestations, hostility and resentment that she expressed to the therapist, she persevered. Reinforcement (in the form of
encouragement and praise) are as important to the mediators of change
in the child (her parents) as to the problem child herself. After all, they
are being asked to change 'addictive' (reinforced) habits, and are in a
learning situation too.

The frequency of the target behaviours decreased gradually. The
record showed that from baseline frequency, non-compliance had reduced by 54 per cent; aggression had fallen by 68 per cent; tantrums by
95 per cent; commanding by 94 per cent; and whining by 100 per cent.
Whining responded most swiftly to systematic ignoring (see Figure 8).

By the end of the programme there was an average occurrence for
both non-compliance and aggression of less than one per day. As Avril's
positive behaviours increased, there were more opportunities for the
parents to 'enjoy' her which in themselves stimulated a high degree of
mutual social reinforcement.

TERMINATION

This phase came at the end of 12 weeks of treatment. Mrs Hayes faded
out the token reinforcement programme but retained the use of positive social reinforcement (on an intermittent schedule – that is, an
occasional basis – consistent with real life) and the occasional use of

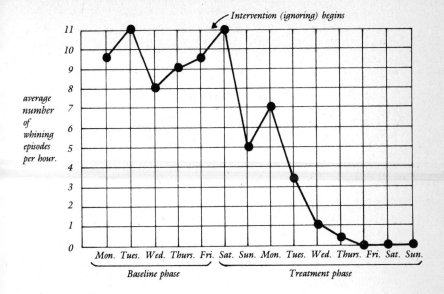

Figure 8. A graphical record of progress in treatment

time-out as a back-up to her now generally effective verbal control. The goals that were selected for treatment were achieved to the satisfaction of both parents. This expression of satisfaction which was confirmed by the monitoring of Avril's behaviours constituted the main criteria for terminating the case. As a by-product of the programme, Avril now gave the appearance of being a far happier child to the therapist (and more important) to her parents and their relatives. Mrs Hayes no longer looked the harrassed woman of the not too distant past. She now had a lightness in the presentation of her personality.

FOLLOW-UP

A series of checks by telephone and visits indicated that Avril maintained her improvement for 12 months (our standard follow-up period). Mrs Hayes felt that she had successfully reintroduced the programme for short periods as and when it was necessary. She experienced a setback when she let her criteria slip and began to take the line of least resistance. A booster programme was contemplated, but within a week of going back to recording, Mrs Hayes found that she had the situation in hand, and the need for an intervention disappeared.

Summary and comment

This chapter outlined the ten steps common to many interventions. There is no one way (or set order) for doing these things – preliminaries, planning and initiation – but they may prove helpful to those who wish to work to a systematic plan. The importance of the key worker is stressed; and the need for sensitivity to cultural nuances illustrated with examples from Asian and African attitudes to birth and death. Resources which are likely to be of help to you and your client are listed.

The chapter contains a case illustration which provides the reader with an insight into what it feels like to be involved in an intervention – in the mother's own words. Many of the details of therapy – the selection of goals, their monitoring, the programme itself and its termination – are provided.

Chapter 9

The 'How' Question: Helping People to Change

This chapter on how to help clients – the question of approaches – is written with several professions (but most particularly social work) in mind. One of the main difficulties for those who work with families is to find a reasonably clear, signposted path through the 'jungle' of claims and counterclaims, contradictions and ambiguities, concerning the best way of going about things. Which approach do I use, and when? There is a bewildering array of choices including: *family therapy* (there are enough variations of approach here to puzzle practitioners); *behaviour modification*; *counselling*; various brands of *psychotherapy*; *cognitive therapy*; *skills training*; and many others. Is it a case of horses for courses? If so, which horse for which course? The literature is not always helpful or easy to get hold of.

Is it best to be eclectic or is eclecticism somewhat disreputable in psychological circles? If it is, it shouldn't be; psychology has been forced to abandon general (i.e. all-encompassing) theories of human action in favour of more modest, middle-range theories dealing with *different* aspects of psychological functioning (for example, learning, cognition, personality). Even these theories tend to be fragmented and contentious. So why should practitioners eschew an *informed* eclecticism? The trouble is that eclecticism so often degenerates into a ragbag, unsystematic approach – a choice of what is fashionable, seems easy, or 'feels comfortable', as opposed to what is theoretically coherent and empirically supported.

The task of helping a family can be a dauntingly broad one, encompassing (for the social worker) concerns ranging from poor housing and the need for day care for a worker, to marriage guidance and 'systematic desensitization' (see page 170) for a phobic child. The practitioner's role might consist of being a resource-mobilizer, helper, friend, adviser, teacher, therapist or counsellor, and possessor of expert know-how of strategies for social action. Such diversification calls for a remarkably flexible response on the part of the practitioner. The scope of the analysis and level of intervention can also range widely, from the large grouping (the neighbourhood or community) through the small group (the family), the couple (parents as partners) to the particular individual (say child).

This is not only a book about social work as such, but there is room to underline the importance in any intervention of mobilizing *human* resources – activating or re-activating helpers, friends and social networks. There is evidence that a network of supportive persons (and the quality and intimacy of the support provided) can mitigate the effects of stress.

MOBILIZING HUMAN RESOURCES

A professional can assist his or her clients by putting them in touch with people, clubs, specialized self-help groups (and, indeed, other resources). Surveys have shown that one important way in which people cope with their problems is to turn to family and friends rather than to professionals for help and they, in turn, act as a buffer against some of the harmful effects of stress. As social networks, ties and contacts promote psychological well-being, it is important for the professional to identify their presence or absence for the client. Ascertain the frequency and intimacy (the meaningfulness/emotional intimacy) of this support for your clients using the rating scale in Table 11.

Intimate or close relationships of the type provided by primary groups (those people with whom one has face-to-face interaction and a sense of commitment) are the most significant sources of support. The supportiveness of relationships is reflected by the availability of:

- emotional support (the expression of liking, respect, etc.)
- aid (material assistance, services, guidance, advice)
- social companionship
- affirmation (the expression of agreement)
- social regulation (appropriate roles support such as mothering, fathering, partnership – husband/wife/companion, etc.).

Different kinds of support are helpful for different life crises. And the particular persons and circumstances involved in a potentially disruptive life event determine what is likely to be most effective. The support of peers and encouragement at work are positively related to well-being in men but not (in general) women; cohesiveness and supportiveness

Table 11. Sources of support and intimacy

	Frequency					Meaningfulness (importance)				
	Never	Hardly ever	Quite often	Often	Always (regularly)	None	A little	Quite a lot	A lot	Of great significance
a partner	0	1	2	3	4	0	1	2	3	4
parents	0	1	2	3	4	0	1	2	3	4
other relatives	0	1	2	3	4	0	1	2	3	4
children	0	1	2	3	4	0	1	2	3	4
friends	0	1	2	3	4	0	1	2	3	4
neighbours	0	1	2	3	4	0	1	2	3	4
colleagues/ work- mates	0	1	2	3	4	0	1	2	3	4
other parents	0	1	2	3	4	0	1	2	3	4
acquaint- ances	0	1	2	3	4	0	1	2	3	4

How often can you expect help and support from:	How meaningful/significant is the help and support you get from:

within the family are positively related to the well-being of women but not men. A confiding relationship with a man is a protective factor for a woman warding off depression in the face of distressing life events.

MARITAL WORK

There has been a lot of research into the adjustments required of married couples, into the conflicts, manipulations and changes that take place in the course of a marital relationship. The emphasis on conflict and manipulation is somewhat misleading. The evident fact is that in many ongoing marriages there is great deal of interaction which is playful, complementary and joyous, as well as much that is hostile. The fact that most marriages survive, and are judged to be happy, indicates that the majority of adjustments are fairly satisfying.

A process of bargaining may underlie some of the similarities in marriages of long duration. It is one of the great platitudes – part of popular wisdom – that marriage is a matter of give and take. We saw, in Chapter 4, that people initiate and prolong relationships of intimacy as long as those relationships are reasonably satisfactory with regard to what are called their 'rewards' and 'costs'. In marital interactions the *social exchange* model helps us to assess (in part) what is going wrong with a partnership. For example, immature individuals are not always able to manage the give-and-take of friendship. What is called 'exchange theory' gives us pointers to why this should be so; it also provides *one* method of improving people's social attractiveness and their relationships. In this theoretical model, social interactions and relationships are compared to economic bargains or the exchange of gifts. All activities carried out by one individual, to the benefit of another, are termed 'rewards', while detrimental activities – hostility and anxiety – are seen as 'costs'.

A notable feature of a partnership that is 'working' is the balance in the relationship that exists between the partners, often called 'status symmetry'. It concerns the mutual respect and lack of dominance and exploitation which characterize intimate and lasting relationships. In friendly or loving relationships there is an overall balance in the influence of each of the participants.

It is useful to draw up a balance sheet. On the debit side, the term 'cost' is applied to deterrents that may be incurred in contacts with another person – such as criticism, neglect, hostility, anxiety, embarrassment, and the like. For attraction to another individual to occur (or to be maintained) the reward-cost outcome must be above the 'comparison level', a standard against which *satisfaction* is judged.

In this model marital discord is dealt with by redistributing (with the help of a contract) prevailing rates of reinforcement (satisfaction) and punishment (dissatisfaction) within the relationship. Individuals are encouraged – following discussion, negotiation and (hopefully) compromise – to maximize satisfactions (the positives) while minimizing the dissatisfaction (mutually irritating behaviours) provoked by the couple. This is where *contracts* can be very useful, not only for marital work but for family relationships that are tense and unhappy. An example of a marital – work contract is given in Figure 9.

FAMILY THERAPY

This is a very fashionable approach in Child and Family Clinics/Centres. There is no one 'family therapy' but several 'schools', such as *analytic*, *strategic* and *structural* family approaches. Family therapy is concerned (among other matters) with helping families to move from entrenched habits of behaving and interacting which preclude them from finding solutions to the problems that are currently confronting them. They are

CONTRACT between James and Nell Small

We: (he) and   (she) have decided together to improve our relationship and with that in view we have jointly agreed to do our level best to put into practice the following rules and to monitor progress. In doing this our goal is (i) to make changes in our behaviours and attitudes; and (ii) to become more aware of our own (and our partner's) point of view. We will make the following changes:

He

1. Be more ready to say sorry,
2. Control my irritability and temper.
3. Show more interest in my wife's appearance.
4. Sit down for a chat for at least half-an-hour when I get home from work.
5. Refrain from making fun of her friends and church activities.
6. Help with jobs around the house.

She

1. Stop interfering when he corrects the child.
2. Be more relaxed about things.
3. Show more interest in my husband's work.
4. Be more ready to forgive and forget.
5. Be willing to make physical contact (e.g. not to pull away when he holds my hand, puts his arm around me).
6. Remember to check that there is petrol in the car.

We do not guarantee 100 per cent success at first, but we are committed to trying to make things work. In the case of rules being broken we agree to sit down and go over the particular disappointing incident *calmly*.

We also agree to keep a record of progress.

Signed --------------------- (He)

--------------------- (She)

Figure 9. A sample contract

encouraged by a variety of therapeutic strategies and homework tasks to think, feel and act differently.

In order to understand the family pattern across the generations (the extended family) and the alliances, conflicts and attachments within the family unit, clients are encouraged to look at themselves from a fresh perspective and to try alternative solutions to their dilemmas. The *structural* approach to producing family change is associated with (among others) the name Salvador Minuchin, and the Philadelphia Child Guidance Clinic. The focus of attention is very much on the developmental tasks faced by the family and its members at various stages of its (and their) life-span. Day-to-day patterns of relationship – communication and interaction – between members are inferred from highly charged or repetitive sequences observed and analysed in the therapy room. You can see from all of this that the therapeutic task is defined in far broader terms than the individual – be it parent or child. The child – brought to the clinic as the 'patient' or 'client' by the parents – would be viewed as one part of a complex network of personal and family relationships.

Family therapists see the total network of family transactions as greater than the sum of its parts, hence their rejection of the parents' labelling of a problem as 'my son's/daughter's problem' as simplistic. The family system is viewed as the total functioning of three subsystems (spouses: parents and children: children alone) – all contained within a defined *boundary* and, in turn, operating within a social-cultural context.

The family changes continuously. For example, as children grow into adolescents they bring new elements into the family system. The peer group gains more influence. The youngster learns that friends' families work by different standards and rules. The teenage culture introduces its values with regard to sex, religion, politics and drugs. Parents, too, are changing in ways that I described in Chapter 3.

The structural family therapist's first step is to 'join' with the family, to participate in its transactions and observe members' roles, their communications, and the boundaries within the family and between the family system and other systems. The family 'organism', like the individual person, moves between two poles: one representing the security of the known, the other being the exploration necessary for adaptation to changing conditions. When the family comes to treatment, it is in difficulty because it is stuck, trying to maintain old ways which no longer meet the needs of a changed and changing set of circumstances. The therapist takes a family (according to Minuchin) 'along the developmental spiral and creates a crisis that will push the family in the direction of their own evolution'.

The approach involves the therapist as an energetic *intruder*. He or she works actively to restructure family organization and channels of communication by modelling, direction and the use of 'action techniques'. The techniques for creating crisis or 'creative turmoil' and for putting the family on to a new and harmonious path (thus enhancing the potential for growth of each of its members) are many and varied.

There is a basic sequence through which family therapy passes. Andy Treacher describes it as follows:

▶ *The Joining Phase*. The family and the therapist are originally isolated from each other. But therapists use their skills so that they become absorbed into the family through a process of accommodation. This process creates a new system – family and therapist. It may take several sessions to create the new system, but since it is essentially a transitory one therapists carefully monitor any signs that family members are going to drop out of therapy and thus disrupt the new system.

▶ *The Middle Therapy Stage*. This is the phase during which the major restructuring 'work' occurs. Restructuring interventions are made during sessions and consolidating homework tasks are set between sessions.

▶ *The Termination Stage*. This phase involves testing the family's ability to 'fire' the therapist and go it alone. The 'ghost' of the therapist is left behind by getting the family to simulate its ability to solve new problems and to deal with old problems if they recur.

▶ *The Follow-up*. A follow-up session after three months, six months or a year enables the therapist to evaluate the impact of therapy and test whether it has been successful in achieving second order change, which means enabling family rules and family functioning to change in such a way that the family generates effective solutions to problems.

Before looking at techniques we need to address the question of the manner in which the family members are seen – all together (on every occasion or occasionally), in differing combinations and permutations, or individually. The emphasis – some would say over-emphasis – on the use of *conjoint* family therapy (i.e. seeing all the family members together) as an exclusive means of therapeutic intervention – arises from a restricted and narrow definition of the systems approach.

Andy Treacher and John Carpenter, in their useful book *Using Family Therapy* (an exploration of family therapy and its various applications) criticize some family therapists for their failure to consider the significance of wider social systems. Such therapists, by their concentration on therapy with nuclear families within clinical settings have allowed their vision of family therapy to become myopic.

The family replaces the individual as the locus of pathology; its social context is ignored, and it is 'assumed that all its problems can be easily revealed to the gaze of a group of therapists who cluster behind a one-way screen'. These authors maintain that such a narrow approach to understanding change within a family system cannot be defended at a theoretical level.

Change is often best effected by an intervention at another system level. For example, a worker who is attempting to produce change in a family which is experiencing many problems may be better advised to assist in the formation of a housing action group, designed to influence the housing department, than to concentrate on a more limited goal of defining boundaries between the members of a family who are crowded into a small, damp and decaying flat at the top of a tower block with no working lifts (page 4)

They go on to make the important point that family therapy and individual counselling and psychotherapy have been unhelpfully polarized. The skills of working *individually* with members of a family are often indispensable to the systems approach – especially when the therapeutic task is to help an individual detach himself or herself from the family system.

Techniques

There is space for only a brief description of a few techniques of structural family therapy:

- *Enactment* is the direct illustration by the clients (as opposed to mere description) of the problems that exist between them. Clients are encouraged, where appropriate, to talk directly to one another rather than to (or through) the therapist.

- *Boundary clarification*. The creation or clarification of boundaries between family members is a feature of structural work. A mother who babies her teenager may hear with surprise her daughter's response to the question 'How old do you think your mother treats you as – three or 13?'

- *Changing space.* Asking clients in the therapy room to move about can intensify an interaction or underline an interpretation being made about a relationship. For example, if a husband and wife never confront one another directly, but always use their child as a mediator or channel of communication, the therapist *blocks* that manoeuvre (called triangulation) by moving the child from between the parents. Here she may comment, 'Let's move Sally from the middle so you can work it out together'.

- *Reframing* is an important method in fulfilling the objective of helping clients change in a covert – less directed – manner. It is an alteration in the emotional or conceptual viewpoint in relation to which a situation is experienced. That experience is placed in another 'frame' which fits the facts of the situation as well (or more plausibly), thereby transforming its entire meaning. Giving people different 'stories' to tell themselves about themselves or about events – stories that are less self-defeating or destructive – is also a feature of behavioural work (see page 165).

Improving Relationships within the Family

All social interaction involves *mutual influence* because of human interdependence and the key role of co-operation in human societies. This influence is most potent when it has its source within a happy and cohesive family. Indeed the presence of family cohesion has a marked effect on the psychological well-being of family members.
- Members spend a fair amount of time in shared activity.
- Withdrawal, avoidance and segregated (separate) activities are rare.
- Interactions that are warm are common and interactions that are hostile are infrequent among members.
- There is full and accurate communication between members of the family.
- Valuations of other members of the family are generally favourable; critical judgements are rare.
- Individuals tend to perceive *other* members as having favourable views of them.
- Members are visibly affectionate.
- They show high levels of satisfaction and morale, and are optimistic about the future stability of the family group.

When these features are absent, the family members who are particularly at risk are those already vulnerable for other reasons: the young, the elderly, those coping with stress such as hospitalization, alcohol dependence, or caring for a large number of children. The list above indicates areas on which you might focus in order to encourage more cohesive activities and attitudes. Contracting – mentioned already and discussed more fully later in this chapter – could facilitate such an objective.

A SOCIAL LEARNING APPROACH TO FAMILY VIOLENCE

Concern about aggression and violence in society, both outside and within the family, has reached such a pitch that a note of despair, and sometimes hysteria, is now common in the media.

As a general principle, we can confidently claim that the maintenance of aggressive behaviour is largely dependent on its consequences (see page 52). Aggressive actions that have 'rewarding' consequences (and this might include 'letting off steam' by a frustrated parent) tend to be repeated, whereas those that are unrewarded or punished are generally discarded.

Coercive Families. In what have been called coercive families the cues or messages are frequently negative ones, with the 'sound and fury' of criticism, nagging, crying, shouting, hitting and so on. Communication between members may not be so much aversive as impoverished or practically non-existent. Sitting down to *negotiate* a contract with members of the family facilitates communications, and introduces them to an important means of resolving interpersonal conflicts and tensions of the kind that arise in the families – discussion, negotiation, compromise.

It is all very well to negotiate a contract, but what goes into it? We have to remember that coercive family systems which permit behaviour control by the use of pain are quite likely to produce children who exhibit frequent ('high rate') aggressive actions. Negative reinforcement is most likely to operate in certain closed social systems where the child must learn to cope with aversive stimuli such as incessant criticism. In such a family a boy (say) will find that his violent actions (e.g. hitting) *terminate* much of the aversive stimulation – teasing, bullying, etc. – from his brothers and sisters (negative reinforcement); in addition, as many as a third of his coercive behaviours are quite likely to receive a positive payoff, e.g. getting his own way.

In planning your contract or some other intervention (see Appendix 4) you must remember that people rarely show aggression in blind, indiscriminate ways. Rather aggressive (or more extremely violent) actions tend to occur at *certain times*, in *certain settings*, towards *certain individuals* (as objects), and in response to *certain forms of provocation*.

Assess these in terms of contemporary (i.e. current circumstances which

- instigate aggression (*viz* physical or verbal assaults, deprivation, frustration, conflict, exposure to aggressive models (bad examples))
- *maintain aggression* (*viz* direct, vicarious and self-reinforcement).

Your choice of approach might include the following:

▶ *Reduce stimuli which set the stage (so called 'discriminative stimuli') for aggressive behaviour*

The absence of a supervising adult may be the signal for a child to threaten or hit another in order to take away (say) his or her toy. This would be a rewarding consequence for the dominant child. Better organized supervision in the playground or home would be one response to this situation.

▶ *Reduce the exposure to aggressive models*

If a child is mixing with a bully who is providing an example of aggressive behaviour it is advisable to detach him or her from this relationship as soon as possible. If parents are modelling (sometimes unwittingly) hostile attitudes and aggressive actions, your target for intervention is as much their behavioural repertoire as that of their offspring.

▶ *Reduce aversive stimuli*

It is crucial to attempt to change the circumstances in which a client's aggressive behaviour stems from frustrating, depriving or provocative experiences instigated by other people or life circumstances. This is easier said than done, but a resourceful professional is often able to mitigate some of the contributory aversive 'triggers'.

▶ *Provide models of non-aggressive behaviour*

If possible, bring children into contact with children who do not adopt aggressive actions to cope with life. You might be able to demonstrate non-aggressive problem-solving by means of role-play or by video demonstrations of similar aged children using such strategies.

▶ *Develop relevant social skills*

There are countless social graces and nuances which make social life easy and pleasurable for all concerned. However, there are many people – children and adults – who lack some of the crucial skills required to cope with life and to solve problems in a constructive and adaptive manner. Aggression may become part of their repertoire for 'righting' perceived wrongs and for getting their own way. Social skills can to an extent, be taught; such issues are dealt with in Chapter 12.

▶ *Apply (if appropriate) methods of desensitization, relaxation and communication training* (see pages 170 and 150).

▶ *Discussion* (see *Groupwork*) if it is honest and defused of rhetoric, can be a potent antidote to misunderstanding and resentment.

In families where parents smack or beat their children for their 'naughty' behaviour, and often as a means of releasing their tensions, there are several things you can discuss with them (assuming that you are assured of the essential safety of the child):
Ensure that the parents' *expectations* of the child are appropriate for his or her age and ability.
Ascertain that their *attributions*, their theories of causation of their child's behaviour (e.g. 'there's a demon inside him'; 'it's her bad blood'; 'she does it because she hates me') are not wildly distorted.
Check whether there are sufficient positive interactions (e.g. play, outings, conversation) and rewards and encouragements.

▶ *Teach the client cognitive self-control strategies* (e.g. self-talk)

Self-talk

Self-talk – a sort of internal monologue – is a major preoccupation of all of us when we are beset with trials and tribulations. 'I can't cope any more . . . I'm in a terrible mess . . . There's no hope . . . Oh, what am I to do?' Such self-talk is accompanied by observable behaviour, e.g. listlessness, weepiness, sleeplessness, social withdrawal, and so on.

To help adolescents (and indeed, parents, at times) we examine and dissect some of the faulty reasoning underlying the self-talk: the exaggeration ('No one loves me . . . there's *no* hope!'), the need to be all-competent, to show no weakness, to be acknowledged and loved *all* the time, to be forever right. Counselling on such illogicalities, the prompting and practising of new self-talk ('I can manage . . . I'm a good mum'; 'Think first, act afterwards . . . keep cool') may bring some relief.

A number of procedures are available for the purposes of controlling impulsive actions; they include self-management by the client of (say) hostile feelings, together with his or her observations of the circumstances in which they occurred and their consequences. You might provide the client with positive self-statements for dealing with anger:

Preparing for provocation

  "This is going to upset me, but I know how to deal with it.
    What it is that I have to do?
I can work out a plan to handle this.
I can manage the situation. I know how to regulate my anger.
If I find myself getting upset, I'll know what to do.
There won't be any need for an argument.
Try not to take this too seriously.
This could be a testing situation, but I believe in myself.
Time for a few deep breaths of relaxation. Feel comfortable, relaxed,
at ease.
Easy does it. Remember to keep your sense of humour.**"**

Reacting during the confrontation

  "Stay calm. Just continue to relax.
    As long as I keep my cool, I'm in control.
Just roll with the punches; don't get bent out of shape.
Think of what you want to get out of this.
You don't need to prove yourself.
There is no point in getting mad.
Don't make more out of this than you have to.
I'm not going to let him get to me.
Look for the positives. Don't assume the worst or jump to
conclusions.
It's really a shame that she has to act like this.
For someone to be that irritable, he must be awfully unhappy.
If I start to get mad, I'll just be banging my head against the wall. So I
might as well just relax.
There is no need to doubt myself. What he says doesn't matter.
I'm on top of this situation and it's under control.**"**

Coping with arousal

  "My muscles are starting to feel tight. Time to relax and slow down.
    Getting upset won't help.
It's just not worth it to get so angry.
I'll let him make a fool of himself.
I have a right to be annoyed, but let's keep the lid on.
Time to take a deep breath.
Let's take the issue point by point.
My anger is a signal of what I need to do. Time to instruct myself.
I'm not going to get pushed around, but I'm not going haywire
either.
Try to reason it out. Treat each other with respect.
Let's try a cooperative approach. Maybe we are both right.
Negatives lead to more negatives. Work constructively.

She'd like me to get really angry. Well I'm going to disappoint her.
I can't expect people to act the way I want them to.**"**
(*From Novaco, 1975 with permission*).

All of the methods described above attend to the 'A' term (antecedent events) in the ABC equation (page 27). The following ones are more to do with the 'C' term (consequent events or outcomes). Procedures based on selective reinforcement (making aggression *unrewarding* or *costly*) can reduce aggressive behaviour. *Some childish aggression (e.g. temper tantrums) may be ignored* (if that is not a dangerous option) when attention has been positively reinforcing. It can be ignored while an incompatible pattern of desirable, prosocial conduct is rewarded and thus encouraged; it may be penalized by methods such as response-cost and time-out (see page 180).

CONTRACTS

Contracts (as we saw briefly on page 138) draw on various ideas and concepts for their rationale. Two theories – exchange theory (which comes from social psychology) and contingency (reinforcement) theory – are most prominent, and give rise to six key concepts.
- Communication
- Negotiation (bargaining)
- Compromise
- Reciprocity
- Expectations (rules)
- Reinforcement

Social psychology tells us that groups which exist for any length of time (and we can think of the family group as a particular example) have a definite communication structure. For example, there tends to be consistency in the number of communications individuals receive, and in the number (and content) of communications they initiate. There is a positive correlation (association) between the frequency of communication ('in' and 'out') and the status of the individual in the group. One can imagine that a powerless member of the family (say, an economically dependent wife) is allowed or able to say very little for herself.

It is important to point out to clients that the *responses* of one individual are the *cues* for the responses of the other, which in turn become cues for the responses of the first. Shout (or whisper) and the other person is likely to shout (or whisper) back. Cues are by definition 'carriers' of information; and transmission of information is the *essence* of communication. So what kind of messages do people give each other – not only in what they say (verbal cues) but what they do or the way in which they say things (non-verbal cues)?

Reciprocal contractual agreements are not unnatural to most people: they exist in families and other groupings, whether explicit or implicit. Many of the problems that arise are due to the arrangements not being reciprocal or explicit enough. Contracts (whether written down or agreed verbally) have the effect of structuring reciprocal exchanges. They specify who is to do what, for whom and under what circumstances; reinforcement contingencies (to take one example) can be made explicit between individuals who wish behaviour to change (e.g. parents, teachers, nurses) and those whose behaviour is to be changed (children, students, clients).

At a time of crisis when marital partners or teenagers and their parents (or indeed brothers and sisters) are at loggerheads, angry and resentful, contracts provide an opportunity for a family to take stock and to break through vicious circles of retribution and unreason.

Contingency agreements are contracts drawn up between two or more people in which a set of mutual expectations is written down detailing reciprocal benefits and the 'costs' or penalties for transgressions. The main assumptions underlying the use of formal verbal agreements or the stronger written form of contract, are as follows:

☐　The publicly endorsed, unambiguous and specific commitment to a future course of action will prove more binding, a better guarantee of compliance, than more casual 'promises' or ephemeral statements of intention (think of those turned-over new leaves at the New Year).

☐　To obtain such results the parties concerned must not feel they have been unduly coerced into their contractual arrangements.

Applications. The following elements of contracting are important for the clients:

• Be very specific in spelling out the desired actions.

• Pay attention to the details of the privileges and conditions for both parties; they should be (a) important as opposed to trivial, (b) functional (if manifested more frequently they will increase the chances of the parties' obtaining from their environment the natural kinds of rewards which most people desire and enjoy).

• If parents wish their youngster (or adults their partner) to desist from certain actions and activities, encourage them to express these in terms of positive change. (For example, if they would like X to stop being so critical and negative they should specify the change they wish to bring about by inviting X to accentuate the positive, the pleasant or praiseworthy. This would then have to be spelled out in terms of specific examples of behaviour – words and deeds). (Reciprocal requirements can be asked of parents or partner.)

- Get parents (or partner) to write down five items of behaviour (actions) they wish their son or daughter (spouse) would do more often.

- Don't let the parties be vague (e.g. 'I wish he'd be more helpful'). Be concrete and specific (e.g. 'I wish he'd help me set and clear the table').

- Parents may want their son to complete his homework and attend school regularly: he, on the other hand, desires more free time with his friends, or more pocket money. A husband may wish his wife would be more attentive; she might like him to be sociable, and so on. Encourage discussion, negotiation and compromise.

See the sample contract.

HELPING YOUR CLIENT AS AN INDIVIDUAL

There are different levels at which you can help your client, ranging from the general (emotional support, information, advice, etc.) to the specific and technical (for example, behaviour therapy). To be in a position to give effective help to your client presupposes
- communication skills
- a good relationship
- mutual trust and understanding
- 'therapeutic' conversational skills.

Communication training. Communication training is one of the more promising of the new behavioural methods which have developed from social skills therapy and assertion training. It is valuable for training professional students in the vital skills of being clear and comprehensible in their work. At the same time it provides them with a method applicable to many of their clients-to-be. The method concentrates on the following:
- A series of exercises which puts the complex skills of communication into their component parts and teaches each of these in a carefully graded sequence to small groups of clients (or trainee social workers).

CONTRACT between Mr and Mrs S — and Anne S —

Mother and father would like Anne to:

1   Let them know about her movements when she goes out at night; Anne will let them know about her movements when she goes out at night by:
    telling them where she is and with whom;
    letting them know when she'll be home.

2   Be less moody; she won't go silent ('sulk') for hours on end when reprimanded or thwarted.

3   Be more ready to say sorry; i.e. she will apologize when she's been in the wrong.

4   Show more concern about her school work (e.g home- work); i.e. she will put in at least an hour per night.

5   Stop being so rude to her father, i.e. walking out when he gives her advice.

Anne would like her father and mother to:

1   Stop criticizing her friends all the time; i.e. stop calling them names and saying they're no good, unless they are making a particular, constructive comment.

2   Admit when they are in the wrong, i.e. they will apologize when they have been in the wrong in their confrontations with her.

3   Give her more pocket money (a sum agreed) and to review the amount every six months in the light of the rising expense and changing nature of her commitments.

All agree

1   That the terms of the contract will not be changed except by mutual discussion and agreement.

2   That disputes will be settled by the witness (grandmother), whom all accept to be objective and fair-minded.

3   That successful execution of the contract for a month will be rewarded by a family treat (first month: an outing to a posh (named) restaurant).

4   That failure to carry out individual terms of the contract will result in a fine on each occasion: an amount of X for Anne; and Y for Mr and Mrs S — respectively. The money is to go in a 'penalty box' (kept by the grand-mother), the proceeds of which will go to a charity of her choice.

Signed Anne ....

Mr S — ....

Mrs S — ....

Grandmother (witness) ....

(*From Herbert, 1987, with permission.*)

- Use of the principles, of modelling, shaping, behavioural rehearsal, and positive reinforcement (see Chapter 11).
- The 'teacher' seeks directly to impart communication skills, to identify blocks in communication, and to overcome these by training clients (students) in more effective methods of interaction.

The good relationship factor. Among the most frequent complaints by parents of the professionals who provide them with services are lack of concern, care and warmth: in other words, the absence of a supportive relationship. This is a particularly sad state of affairs as it is widely held that among the most important qualities associated with 'healing' properties are the therapist's understanding, respect, acceptance, genuineness, empathy and non-possessive warmth. These attributes are stressed in the counselling (client-centred) literature and their effect is related to aspects of the client's well-being or self-esteem.

Whether a trained professional has a monopoly of these qualities (or some unique deployment of them) is thrown into doubt, surely even for those who give most weight to the relationship factor in therapy, by the absence of significant differences in the results of professional as opposed to non- or para-professional helpers. The consistency of positive findings supports the potential value of non-professional assistance. This is good news for those social workers who believe in utilizing community resources (parents and other non- professionals) in the helping endeavour.

Therapeutic conversations/communications. The art of talking (therapeutic conversations or communications) is highly valued in the difficult task of encouraging change in the understanding and actions of adult and young clients. Helping people to discover insights into their mental processes and behaviour, is a well-known feature of therapies.

Psychotherapy. The word psychotherapy means literally 'the treatment of problems of the mind'. The term also implies that treatment is carried out by psychological methods rather than by the use of physical measures such as drugs. Clients do a lot of talking about their lives, their present and past, their personal relationships. Psychotherapists, to a greater or lesser extent, also talk, offering interpretations, reflecting back to the clients their feelings, providing reassurance. Some analyse the so- called transference feelings, that is to say the client's feelings that have their origins in past experience and relationships, but are now displaced on to the person of the therapist.

It is difficult to define psychotherapy in any tidy fashion because so many different theories of personality and viewpoints about the nature of mental problems determine the approach of the particular therapist. One clinician may be a psychoanalytic psychotherapist but even then he or she could be trained in the Freudian, Jungian or some other school. Another may be influenced by the Rogerian ideas of client-centred therapy. Typical problems dealt with by psychotherapies include:

- an avoidance of situations/people/objects one should not have to avoid;
- a sense of emotional turmoil (anger, fear, anxiety, dread, guilt, depression, disgust);
- a feeling of helplessness, of not being fully in control of one's life;
- feelings of unhappiness, distress, misery; vague feelings that life is not being lived as meaningfully, effectively or joyfully as it should be;
- a feeling of having lost control;
- a loss of ability to make decisions;
- a loss of the ability to make choices;
- a loss of the feeling of being real, vital, committed to or enthusiastic about life;
- a sense of conflict, apathy, aimlessness;
- a sense of alienation (with self and/or society);
- a sense of being compelled to do things against one's will.

These problems also lend themselves to an expert behavioural approach. It is crucial in behavioural assessment and treatment to reformulate these complaints in operational terms, i.e. in overt terms of what the client says and does, and in a manner that lends itself to the quantifying of the problem. Such problems are also the 'bread and butter' of counsellors.

Insight. The therapist using insight therapy with older children and adolescents engages in procedures which will give the clients insight into the unconscious meaning of their symptoms, and into the relationship between their motivations and their behaviour. It is assumed that this insight will give greater control over the behaviour. Many of our motives are thought to be unconscious and it is impossible to come to terms with an 'invisible enemy'. The therapist tries to make the invisible visible, the unconscious conscious.

An illustration
"*A problem in which short-term psychotherapy utilized insight and 'ventilation' (the release/expression of suppressed emotion) is the case of Jason who acted in an extremely rebellious, disobedient and aggressive*

manner. His parents could not cope with him. When his innermost thoughts and feelings were tapped by analyzing projective material (his stories and paintings) and by observing his repetitive games with the 'family-group' of dolls, it became apparent that he believed his parents had stopped loving him when his brother was born. He had been the only child for five years and had little understanding that love can be shared rather than monopolized. He had the idea that his mother and father got angry with him and punished him, not because he was being difficult and negativistic, but simply because their feeling toward him had changed and they no longer loved him. His intense jealousy of the baby was not apparent on the surface. His over-zealous attention to the infant — as it appeared — covered feelings of hatred and envy. Not realizing this the parents were not able to cope with the situation. In this case the function of the treatment as it was seen by the therapist was not only to release and interpret the child's feelings, and to educate him about the inclusiveness of love rather than its exclusiveness, but also to help the mother to understand and tolerate the source of her child's anxieties and aggressions 99

If the child is very young, conventional methods of psychotherapy as used with adults are not very suitable. The child is not always able to put anxieties into words. He or she is not always interested in exploring past life or attitudes. Play is a familiar mode of expression for the child and it is deployed by some child psychotherapists as a part-equivalent to 'talking-therapy'.

Play. Whatever the theoretical framework of a particular clinic, it is fairly common practice for children to be made to feel at ease in a playroom in which they can paint, construct things on a sand tray with miniatures, act out dramas with dolls and puppets, be aggressive with guns and choppers, and in fact, give expression to a wide range of feelings and fantasies. The skilled therapist may detect recurrent themes in the child's play, preoccupations which point to conflicts or areas of tension in the family, at school or in some aspect of the child's life which are blocking development.

In its simplest form play therapy is a modifying or reshaping of attitudes and feelings. But the therapist cannot simply sit down with the child and explain the self-defeating nature of his or her attitudes towards self and the environment. The child must come to see for him or herself and to feel within that what he or she is doing is self-defeating and unnecessary. This is not usually achieved over-night. The child's attitudes need to be analysed carefully and on a broad front and not with a superficial, facile and 'pat' formula. Genna, who had a dread of going to school (school phobia) appeared to be afraid of a harsh teacher and a bully in the school. A careful analysis of her personality and home and school background revealed that the problem was more a fear of *leaving home* rather than *going to school*. The mother, an anxious woman, whose mothering style was overprotective, was having marital problems, and the child overheard her saying to her husband that his infidelity was 'killing' her. The child was afraid that her mother might die when she was not at home to keep an eye on things. There were other issues to this case and a good deal of time was required to right matters and get the child back to school.

Virginia Mae Axline, in her book *Play Therapy*, describes the non-directive form of play therapy. Her approach is based upon the fact that play is the child's natural medium of self-expression. An opportunity is given to the child to 'play out' feelings and problems just as, in certain types of adult therapy, an individual 'talks out' his or her difficulties. Non-directive therapy with children is based upon the assumption that the individual has a growth impulse that makes mature behaviour more satisfying than immature behaviour. The basic principles which guide therapy are as follows. The therapist

- Endeavours to develop a warm friendly relationship with the child.
- Accepts the child exactly as he or she is.
- Establishes a feeling of permissiveness in the relationship so that the child feels entirely free to express his or her feelings.
- Is alert to recognize the feelings expressed by children and to reflect those feelings back to them in such a manner that they gain insight into their behaviour.
- Maintains a deep respect for the child's ability to solve his or her own problems if given an opportunity to do so. The responsibility for making choices and for instituting change is the child's.
- Does not attempt to hurry therapy along. It is a gradual process.
- Does not attempt to direct the child's actions or conversation in any manner. The child leads the way and the therapist follows.
- Establishes only those limitations to the child's behaviour that are necessary to anchor the therapy to the world of reality and to make the child aware of his or her responsibility in the relationship.

Talking to and guiding young people

Haim Ginnott (author of two excellent books on children and adolescents respectively) is concerned that the two-way nature of good communication between adults should also form the basis of conversations with young people. A dialogue with a child or teenager requires respect and skill. Ginnott advises adults to listen carefully to what young people say. Messages should preserve their own and the youngster's self-respect.

There is a myth around that says that adolescents are beyond help. They may not be easy to help, indeed there may be an initial reaction of prickly disdain; but teenagers who experience problems *can* be helped by sharing knowledge and hard-won experience. When they face really tough decisions, most *are* open to sensitively and sensibly proffered guidance. People are most susceptible to help during periods of rapid change, and adolescence is a period of flux. At times of crisis parents are receptive to advice. Yet high on their list of complaints about professionals are failures of communication. These failures involve;

- insufficient information
- inaccurate information
- an overload of information at any one time
- information that is difficult to comprehend because of technical jargon or poor presentation.

Providing information

This then is another way of helping your client by providing the factual data, or know-how about how to get access to information. That information should help them to make informed choices and decisions. You may know people who can offer objective, matter-of-fact information or guidance to your client because of their special expertise.

Within therapy, the therapist may influence the client by providing information or interpretations; by changing clients' attitudes, values, behaviours and perceptions; by teaching problem solving and social skills; by altering the client's pattern of interests, attitudes and understanding.

COUNSELLING

Counselling has, as its main aim, the production of constructive behavioural and personality change. Such change emerges from a relationship of trust, one which emerges from confidential conversations between the professionally-trained counsellor and the client.

Carl Rogers has played a major part in developing the client-centred, non-directive approach to counselling or therapy. In the Rogerian 'client-centred' approach, the goal of the intervention is to work in such a facilitative, non-intrusive manner as to remove the incongruence the individual has developed between the experiencing inner self and the self he or she presents to the outside world. In this way it is hoped to increase positive self-regard and self-direction.

Rogers comes from an academic background in counselling and is less influenced by psychoanalytic thinking than most others in the so-called humanist-existential (or ego psychology) strand of psychological work.

Framework for counselling

☐ Verbal exchange is the means of influence.

☐ The basic assumptions about the nature of man and woman are not pessimistic (fatalistic?) like Freud's.

☐ Rogers has a clear notion of the wholeness of the self. The person is essentially good, rational, realistic, social, forward-looking.

☐ He or she may need help with their basic impulse to grow. As he puts it: 'It has been my experience that persons have a basically positive direction' that is 'constructive, moving toward self-actualization, growing toward maturity, growing towards socialization.'

The counsellor should feel warm and positive toward clients, accept the experience that they are experiencing (empathy), and evince 'unconditional positive regard'.

The therapeutic process is akin to good education or socialization, and is seen as a freeing of the 'growth capacities' of the individual, which permits him or her to acquire 'more mature' ways of acting and reacting, ones which are less fraught with anxiety or conflict. Rogers is talking about a learning process, within a humanistic rather that behaviourist context. The attributes of the counsellor which facilitate such learning are thought to be:

Genuineness and authenticity: the conveying of 'realness' to clients.

Non-possessive warmth: the attitude of friendly concern and caring.

Accurate empathy: the capacity to see things from the clients' point of view, to 'feel with' them, so that they feel they are understood.

Counselling – within this framework – involves the painstaking exploration of problems; there is an attempt to clarify conflicting issues and discover alternative ways of describing them and/or of dealing with them. Counselling helps people to help themselves. This helping method (like the problem-solving approach but unlike some of the other methods) emphasizes the 'self-help' element, the need to call on the inner resources of the person who is in difficulties. To this end, the counsellor provides a supportive relationship which enables the individual to search for his or her *own* answers – to rely on their own resources.

Non-directive counselling and therapy is based upon the assumption that the individual has, within, not only the ability to solve his or her own problems satisfactorily, but also a growth impulse that makes adult behaviour more satisfying than childish behaviour. This assumption puts the non-directive approach well toward the 'consumer' model of service delivery described in Chapter 1.

Counselling in a crisis

In your work with children and their parents you will be called upon to disentangle what look like insuperably knotty problems. The tempo of your work is *relatively* unhurried; after all these difficulties have been around a long time. They require a painstaking assessment and a lot of thought. But emergencies come along – acute crises – and your task is to respond quickly to alleviate the *immediate* impact of disruptive stressful events. There are many potential crises in family life:
Child diagnosed as mentally/physically handicapped.
Separation/divorce.
Loss of a member of the family (bereavement).
An attempted suicide in the family.
Physical illness or injury.
Mental illness (e.g. schizophrenia, depression) of a member of the family.
The discovery of sexual abuse of a child/adolescent in the family.
Police involvement (a child's delinquent acts)/a Court appearance.
Drug abuse discovered.
Anorexia nervosa diagnosed.
Youngster abandons home.
School refusal.
Family violence.

There is no substitute in an emergency for *common sense*. All the crises described above have attracted a specialist literature. But for our purposes we shall look at a few general, common sense responses for the professional.

- Remember that during a crisis most people (because their defences are down) are receptive to the right sort of help.

- Do not perceive yourself in *this set of circumstances* as a long-term therapist or a specialist in (say) bereavement counselling – although such a role, or person, may become necessary if the client doesn't seem to be regaining his or her equilibrium.

- You are not there to identify or resolve *all* of the stresses and complications brought about by the crisis.

- Being aware of the *stages* of a crisis allows you to assess whether the client is 'stuck' at a particular point in what theoreticians call the 'crisis work' – thus hindering the mastering of the emergency, and delaying its final resolution. Although active crisis states vary in duration, the actual condition of intense disequilibrium is limited usually to between four and six weeks. Stages in crises of different kinds will vary (see Further Reading), but here is one example. Colin Parkes has charted the course of grief following bereavement: it encompasses pangs of grief and pining for the lost one, also a process of searching and yearning for the departed person which may look quite irrational to the observer. Parkes also described the anger that may flare up (and the guilt) – feelings which may give way to apathy and depression.

- Simply *identifying* for a person in crisis what is happening, or for concerned relatives *explaining* the normality of such events, provides untold relief and a sense of security. The *unknown*, especially the apparently irrational, bizarre happenings (to oneself or others) in times of crisis, add to the burden of the trauma itself. *Reassurance* is one of the most potent therapeutic remedies available to the emergency counsellor.

- Understanding is the other remedy: providing the client with a non-judgemental, sensitive ear and voice – listening and responding to his or her anguish. This is not the time to be coldly logical, expertly clever or coldly objective.

Summary and comment

We have examined several approaches – group and individual – used in the helping process. *Change* is the key word in all of this, be it facilitated by contracts, direct advice, counselling or psychotherapy. Therapies are many and various. Many social workers, psychologists and psychotherapists call themselves 'eclectic', drawing what they regard as the best or most valid from the various systems of therapy.

Some theorists assert that the technical claims of the diverse schools of therapy have never been adequately vindicated. Some comparative studies show little difference in the outcomes of diverse approaches even though a particular therapy, by itself, can be shown to have significant effects when compared to the absence of treatment. Such an assertion that there are insignificant differences between therapeutic approaches with regard to outcome, would be hotly disputed by behaviour therapists. Nevertheless, it is just such an assumption which leads Jerome Frank, author of *Persuasion and Healing*, to argue that the effective factors are the same for all therapies and they can be identified with the common components of all types of influence and healing – warmth, respect, kindness, hope, understanding, and the provision of explanations.

If it is agreed that psychotherapy is to a significant extent carried out within the framework of a 'good' human relationship, questions must be put and hopefully answered about the nature of the psychotherapist's contribution over and beyond the offering of a helpful human relationship.

This chapter touched upon family violence, but the problems of emotional and physical abuse are far too complex and too technical to be dealt with adequately in a generalist text such as this one. The point to be made here is that there are specific preventive and long-term change-orientated methods to consider in addition to the *crisis-procedures* adopted by a particular agency. Groupwork and behavioural methods (dealt with in the following chapters) are of proven value.

Chapter 10

More Methods and Techniques

The methods described in this chapter include broadly-based and nar-row-range ways of working with parents and children. At the broadest level you have the choice of working with parents in groups by means of discussion; then there are various training methods, therapies or specific techniques to be applied to either families or individuals. Group methods of training parents may be combined with individual casework; a mar-riage might be the subject of an intervention *at the same time* as a programme for a child's behaviour problems is being implemented.

GROUPWORK

There are several advantages in working with a group manifesting similar difficulties. They include the following functions:

(a) experiential
(b) dynamic
(c) social
(d) didactic.

Many adults feel that they have failed miserably as parents, and that their child is *uniquely* difficult to understand and manage. Sharing experi-ences with other parents can be comforting, indeed reassuring. Swap-ping 'horror stories' is fine up to a point, but must not go on too long, thus engendering a mood of pessimism.

The opportunity to express feelings of apprehension, resentment and anger (the latter aimed – not uncommonly – at the helping agencies) in a group setting, can be beneficial if handled sensitively by the group organizer. Let us look more closely at this method.

Discussion groups are a popular and economical means of providing clients with learning experiences, and also the opportunity to share experiences and to engage in mutual problem solving. Parent training groups involve all three of these purposes.

You need to plan and organize your group carefully if it is to be effective and not degenerate into a pleasant, but essentially unproductive, 'talk-shop'. There are several basic procedures for discussion groups. David and Frank Johnson, authors of *Joining Together*, make the following suggestions which I have paraphrased (giving examples from my work with parent groups – see Appendix 2).

► **Define terms and concepts**
A group requires a shared language in order to hold a fruitful discussion. Study new terms; try to find agreement on complex, contentious or ambiguous words (e.g. words like discipline, 'problem child', punishment, trust, spoilt, bribery, reinforcement, time-out). Give examples wherever possible to illustrate a word or concept's meaning.

► **Negotiate and/or establish goals**
Clarify the goals (or objectives) for every session (themes might cover child development; what do you do when a child cries?; discipline; sex education; control v. caning; adolescent risk-taking). Handouts which prepare discussions for a topic, or summarize the previous meeting, are appreciated. Break down major topics into sub-topics.

Spread your time over sub-topics in order of importance so that items of significance are not lost. Allow time to review homework tasks if they are part of the agenda (e.g. keeping records or a diary for discussion).

► **Encourage free and fair discussion**
Encourage individuals in the free (but fair) expression of ideas, feelings, attitudes, openness, reactions, information and analysis. Do not allow (a *few* ground rules for the group could be useful here) the scapegoating or 'bullying' of any one member.

► **Integrate the material**
Relate current themes to past topics; make connections, where they exist, between issues. Fragmentary impressions from several discussion sessions are unlikely to add significantly to a parent's understanding of children and confidence in his or her parenting skills. In parents' groups (see Appendix 2) it is important to try out practical ideas such as time-out by means of role play or homework tasks. This leads on to an important point:

► **Encourage the application of the discussion material**
Ask group members to attempt to identify the implications of the

material for their own lives, the activities they engage in, and their relationships with other people. Encourage them to apply the positive things they have learned and report back to the group the 'feedback' they received from this tryout.

▶ **Evaluate the quality of the discussion**

Ask group members to take a critical look at their performance as a group and as individuals contributing to a group.

The role of Course Organizer

Your coordinating or leadership role is absolutely vital if the group is to work. Here are a few more tips.

Set up the room so that all members can see and hear properly. They should be comfortable and facing each other. An approximate circle is ideal. With a family group session, it is illuminating sometimes to ask the group to arrange the room themselves to their own preferences. Stimulating material such as films, case examples, television programmes and magazine or newspaper articles can be used to initiate discussion. The discussion will 'spark' if you negotiate clear themes and objectives. You can lead a group through a complete topic in a logical sequence by presenting new points to the group when necessary. It is important to 'hold back' those individuals (say a father) who try to dominate the discussion. Have agreed rules for the sessions. Provide opportunities for quiet or timid members to speak; attempt to draw them out. You should ensure that everyone has the right (if they wish) to a 'say'. Ask clarifying questions, and sum up discussion at regular intervals as well as at the conclusion.

According to the Johnsons, a group intervention will be effective if it meets the following criteria:

☐ The group *climate* should be warm, accepting and nonthreatening – vital if people are to engage in controversy, expose their vulnerability, show their ignorance, take risks with touchy subjects.

☐ Learning should be conceived as a *cooperative* enterprise – impossible if the participants 'come over' as hostile, competitive, ridiculing, arrogant or judgemental.

☐ *Learning* should be accepted as the primary purpose of the group – a desideratum that requires painstaking and imaginative preparation of the material and sensitive but firm management of the group.

☐ Every member of the group should *participate* in discussions – a function, again, of a skilful, facilitative group leader.

☐ Such leadership functions might usefully be shared out for certain themes and/or sessions.

☐ Group sessions don't have to be endlessly solemn or heavy-going. They should be stimulating and thus *pleasurable*, and (at times) sheer fun.

☐ *Evaluation* should be viewed as an integral part of the group's activities. Group skills can be improved by constructive, critical evaluation.

☐ Members should *attend regularly* and come prepared – and the importance of mutual responsibility for the well-being of the group may be underlined by drawing up *contracts* with participants.

INDIVIDUAL HELPING

There are several ways in which you can support a client through a difficult patch on a one-to-one basis. Sometimes you may be able to do something *directly* on your client's behalf – for example, acting as a mediator in a quarrel, or as an 'advocate' in their pursuit of assistance from an impenetrable agency. You may be able to change the external circumstances (perhaps by improving other people's attitudes or by mitigating the aggravating circumstances) which are the cause of your client's difficulties.

If you cannot change the circumstances, you may have to rely on modifying the client's perception of or reaction to the situation. Other methods are described in the following pages. These approaches are *not* mutually exclusive; they overlap in practice and, indeed, converge in the 'behavioural approach'.

Persuasion. Persuasion rests on practical knowledge or practice wisdom. It offers reasons why the client should change his or her beliefs and/or behaviour. This does not eschew the arts of persuasion. Subject to ethical constraints and the process of negotiating goals with clients, it is an important component of therapy to voice clear opinions based upon valid information and knowledge of the developmental literature and of hard-gained practice, wisdom and experience.

Providing instruction. Teaching entails skills of 'doing'. The client may not be able to act without instruction, training and monitoring. Because some actions (e.g. child-training techniques) are so ingrained in parents' repertoires (being anchored by ideology or habit, or constrained by lack of skill), it is not usually good enough to simply *advise* parents to change. Demonstrations, rehearsals, instructions and practice may be required in order to provide clients with the equipment for change.

Providing explanations. You may be able to offer explanatory 'stories' (cognitive restructuring), which help clients to re-order their beliefs about the nature of their problems. Attempting to change a person's beliefs, desires and actions is a commonplace activity in ordinary life. The therapist is particularly interested in providing helpful explanations ('stories') or changing existing belief systems which he or she considers to generate distressing, self-defeating actions on the part of the client. Insight, then, is not rejected as a facilitative therapeutic agent.

Giving advice. Guidance is most likely to be effective if it is requested. Advice offered (you might remind parents) in a hectoring or self-righteous tone of voice, with a long-suffering or patronizing expression, or by an ill-chosen turn of phrase, can sound like a command. ('Take it or else . . .' seems to be the implication).

Offer your *opinion* in a cool, concerned but measured way about what you consider the best course of action, in the light of what you know of the situation. Remarks indicating understanding, such as 'I know just how you feel. It's a real dilemma you face, isn't it?', should (when appropriate) precede advice or opinions. You might also ask: 'What do *you* see as your options/alternatives?' This approach helps to defuse anger, resentment and irrationality from fraught situations, so that *reason* can be allowed to function.

Advise parents on how to advise their children:

- Although advice is best given when invited (even when your child may want to confirm what he or she has already decided), you can't always wait for an invitation to make a comment.
- Unsolicited advice requires particular diplomacy.
  Don't pull rank ('Of course, I've been around a long time, so I know best') when giving it.
- Advice can be followed, or *not* taken. If you don't see it that way, then it is a command, not advice, that you're giving.

It *is* a time to be warmly reassuring, solid and safe. At the 'Centre for Behavioural Work with Families,' the imparting of information and advice on child development and childhood problems would be seen as an important part of our work. This might be done on a one-to-one casework basis or in a group setting. The following illustration gives you the flavour of this sort of approach when focused upon children's developmental 'problems'.

Individual advice

MH (Therapist) and Mrs Sally Smith (discussing Penny, aged 7).
Being left in the dark, or waking up in the dark, is not initially or necessarily an unpleasant experience for a young child. And this is precisely what puzzled Sally Smith about her daughter. 'Why,' she asked me. 'should Penny develop fear when she's nearly eight?'

T: 'Has Penny woken in the past and called out to you, perhaps because she felt ill or had a bad dream?'

Sally: 'Yes, funny you should ask that. About a month ago she screamed out in the night. She'd had an awful dream about death and monsters. I'm afraid she watched a monster TV film when she spent the night at her friend's home.'

T: 'Did you go to her room?'

Sally: 'Yes, I went in, sat on her bed and reassured her.'

T: 'Did you put the light on?'

Sally: 'Yes, of course. Why, was that a mistake?'

T: 'It is only a possibility, of course, but a child can easily associate darkness with distress, and light with positive feelings in the form of consoling, comforting nurture – your presence in this case.'

Sally: 'I hadn't thought about that?'

T: 'It is preferable, in future, to enter the room, chat to her and reassure her in the dark. Try to ensure that there is no direct and recurrent relationship between your arrival and the light. Take her back to bed when she comes to you, and stay with her until she is calm. Don't let her stay in your bed, otherwise this will soon become a habit.'

Sally: 'I'm afraid I've got so fed up with her fears of the dark and monsters and disturbed nights that I recently started to punish her. I feel bad about it, so I suppose it was a bad move.'

T: 'There is no way you can punish a child out of her fear. What you might succeed in doing is punishing her into submission, so that she hides her fears from you but suffers them nevertheless. You wouldn't want that I'm sure; and it would imply a loss of confidence in you.'

Sally: 'So what should I do? I'm at my wit's end'.

T: 'You could leave the light on until Penny goes to sleep, then switch it off and leave the door open with a light on outside so that if she does wake up she will not find herself in total darkness. To avoid sudden distress on the child's part you could explain the game to her and make sure that she knows how to switch on the light for herself should she wake up and want it on. When she is asleep, you can turn the light off again. Because the situation is under the child's control there will be no call for panic reactions. Given sufficient patience on your side, she will eventually get tired of leaving the comfort of her bed in order to switch on the light, and will decide that there is more sense in going back to sleep with the light off. The essence of the operation is that you should in no way suggest that you are putting the light off in order to punish your child. Once it becomes a contest of wills, you have defeated your original purpose of enlisting her own energies in coping with fear.

If Penny comes to your bed, insist that she goes back to her own room – and take her back yourself if necessary. Award her a star or point on her very own 'bedtime chart' which is marked out in squares for every night of the week. If she doesn't come to your bedroom, give her *two* stars the next morning and lots of praise. Let her stick the stars herself. Count up the stars at the end of the week, and if they reach an agreed number exchange them for a promised special treat. Fortunately, children's fears tend to be transitory anyway, but this method should hurry along the process of clearing it up.'

Settling differences

The organizers of an Open University course entitled *Parents and Teenagers* have suggested a step-by-step approach to settling differences of opinion between parents and adolescents. Here is a parent (Mrs Brown) working through a potentially fraught situation. She hates motor bikes and her son, Mike, wants to buy one. She asks herself '*Why must he have a motor bike?*' Here is a list of answers:

There is no public transport worth speaking of.

He can't afford a car.

He says his friends go on outings, and without transport he is excluded.

He claims to be 'grown-up' and therefore 'responsible' and free to make choices.

Why should he not have a motor bike?

He may have an accident . . . get hurt . . . get killed. Motor bikes are associated with rough types.

Step 1. **Working out feelings and attitudes about the situation.**

(i)   I feel . . . . . (e.g. resentful).
(ii) When he . . . . . (e.g. keeps pestering me for a motor bike).
(iii) Because . . . . . (e.g. he knows it upsets me).

Step 2. **Deciding whether the particular situation is worth bothering about**.
Reasons for: High risk.
Reasons against: There'll be an awful row if I give a final no.

Step 3. **Making an approach**.
(i) Expressing one's own feelings in an unprovocative manner.
(ii) Listening carefully to the reply. Clarify one's understanding of the other's position.

Step 4. **Working out a practical agreement/compromise**.

You might provide the parents with the following guidelines.
► They should work out what is at stake. Deciding whether or not to take (or sanction) a risk depends on:
– How likely they believe the feared outcome might be.
– How important/damaging the possible outcome is.
– How much they/their teenager has to lose.

Remind them:
► to bear in mind that risk-taking is an important (if worrying) feature of adolescent development;
► to ensure that they and their teenager are well informed (e.g. that a potential motorbike rider has a good machine and is well trained in driving and roadcraft);
► to discuss risk-taking with their son or daughter, try to agree what he or she can do to make the experimenting relatively safe, think about what they can do to make it so;
► to try reaching a compromise or give way on one (lesser) risk so as to obtain their teenager's agreement to forego another one.

Role play

Role play is an activity we have all indulged in at different stages of our lives, beginning as children playing doctors and mummies and daddies. Role play is also an educational technique which brings a specific skill and its consequences into focus. It is a vital tool for experiential learning as it allows the participants to play themselves in different or worrying situations, such as adolescents preparing for job interviews; or to play the part of another person in a known situation, such as reversing roles so that parent becomes child, child pretends to be parent. Role players do not have to be good actors. They put themselves into a *situation* (or *scenario*) which is spelt out, and 'acted out' on the basis of certain *assumptions* which have been carefully discussed.

By using role play as an educational technique insights can be obtained – emotions, reactions, thoughts, behaviours, attitudes and values can be explored. At the end of the role play, participants can reflect on the experience, and gain greater understanding of the role-played situations. Role play can be used as a vehicle for discussion; it can increase communication skills and self-esteem; it illustrates novel situations and ways of dealing with them; and it allows participants to see how others feel in a particular situation. Here are some guidelines:

▶ When using role play, have clear and well-defined objectives.
▶ Ask participants to *volunteer* for the various roles.
▶ Use props to identify participants in their roles if this is felt to be helpful.
▶ Encourage participants to identify with the role they are playing. If they are playing an unknown character, ask them to respond in the way they think that person would. If they are playing themselves in an unknown situation, ask them to respond as honestly as possible to that situation.
▶ You should stage manage and direct the role play.
  Remind participants to come out of role at the end of the session.
▶ Debrief the participants. Debriefing is the period when reflection and evaluation occurs. Ensure there is sufficient time for this. As themselves, the players discuss what they learned from the experience; encourage general discussion about the relevance of the situation to their lives.

Teenagers (and their parents) can be helped to resolve conflicts by the use of role play. The method is used to teach clients basic skills, to help them become more effective in their interactions, and to help them to become more confident when extremely anxious (for example, through enacting scenes such as using the telephone, going to an interview with an employer, or dealing with provocation).

Overcoming fear. Methods found most effective in helping young people to overcome fears include:

• Helping them to develop skills by which they can cope with the feared object or situation.
• Taking them by degrees into active contact and participation with the feared object or situation.
• Giving them an opportunity gradually to become acquainted with the

feared object or situation under circumstances that at the same time give them the opportunity either to inspect or to ignore it.

Exposure training

Behavioural methods have provided the cornerstone of treatment for phobias. The aims of treatment are fourfold:

- to reduce levels of both general and situational anxiety
- to relieve disturbing physiological symptoms
- to reduce avoidance behaviour
- to prevent interference in daily living.

The fearful youngster may be exposed to the phobic object (say, a dog) or situation (say, going to the dentist) in fantasy, in pictures or in real life. Exposure may be graded, by means of an initially easy but then increasingly difficult series of situations. This gradual mastery of fear-provoking events is also referred to as *systematic desensitization*.

Self-control training

Self-control procedures are designed to give the client a more effective means of manipulating the eliciting, reinforcing and discriminative stimuli which affect behaviour. The worker's role is first to carefully examine the antecedents and consequences of a piece of behaviour over which the client wishes to have more control and then to suggest ways in which these events may be altered. They may be altered by either physical or cognitive changes in order that the client may achieve a greater degree of control over her behaviour.

An example

CC *Sue was heavily overweight and was anxious to control her eating behaviour. She was asked to carefully record everything she ate or drank and the time at which it was consumed over a two week period. From this data it became evident that her overeating was restricted to certain types of food and occurred during only the latter part of the day. Further investigation revealed that the sorts of food Sue ate to excess were packets of sweets, cakes and biscuits which she usually bought at a local shop on her way home from work. She never overate in company, only when alone.*

A self-control programme was designed in order to help her resist the temptation to overeat. She was instructed to take a different route home so as to avoid the shop she usually called at; and if she was to be alone in the flat, was told to change immediately from her day clothes into a housecoat to help discourage her from popping out to the shops later in the evening. Her flat-mates agreed to help by not bringing any forbidden cakes or sweets into the flat when Sue was around and they also made an effort to ensure that she was not left alone in the evenings. Sue was allowed to reward herself for sticking to her diet by having a favourite cake or sweet at the end of each 'successful' week. When tempted to cheat she was told to visualize an unpleasant and humiliating scene where a group of boys made rude and teasing remarks about her size — a hazard which she would do anything to avoid. **,,**

Stress management

A British clinical psychologist, Reginald Beech, in his book *Staying Together*, makes the point that life stresses are the enemy of personal relationships. It *is* possible to reduce the impact of stress on our lives, so his list might be useful to your client. I have paraphrased the items you might wish to put to them:

- Keep a running check on stresses in your life. Even the apparently trivial ones, when they accumulate, can become an excessive burden.
- Positive self-talk helps us to keep the stresses and strains in our lives in more reasonable proportion. (I dealt earlier with this technique.)
- Don't try too hard to solve all your problems and expect to erase them altogether. This is usually a vain hope. Concentrate, instead, on *reducing* stress. Even a small reduction in each stress can lead to a big difference in our ability to cope.
- Don't try to be all things to all people all the time. Ration yourself by taking a sensible view of your commitments, not forgetting to leave time for yourself and for some privacy.
- Don't be at the mercy of your environment. You really *can* rearrange your world – if the will is there – to fit in with what you would like to happen.
- Learn to say 'No'. You don't have to say 'Yes' to the unreasonable (and even some of the reasonable) tasks that are foisted on you. Examine your needs and priorities in what is being dished out and feel free to refuse sometimes.
- Cut down on the 'have to'. Question what you tend to take for granted; don't just go ahead and do it because you have always done so.
- Don't set out to win everything. When it really doesn't matter then take a philosophical, relaxed approach. Many so-called confrontations aren't worth a candle.

- Delegate. It doesn't always have to be *your* job. Spread the load more.
- Slow down. Don't set impossibly tiring or tedious schedules for yourself. Introduce rest pauses, moments of reflection and pleasure, into your day.
- Get some balance into your day. Find time for leisure, hobbies, social life, family life, yourself and your work/studies.
- Curb aggression. Try to plan your way through problems (we will come to problem-solving strategies). You'll end up by feeling better.
- Learn to relax. Practice makes perfect. (Relaxation training tapes are available on cassettes and are an important part of a professional's equipment these days. See Ollendick and Cerny (1981) for a training script.)
- Concentrate on staying calm. In an emergency take a deep breath rapidly but quietly; clasp your hands and press them hard against each other. If sitting, brace your leg muscles, pull in your stomach muscles, clench your jaw and hold the muscular tension for five seconds. Now exhale slowly, feel the tension go out of you, saying the word 'relax' to yourself.

If you happen to be standing, take a deep breath, clasp your hands behind you, pressing them hard together; force your knees back to create leg muscle tension – pull in your stomach muscles and clench your jaws. Maintain the tension for five seconds, then let it go slowly, exhaling and saying the word 'relax' to yourself.

Don't exaggerate the muscular tension but make sure you can feel it. Fix your gaze on something so that you appear to be preoccupied or deep in thought for a few moments, so as to conceal the stress you are controlling.

Repeat the exercise if necessary.

Summary and comment

The methods and techniques described in this chapter represent only a small selection of those available. It is vital that you do not rely on techniques like items in a cookbook recipe. They should come out of a clearly formulated theory of human behaviour, a careful assessment, and a coherent conceptual framework for producing change.

The chapter outlines the various advantages of working in groups and provides detail of the organization and implementation of groupwork. Individual helping methods – persuasion, instruction, the provision of explanations or insight, giving advice, settling differences, role play, stress management and self-control training – are described, with examples.

Chapter 11

Child Management and Behavioural Methods

Behavioural methods are very much concerned with *contingencies*, which is a technical way of referring to rules. Before we look at specific applications let us consider a perennial issue in child-rearing – that of discipline – and one that is concerned with rules and routines.

RULES AND ROUTINES

Why should children learn to follow rules and routines? Is it reactionary, indeed Victorian, to *insist* on obedience and conformity to rules as part of child-rearing? The answer is a resounding 'No!' Setting limits *is* crucial but the limits should not be defined too narrowly. As with all things in child development, there is a balance – a golden mean.

This is where you can help parents: to work out their priorities and how to achieve them (see page 31). Failure is costly for parents. Disobedience and defiance are common problems, and their consequences are frustrating, irksome, even exhausting and debilitating for parents. When they persist they can sometimes prove dangerous (in homes at risk of child abuse). There are other potentially serious consequences. Obedience is critical if the complex processes of socialization are to work (see page 17). Parents have the task of turning helpless, unsocial and self-centered infants into sociable children and eventually into reasonable and responsible members of the community. In the early years – from birth to seven or eight, or thereabouts – compliance to parental requests and instructions is vital if the child is going to learn all of the social, intellectual and physical skills he or she will require for a reasonably smooth and contented journey toward maturity. The toddler period is particularly sensitive if social training is going to proceed smoothly.

Among the reasons for enforcing certain rules are:

- the need for safety – the child has to learn to avoid dangers;
- harmony within the family – a disobedient 'brat' sets the scene for an unhappy home and disharmony between the parents;
- the social life of the family – 'spoiled', noisy, aggressive, destructive children are not welcome in other people's homes and contribute to the social isolation of their parents.

Parents achieve compliance partly through example because their children (usually) love them, seek their approval and want to be as much like them as possible. It is also achieved by consciously steering the child in the way he or she should go. A firm but loving framework of discipline helps children to develop their own guidelines and controls symbolized by what we call 'conscience', so that they can look ahead to the consequences of their actions and 'discipline' themselves.

You will find that most parents find discipline one of the most difficult parts of their job; so be forewarned and forearmed. They are quite likely to ask you not only awkward questions, but also for specific advice. It does not help matters to find yourself in an area, not of scientific facts, but of value judgements. *Guidelines*, rather than 'formula' prescriptions, will be among the more useful aids you can provide them with. Better still, you might help them to work out their strategies for themselves, by teaching them how to solve problems.

Preparing the child for life

A list of guidelines has been provided on pages 105–108. Here are some additional points to note in connection with Guidelines 3 and 4, the two which require broadly compliant responses from children.

The point was made there that most routines are useful short-cuts to living. Those routines, carried out on 'autopilot', help a child to undertake daily tasks *around the clock* with minimum effort or fuss – once the habits are learned. In unhappy homes with a disobedient child you can predict fairly safely that one or more of the following situations will be sheer purgatory for the hapless parents (most likely the mother).

- Getting the child up in the morning.
- Washing self, getting dressed.
- Eating (breakfast, and later in the day, other meals).
- Getting the child off to playgroup or school.
- Obeying requests/instructions during the course of the day (e.g. 'Put your toys away'; 'Don't keep switching the telly on and off'; 'Stop

teasing your sister'; 'Put that chocolate back on the shelf'; 'Don't go out on the road').

- Defiance of house rules (e.g. breaking rules about playing with matches, about not switching on the TV before the children's programmes begin, about sitting at the table until the meal is finished, or about not taking food out of the fridge without permission).
- Interrupting (by pestering) mother when she is in the toilet, on the telephone, cooking a meal, etc.
- Disrupting shopping trips by incessant 'I wants', pulling items off the shelves, tantrums, etc..
- Quarrelling, fighting incessantly with brothers and/or sisters, teasing, etc.
- Going to bed when asked; staying there for the night.

You may be asked to suggest *practical* strategies for managing these situations. The later section of this chapter should prove helpful.

The compliance that underpins the learning of rules, routines and good manners can be facilitated by working with parents on the following themes: ensuring that rules are clear and reasonable; that obedience or disobedience is sanctioned consistently; and that the requests and commands that give effect to rules are precise and comprehensible. If there are difficulties with the latter:

- Model how (i.e. demonstrate and check on the client's performance) to make effective requests and commands.

Alan Hudson recommends the following steps:

- Use the child's name.
- Give a *specific* direction.
- Include a mention of time (e.g. 'right now' or 'when you have finished the chapter').
- Say 'please'.
- Get all the words together (in the form of a statement, *not* a question). Do not say: 'Sandy, will you get dressed for mummy? Do say: 'Sandy, I would like you to get dressed now, please'.
- Make the request standing *close* to the child; with a small child get down close to the height of the little one.
- Use a pleasant but *firm* tone of voice (no pleading, cajoling, wheedling!).
- Try to be looking at the child. It may be helpful to say: 'Sandy, look at me now, please' and then give the desired command.
- If the child obeys or disobeys – ignores/refuses – within (say) ten

seconds, follow the behaviour with clear and predictable *consequences*:
  (a) Obedience is followed by positive consequences (e.g. praise).
  (b) Disobedience is followed by negative consequences (e.g. loss of privileges, time-out (see page 180). Discourage parents from smacking or shouting.
- In the case of special circumstances (shopping, visiting) or places (church, restaurants), help parents to preempt problems by working out a scenario.
  (a) Explain to the child what is going to happen.
  (b) Promise a treat/privilege if the child behaves well (specify).
  (c) Engage the child in prosocial behaviours that compete with the unwanted behaviours (e.g. helping mum to pack the shopping box rather than taking items off the shelves at the check-out counter).
  (d) Use response-cost (as a penalty) for transgressions (see page 182).
- Do not keep repeating the requests! (Don't nag.) Follow noncompliant actions with a penalty.

Behavioural methods. The discussion of rules and requests (above) has been a necessary exercise in setting the stage for a discussion of behavioural methods, many of which are potent in correcting the *extremes* of noncompliance. Of course, parents need some principles *and* practical techniques for encouraging and maintaining, not only compliant, but also other prosocial behaviours.

Here are some of the main methods couched in a form that can be presented directly to parents for use with their children. Some of the methods are illustrated by means of brief vignettes drawn from case material.

STRENGTHENING NEW PATTERNS OF BEHAVIOUR

Principle 1: **Operant learning**
Those methods of intervention, based on operant conditioning, attempt to influence or control the outcome of certain behaviours through the use of positive reinforcement, i.e. pleasurable consequences. (Voluntary actions ('operants') that are followed by favourable outcomes for the individual are likely to be repeated.)

A social worker using operant methods can analyse a family system and find out how the various members reinforce undesired behaviour in some members and intentionally or unintentionally ignore or punish desired behaviour. It is then possible to make beneficial alterations in such distressed systems by planning with the family systematically to rearrange the consequences of behaviour so that all (or certain) members of the family receive social reinforcement for desired behaviours (see Chapter 8 for adult application).

Instructions to parents. In order to improve or increase your child's performance of certain actions, arrange matters so that an immediate reward follows the correct performance of the desired behaviour. You might indicate your intentions by saying, for example, '*When* you have put your toys away, *then* you can go out'. When the child has learned a behaviour it is no longer necessary to give rewards regularly. Remember that words of praise and encouragement at such a stage can be very reinforcing.

Principle 2: **Modelling**
To teach a client new patterns of behaviours, give him or her the opportunity to observe a person performing the desired actions. Social workers and others in the helping professions are very important as models in shaping behaviour.

Modelling is used effectively in at least three situations:

- to acquire new or alternative patterns of behaviour from the model which the client has never manifested before (e.g. social skills, self-control);
- to increase or decrease responses already in the client's repertoire through the demonstration by high prestige models of appropriate behaviour (e.g. the disinhibition of a shy, withdrawn client's social interactions, or the inhibition of learned fears – e.g. avoidance of gym – or the suppression of impulsive antisocial behaviour which gets in the way of social relationships) and
- to increase behaviours which the observing client has already learned and for which there are no existing inhibitions or constraints.

Three variations of modelling – *filmed modelling, live modelling and participant modelling* – tend to be used in clinical practice. Alan Hudson describes nine steps in the therapeutic use of modelling:

▶ Provide instruction to the learner (say the parent) about the relevant aspects of modelled behaviour to attend to. (You might be training her to give clear, firm instructions to her child.)
▶ Ask the learner to repeat those relevant aspects to be attended to.
▶ Model the behaviour.

▶ Ask the learner to report on relevant aspects of the behaviour attended to.
▶ Reinforce the learner for reporting.
▶ Repeat the modelling, reporting – reinforcing if necessary.
▶ Ask the learner to imitate modelled behaviour.
▶ Reinforce the learner for imitating the modelled behaviour, correcting as necessary.
▶ Repeat imitation and reinforcement until the behaviour is displayed with 100 per cent accuracy.

An adult example

❝*Jenny was a quiet, shy woman in her late twenties who found it difficult to cope with her bright, forceful four-year-old daughter and was also experiencing feelings of frustration and anger about her unsatisfactory marital relationship, feelings which she had not dared to communicate openly to her husband. Assessment revealed that Jenny had almost no self-confidence and a very poor self-image, mainly due to past unhappy life experiences. Jenny was well aware of the reason for her self-deprecation and self-doubts but this insight did not seem to affect her behaviour. At the Centre we began an informal programme involving role-playing situations in which she felt unable to assert herself. By modelling appropriate reactions and using relaxation to allay her anxiety we were able to teach her to be more assertive – behaviour which reduced her feelings of helplessnes and frustration and gave her confidence to make a realistic appraisal of her marriage and exert more control over her life.***❞**

ELIMINATING/REDUCING INAPPROPRIATE BEHAVIOUR

Principle 3: Satiation
To get a child to desist from acting in a particular way, allow him or her to (or make them) continue performing the desired act until he or she tires of it. Of course this would not be appropriate if the act was dangerous or seriously antisocial. (If the child tears up your curtains give him or her bundles of newspapers to tear up ad nauseam.)

Principle 4: Extinction of inappropriate actions
To stop a child from acting in a particular way, arrange conditions so that he or she receives no rewards following the undesired acts.

Instruction to parents: Ignore (in other words, pretend not to notice) minor misdemeanours such as whining, pestering, tantrums. If a child grabs toys or other goodies from his or her small brother, try to ensure the grabbing has no rewarding outcome. Return the toy to its owner. (You could combine training the older child that grabbing is unproductive, with teaching the little one to share. Encourage them to take turns.)

Withhold reinforcements such as approval, attention, and the like, which have previously and inappropriately followed undesirable behaviour. Remember: your child may 'work hard' to regain the lost reinforcement and thus may get 'worse' before getting 'better'. If the problem behaviour has been continuously reinforced in the past then extinction should be relatively swift; after all it is much easier for the youngster to recognise that he or she has lost reinforcers than it is for the child on intermittent reinforcement. In the latter case, extinction tends to be slow.

Planned ignoring – for behaviours such as temper tantrums and whining – includes the following:
- as soon as the misbehaviour begins, turn away or walk away from your child;
- say nothing and try not to show any expression at all;
- resist getting into any debate, argument or discussion with your child while he or she is misbehaving;
- if you think he or she deserves an explanation for whatever is upsetting him or her, then say 'when you have calmed down we will talk about it.'

Example of planned ignoring

CC *Suzy was a nine-year old spastic girl, the only child of rather anxious and over-protective parents. They were very concerned at her difficult behaviour during mealtimes when, although perfectly able to feed herself, she would refuse to eat unless fed, would throw food and utensils on the floor, and often refuse food entirely. Assessment revealed that at school lunches the child showed none of these behaviours. Nor were they displayed at home when she ate informally in front of the television in the evening. Her problem behaviour was specific to family lunch at weekends and holidays, the only occasions when the whole family sat down together at the table. It appeared that this setting was providing Suzy with an audience to which she gladly reacted.*

In order to combat this, her parents were instructed to ignore any 'naughty' behaviour and only to speak to Suzy when she was eating properly. They were not to feed her or coax her, and any food refused was to be removed without comment. Between meals snacks were forbidden and the dining room table was rearranged so that Suzy's parents were not directly looking at her. In order to help them ignore her, which they found very difficult at first, they were told to talk to each other, and thus take their minds off Suzy. Within three weekends Suzy was eating normally and has continued to do so. Her parents also used behavioural principles in encouraging self-help skills and have themselves become less over-protective **"**

Principle 5: **Time-out from positive reinforcement**

The well-known 'time-out' procedure is intended to reduce the frequency of an undesirable behaviour by ensuring that it is followed by a reduction in the opportunity to acquire reinforcement or rewards. In practice one can distinguish three forms of time-out:

- Activity time-out, where a child is simply barred from joining in an enjoyable activity, but still allowed to observe it – for example, having misbehaved, he or she is made to sit out of a game.
- Room time-out, where the child is removed from an enjoyable activity, not allowed to observe this, but not totally isolated – for example, standing outside a classroom having misbehaved.
- Seclusion time-out, where he or she is socially isolated in a situation from which voluntary escape is impossible.

Time-out sometimes leads to tantrums or rebellious behaviour such as crying, screaming, and physical assaults, particularly if the child has to be taken by force to a quiet room. With older, physicaly resistive children the method may simply not be feasible. So the procedure and its choice require careful consideration.

When the behaviour to be eliminated is an extraordinarily compelling one that all but demands attention (reinforcement) from those present, or when time-out is difficult to administer because the child is strong, the mother (i.e. a major source of reinforcement) could remove herself, together with a magazine, to the bathroom, locking herself in when the child's temper tantrums erupt – coming out only when all is quiet.

Instructions to parents. The child is warned in advance about those behaviours that are considered inappropriate and the consequences that will follow from them. Time-out may last for five minutes (no more). Three minutes is sufficient for younger children.

In practice 'activity' or 'room' time-out should always be preferred before any form of 'seclusion' time-out. Techniques such as time-out, which are designed to eliminate inappropriate or undesirable behaviour, are unlikely to succeed unless supplemented by the reinforcement of an alternative and more appropriate behaviour pattern.

A critical determinant of the effectiveness of time-out is the extent to which the child actually enjoys the situation from which he or she is removed. If that situation is positively frightening, anxiety-provoking or boring, it is possible that the time-out procedure might involve removing the child to a less aversive situation and thereby actually *increase* rather than decrease, the frequency of the inappropriate behaviour.

Example of time-out

❝ *Gary was six-and-a-half years old at referral and was described as a very unlovable child. He constantly screamed and shouted abuse at his parents and had violent temper tantrums when he would indulge in physical aggression, hitting and punching people and furniture, and screaming at the top of his voice until he got his own way. He was also persistently defiant and disobedient and seemed to enjoy provoking confrontations with his parents. Observation and assessment confirmed that Gary was indeed showing all these behaviours but also revealed that they were being heavily reinforced by attention from his parents and by the fact that the shouting and temper tantrums usually resulted in Gary's getting his own way and were therefore highly functional for him.*

Not surprisingly, against this background, family relationships were very strained and Gary was so unpopular that on the rare occasions when he did behave appropriately it went unnoticed and unattended to, which meant he was only getting attention for anti-social behaviour.

To deal with the shouting and temper tantrums his parents removed Gary from the room as soon as he started to shout. This use of 'time-out from positive reinforcement' was designed to eliminate the possibility of his receiving reinforcing attention for anti-social behaviour and also insisting that he complied with the original request on his return. The parents were able to eliminate these outbursts almost entirely. At the same time great emphasis was placed on rewarding Gary for pro-social behaviour with tokens which he could then exchange for a privilege (such as staying up late) or a treat (such as a favourite play activity with his parents).

This programme was designed to improve their relationship with Gary by providing opportunities for mutually reinforcing activities. By the end of the programme Gary was much happier, showing much more pro-social behaviour and getting on a good deal better with his parents. **❞**

This case illustrates how by changing behaviour one can also affect attitudes, and our experience at the Centre is that by modifying children's more difficult behaviour they become more rewarding to their parents, and mothers who have been at the stage of rejecting and even abusing their difficult children find they can see more positive sides to the child and start to enjoy the experience of being a parent.

Penalizing undesirable behaviour

Principle 6: Response-cost

The use of *response-cost* procedures involves a penalty's being invoked for failure to complete a desired response. This may involve the forfeiture of rewards currently available – as for example, when failure to complete homework results in the loss of television privileges.

Instructions to parents. To stop a child from acting in a particular way, arrange for him or her to terminate a *mildly* unpleasant situation immediately by changing the behaviour in the desired direction. (For example, every time he or she throws a toy in a dangerous manner the offending toy is locked away.)

Example of response cost

"*A hyperactive boy, Darren, was extremely disruptive and noisy. He made life miserable for his older brothers and sisters, whilst they read or watched television, by constantly interrupting them – making loud humming and wailing noises and also banging things. An extension of the range of rewards for therapeutic interventions is enshrined in the Premack principle or 'Granny's Rule' – where a preferred behaviour is made contingent on correctly performing a non-preferred behaviour. This principle worked well with Darren. A bottle of marbles representing his pocket money plus a bonus was placed on the mantelpiece. Each transgression 'cost' a marble (or penny). As always, sanctions were balanced by rewards. Punishment alone tells children what not to do, not what they are expected to do. He was required to play quietly for set periods – timed with a kitchen timer and if he did this successfully he was rewarded by tokens. These tokens could then be exchanged for treats – for example, he could loudly blow his sister's trombone for five minutes: something he had always wanted to do and something he found a great incentive.***"*

Encouraging competing behaviour

Principle 7: Overcorrection

Instructions to parents. Require the child to correct the consequences of his or her misbehaviour. Not only must he or she remedy the situation caused thereby, but also 'over-correct' it to an improved or better-than-normal state. In other words, you enforce the performance of a new behaviour in the situation where you want it to become routine.

Get the child to practise positive behaviours which are physically incompatible with the inappropriate behaviour.

An example

“ *Gavin, who stole and broke another youngster's penknife, was required to save up enough money not only to replace the knife, but also to buy a small gift betokening regret. He was praised at the completion of the act of restitution. When he deliberately punctured another child's bicycle tyre he not only had to repair the tyre but also to oil and polish the entire vehicle.* **”**

This involves positively reinforcing a particular class of behaviour which is inconsistent with, or which cannot be performed at the same time as, the undesired act. In other words, to stop a child from acting in a particular way, deliberately reinforce a competing action.

Summary and comment

Behaviour therapy (modification), unlike psychoanalysis (which is the domain of a very small group of specialists), is increasingly being used not only by clinical psychologists but also by psychiatrists, social workers, nurses and teachers trained in the approach. Sadly, appropriate training is still hard to come by in the UK, although it features increasingly in the curricula of courses for various helping professions.

There is a grave shortage of professional people with relevant training. This can be mitigated by the fact that clinicians do not have a monopoly of helping skills or such therapeutic qualities as common sense; by providing non-profesionals and para-professionals with skills to cope with future problems, behavioural work has moved the focus of therapy towards a preventive model of mental health.

This behaviour modification approach has been taught to parents (see Appendix 2); persons without a considerable amount of psychological knowledge can grasp the concepts; many persons can be taught at one time; a relatively short training period is needed. The long-term purposes of training is to help parents to become more systematic in their own behaviour, so as to be more effective in managing their children.

Parents often prefer a view of problem development that does not assume 'sick' behaviour based on a medical model (see Chapter 1). In addition, many childhood problems consist of well-defined behaviours that are conducive to behavioural treatment. Various methods were described in the chapter.

Chapter 12

Using Life Skills Training

After many years of working with families with a seriously problematic child (or children) I am not surprised when I discover a socially isolated family in which parents seldom go out, the circle of friends has shrunk, and for the mother there has been a loss of social confidence and self-esteem. In some instances the parents were (or felt) unskilled from the beginning; in others a difficult (perhaps handicapped) baby made them feel deskilled.

Whichever it may be, among the skills which assist individuals in the many and varied 'life-tasks' which become salient at different stages of life, social and problem-solving competencies are high priority items.

The self-efficacy theory (as we saw on page 13) attempts to explain the interacting and mutual influence of people's self-perceptions and their behaviour. You may remember that self-efficacy is a belief in oneself, a conviction that one can produce positive outcomes through effort and persistence. People high in their possession of self-efficacy are convinced of their own effectiveness; those who are low in it believe that their efforts are doomed to failure. Parents with a history of failure in certain situations (say, social situations) begin to believe that they cannot succeed. Their pessimism leads them to avoid the source of their fear, and avoidance further handicaps them and their children.

For example, there is no opportunity for the child to develop new social skills, let alone practise old ones if the mother doesn't speak to people at the park, take the child to parties or friends' homes. And if unskilled patterns of behaviour are allowed to continue uninterrupted children may never learn how to cope adequately with their social environment; this leads to a sense of isolation, unhappiness and (not infrequently) 'acting out' reactions.

The rationale for social skills assessment and training is to help children (and their parents) to become more flexible and socially competent, so they may have less recourse to self-defeating behaviours and feelings.

In the current enthusiasm for social skills training (SST) as a 'package' it is important to remember the need for an ABC analysis and *comprehensive* assessment in each case of 'problematic' behaviour (see Chapter 2). 'Cookery book' applications of SST without such individualized assessments are likely to fail, mainly because of the multi-causal nature of children's problems.

A careful analysis should be made of the types of social situation which upset the child. Parental attitudes (such as over-solicitous concern about the child) foster timidity, providing a cue for the child to behave in a dysfunctional manner when in the company of others. Parents thus become part of the intervention. It may be they themselves who, by excessively authoritarian discipline or excessively demanding attitudes, produce negative self-attitudes in the child. Children may feel unwilling or unable to do what is required of them by their parents, and this may transfer to social situations where they feel they are on display.

If parents themselves lack social skills and graces, they may fail to provide adequate models for their children to identify with or imitate in social situations. Again, parents who are inconsistent in their demands on their children may engender timidity in them because they never know whether what they are doing is right.

The interference model. The interpretation here is that specific skills are, in fact, present but not employed because emotional or cognitive factors interfere with the performance of their skills. The 'process' of working out appropriate goals and strategies, of monitoring and setting standards, and then adjusting and controlling one's actions, may be faulty. This could result from severe anxiety, faulty self-attributions and low ('I can't do it; everyone's looking at me') self-esteem.

SOCIAL SKILLS TRAINING

This approach involves a structured learning experience for developing skills for interacting with people. It aims to change specific person-to-person behaviours that influence the quality of relationships, such as:

- assertiveness
- the ability to listen
- conversational skills (plus greetings and partings)
- non-verbal skills
- the ability to be rewarding

- observational skills (reading social signals, getting information, asking questions)
- problem-solving skills (the ability to work out solutions to novel and thorny social problems).

Even young people with poor social skills are likely to have several effective *components* of socially-skilled behaviours. These can be built on, improved and integrated smoothly, by instruction, or by feedback and prompts, during role rehearsal. Role rehearsal allows you to comment on the client's performance. It is a gradual process – building up skills by means of working out the various component tasks making up a particular skill. This 'pretend' sort of rehearsal provides an intermediate step in changing behaviour and developing new and more effective strategies. The end-point is when the client tries out the new skill or role in real life.

To take one application: the self-effacing, timid youngster may overcome these difficulties by training in assertion. A young girl, say, practises asserting herself in an imaginary confrontation with (say) a shopkeeper who has given the wrong change or by asking a boy to a party. The difficulty of the situation is gradually increased. The youngster then asserts herself in relatively easy real life settings, before tackling more challenging circumstances.

The basic SST technique is *role playing*. Michael Argyle and Monika Henderson describe a three-stage sequence:

▶ Lectures, discussions, demonstrations, videos or films about particular aspects of the skill. The demonstration and explanation phase is most usefully conveyed by *modelling* (see page 177).

▶ A problem situation is carefully defined, and 'stooges' are introduced with whom trainees role play from 7 to 15 minutes each. The stooges are briefed about the circumstances and about which problems to introduce.

▶ Next there is a feedback session, consisting of verbal comments by the trainees, discussion with the other trainees and playback of audio- or video-tapes.

Sometimes a fourth session of practice is allowed for so that the trainee can rehearse the lessons he or she has learned.

This basic sequence can be expanded to include training in:
- analysis of difficult social situations
- conversation
- presentation of self
- rewardingness.

Rewardingness is a vital quality in the enhancing of relationships. Intimacy and supportiveness are foundational elements in 'coming over' as rewarding to others. The following indicate the manner in which people reflect intimacy:
- addressing the other person by their first name
- showing an interest in their activities
- sharing news of success
- showing positive unconditional regard
- trusting and confiding in the other person
- acknowledging birthdays and other special occasions
- striving to make the other person happy while in each other's company
- inviting them to family celebrations or other intimate affairs
- making them welcome
- showing affection
- discussing intimate subjects such as religion or politics, sex or death.

COGNITIVE APPROACHES

If psychological treatment can boost a client's perceived self-efficacy, then the client (according to the evidence) should approach formerly dreaded situations with new confidence. Much SST training is content oriented, i.e. the teaching of specific, complex skills. A cognitive approach tends to be more process orientated (e.g. problem-solving) although children's knowledge of social exchange norms and awareness of their own special impact upon others would be seen as crucial to their ability to 'read' social situations realistically and with sensitivity.

But we know that negative beliefs and unrealistic expectations may lead to disharmonious social interactions. Such matters would certainly be high among the concerns of the cognitively-oriented behaviour therapist. He or she would be committed, too, to helping the child to 'unravel' knotty social situations, to analyse them and to generate alternative solutions to the self-defeating strategies so far adopted. Those adopting a cognitive-social learning model, view effective social functioning as being dependent upon the client's
- knowledge of specific interpersonal actions and how they fit into different kinds of person-to-person situations;
- ability to convert knowledge of social nuances into the skilled performance of social actions in various interactive contexts; and
- the ability to evaluate skilful and unskilful behaviour accurately and to adjust one's behaviour accordingly.

PROBLEM SOLVING

Life is full of crises, problems, and decisions, but many people do not have the appropriate skills to manage them. Much of what we think of as problematic behaviour in a client, can be viewed as the consequence of ineffective behaviour and thinking. The individual is unable to resolve certain dilemmas in his or her life; the unproductive attempts to do so have adverse effects such as anxiety and depression, not to mention the creation of additional problems such as confrontations and interpersonal conflict. For the professional the way to decode the client's sometimes incomprehensible actions, is to ask yourself what he or she is trying to 'achieve' – seen from their point of view.

Often, what the client is trying to achieve is the narrowing of the *discrepancy* between his or her *actual* state of affairs and his or her *desired* (or *ideal*) state of affairs. The discrepancy *is* the problem and the client's solutions may be making things worse. Problem solving aims to reduce or eliminate this gap. Of course the desired or ideal state may be unrealistic, and require some modification – perhaps a compromise position. Most often as problem solvers we try to improve the actual state of affairs by finding an answer to a difficulty, a solution to a problem.

The process of problem solving involves you in the following activities:

- *Define the problem and its severity* as precisely as possible. This entails:
  - (a) assessing the current (actual) state of affairs, and
  - (b) specifying the desired (ideal) state of affairs (goals) (see Flow Chart 1).
- *Assess the nature and magnitude of the problem*. This entails:
  - (a) listing the 'forces' *helping* the client move toward the desired goal;
  - (b) listing the 'forces' *hindering* the client from moving toward this goal.

In 'force field analysis', as it is called, the problem is viewed as a balance between forces pushing in opposite directions.

Current State of Affairs
(Sally's school refusal)

(a) Get your client (it may be a family group) to use brainstorming to construct a list of helping (+) and hindering (−) forces.

Helping Forces	*Hindering Forces*
The family's behind her.	Perhaps we put too much pressure on her.

Sally wants to return to school.	She gets panicky when she tries.
The teacher is sympathetic.	Her schoolmates tease her when she appears.
	There is a bully in her classroom.

(b) Rank the forces in order of their significance in influencing the present situation. Rate the importance of forces according to the relative ease with which they can be resolved. Do not waste time on unrealistic ideas.

▶ *Formulate alternative strategies.* This entails working out the various means of moving the client (individual or group) from the actual to the desired state of affairs. Creative and divergent (unconventional) thinking, inventiveness and critical ability are all helpful at this stage. You have to change the helping forces (strengthening them) and the hindering forces (reducing or eliminating them) in order to alter the current state of affairs.

▶ *Now decide on and implement the strategy.* This entails:
   (a) selecting the alternatives that seem most likely to succeed,
   (b) specifying the knowhow, methods and other resources required to implement the chosen strategy.

▶ *Evaluate the outcome of applying the strategy.* This entails:
   (a) defining what a successful outcome means – in terms of explicit criteria,
   (b) specifying what the effects or consequences of the strategy were.

Group problem-solving is generally more fruitful than individual effort, although there is no guarantee of this in particular instances.

In the problem-solving approach 'small' is not so much 'beautiful' as 'manageable'. Problems are not manageable when they are conceived in large global terms. ('*Everything* is going wrong'; 'He will *never* change'; 'There is *no hope*'; 'I seem to have the world on my shoulders'.)

You break through this rhetoric by trying to establish and obtain the relevant facts – attempting to 'unpack' the complicated-looking dilemma. The more your clients can adopt a *mental set* that they *can* cope with a problem, the greater is the likelihood that with your help they will come up with a solution to it.

The feeling of being in control (and conversely, *not* helpless) is vital to the successful working through of difficult situations and is invaluable when you are involved in crisis interventions. You 'relabel' the problem for the clients, defining what they once thought of as impenetrable as 'manageable' – given thought and calm application of a series of interpersonal problem-solving strategies.

The development of problem-solving skills

Interpersonal problem-solving skills are learned from experiences beginning in the family and wherever the child interacts with others in situations which give rise to interpersonal difficulties. How well the developing child learns these skills is thought to reflect the extent to which the child's caregivers (say parents) manifest these abilities themselves; also, the degree to which parents communicate in ways that encourage the exercise of such thinking in the child.

The emphasis is very much (but not exclusively) on *how* the person thinks; the goal in therapy or training is to generate a way of thinking (this applies to parents as well) – a way of using their beliefs and values in making decisions at such times that problems arise.

George Spivack and his colleagues have defined a number of differing interpersonal cognitive problem-solving skills. They suggest a series of skills rather than a single (unitary) ability. The significance of each of these abilities in determining the degree of social adjustment is said to differ as a function of age.

The interpersonal cognitive problem-solving skills include:

• *Problem-sensitivity*, which is the ability to be aware of problems which arise out of social interactions and a sensitivity to the kinds of social situations out of which interpersonal difficulties may arise. It also involves the ability to examine relationships with others in the here and now.

• *Alternative solution thinking*. A close parallel to this is 'brainstorming'. The key feature is the ability to generate a wide variety of potential solutions to the problem. Judgment about what is best is suspended and the skill is to draw from a repertoire of ideas representing differing categories of solutions to a given problem.

• *Brainstorming* is the creative art of generating the greatest number of ideas in the shortest possible time. It is ideally suited to group participation as well as individual application.

There are some simple rules you apply to your chosen topic:

(a) Accept every idea that the topic or issue gives rise to *uncritically*.
(b) Aim for quantity of ideas rather than quality.
(c) At this stage do not initiate any discussion.
(d) List the ideas (e.g. write them on a blackboard or flip-chart).

(e) Set a time limit.

(f) Code the ideas when the brainstorming session is over.

For example: (i) underline those that are not clear/understood; (ii) put a cross next to those that are impossible; (iii) put an asterisk against those that look useful and/or are worth exploring further.

Work out with the client the likely consequences of the better courses of action you have put forward. What is the utility of these consequences in resolving the problem as it has been formulated? For example, with regard to the proposed solutions put forward by Mrs Hayes for managing Avril's tantrums:

(a) Punishment doesn't seem to work, in fact it seems to make her more intractable.

(b) If I ignore her she'll probably follow me around, yelling more loudly. Like me she can be very stubborn.

(c) The idea of trying to reason with Avril sounds good, but I find it so hard to keep cool. And we may not be able to resolve things in the heat of the particular confrontation.

(d) My husband won't thank me for insisting that he back me up; he'll say 'It's your problem'.

(e) Putting Avril in time-out (see page 180) may work but it could also generate trouble, more sulking and tantrums.

(f) Trying to find occasions to praise Avril (mind you, they're rare) should be a possibility; Avril can be reasonable when she's in a good mood – the trick is to catch her at the right time. She is vain and enjoys praise.

- *Means–ends thinking* reflects the ability to articulate the step-by-step means necessary to carry out the solution to a given interpersonal problem. The skill encompasses the ability to recognize obstacles, the social consequences deriving from these solutions and a recognition that interpersonal problem solving takes time.

- *Consequential thinking* involves being aware of the consequences of social acts as they affect self and others and includes the ability to generate alternative consequences to potential problem solutions before acting.

- *Causal thinking* reflects the degree of appreciation of social and personal motivation and involves the realization that how one felt and acted may have been influenced by (and, in turn, may have influenced) how others felt and acted.

Any decision to change is likely to involve both benefits and 'costs': benefits for the client (hopefully), for significant others, and for his or her network. There could also be costs to the client, to others and to his or her social setting. You might construct a list – with your client's help – of the likely benefits and costs of a particular planned change, in terms of these six categories.

Summary and comment

Many, perhaps a majority of, clients who come for help to social workers and related disciplines, are deficient in life skills – most notably social and problem-solving skills. Fortunately there is a growing literature – theoretical and practical – for improving these skills. It is important not to think of them as a panacea – the answer to all social problems. It is also vital not to use them in cookbook fashion without a full and rigorous assessment.

EPILOGUE

I am conscious at the end of this book of a paradox for the reader, be he
or she a student or an experienced practitioner. These pages contain so
much about families, parents, children and others . . . and, yet, so little.
The subject is so vast that we have only scratched the surface. This is not
simply a matter of the limited space available in one guide; it is intrinsic
to the topic. We have so much to learn, so much research to initiate.
Fortunately, there is no reason for an attitude of pessimism or helplessness. We know enough to be of service to those of our fellows whose
family life is floundering, whose children are in distress, and who,
consequently, are calling for help.

APPENDIX 1

Family Centres

Family centres are increasingly popular as a new way of providing services for families and young children. Broadly speaking – despite their individual differences – they attempt to facilitate all or some of the following objectives:

- *Community-based preventive social work practice.*

  Preventing family breakdown and social reception of children into care by supporting families to alleviate stress, teaching practical skills, and attempting to improve the quality of parent-child relationships. Preventing the deprivation of parental care and the fragmentation of families.
- *Complementary education (educational outreach).*

  Developing parents' understanding of the educational context of the home and the community and their educational role in relation to their child; this is the idea of parents as 'complementary educators', as the first teachers of children.
- *Supporting self-help groups.*

  Providing amenities for small self-help groups set up by local people to meet their own needs for friendship, mutual support or child care.
- Making initiatives to counter local unemployment.

A detailed bibliography is available in J. A. Macfarlane (ed.) (1986) *Progress in Child Health, Vol. 3*, Edinburgh: Churchill Livingstone; Chapter 14, by Teresa Smith, 'Family Centres: Prevention, partnership or Community'. A valuable chapter by Dora Black (Chapter 12) on child guidance and child psychiatric services is available in the same book.

APPENDIX 2

Parent Training

You may find it useful to train parents in behavioural methods and child management in a group setting (see Further Readings). Here are some questions and answers on the choice of content of training programmes:

- *Should parents rehearse or practise the skills they learn?*
  In principle the practice of child management skills would seem highly desirable. On balance the safe answer is *yes*, but there is no evidence to suggest that actual practice is a *necessary* or *sufficient* condition for helping parents develop such skills.
- *Should parent training focus on specific target problems or develop their knowledge of general behavioural principles?*
  It does seem that the latter is more cost-effective as it facilitates the implementation and generalisation of newly acquired child management skills in situations.
- *Should parent training programmes begin with easy or difficult problems?*
  There is no simple answer; problems are easy:
  (a) if they occur under conditions that permit ready observation by parents
  (b) if they occur with relatively high frequency
  (c) if they are maintained by stimuli from parents rather than others, and
  (d) if they occur naturally at a specified time (i.e. mealtime, bedtime, and so on).
- *Does early reinforcement arising from success with easy problems increase cooperation?*
  Beginning treatment with more or less difficult behaviour problems does not seem to affect parental cooperation, but there is still some doubt about this issue. It may, however, increase parents' sense of self-confidence or competence (self-efficacy).
- It seems probable that parents will maintain their enthusiasm and interest for the programme as long as they perceive some progress in managing their offspring's actions, regardless of how difficult these behaviours are to deal with, in the therapist's opinion.

Telephone contact and carefully-timed home visits also increase parents' cooperation.

☐   Teach only those behaviours which will continue to be reinforced after training.

☐ The parents' aim in using behaviour modification procedures is to introduce the child to behaviours which are either intrinsically reinforcing or which make reinforcements available which he or she was not previously experiencing.

☐ In a sense there are two therapeutic objectives in training parents, and through them, their offspring:

(a) to enhance a child's responses to the controlling factors in his or her environment without deliberately altering the latter. Assuming a family environment to be essentially satisfactory, one might attempt to adjust a child to it, or

(b) to change the controlling factors in an unsatisfactory learning environment as a means of modifying problem behaviour.

Where the latter strategy is predominant the therapeutic objective is to programme the environment so that it sustains the child's (and parents') 'improvement' after the formal programme is terminated.

At the 'Centre for Behavioural Work for Families', Sue Milner and I have used the following programme for training parents in groups – families referred by Social Services with multiple problems.

Content of the sessions

Introductory home visit
- Introduce ourselves.
- Explain the nature of the programme.
- Give time and place of the group, sort out arrangements for getting to the venue.
- Make a Contract.
- Complete baseline measures (e.g. Home Situation Questionnaire, Attitude to Child Questionnaire).
- Observation of child interacting with family members (see page 43).
- Leave a handout about the Centre's approach.

Each session lasts two hours and includes a 20-minute coffee break.

Session 1
- Introduce ourselves and the other parents.
- Explain the nature of the programme; discuss how other parents have similar problems with their children.
- Video of 'Claire' – one of our training tapes; a family mismanaging a disobedient toddler.
- Discussion of tape and what constitutes a problem.

- Discussion of the specific behaviours manifested by their children that cause them concern.
- Explain red, green and amber code (see page 78).
- Small sub-groups to specify what each parent's *priorities* are (discipline/child-rearing).
- Fill in parent rating scale individually (see page 71).
- Parents individually choose two problem behaviours to work on; parents also describe two prosocial behaviours to record.

Homework: Parents are given a recording sheet and are asked to record the frequency of prosocial behaviours and the chosen problem behaviour. Parents are asked to bring the records with them next week.

Session 2
- Greetings.
- Discussion of successes and difficulties of the previous week.
- Collect data from previous week.
- Video of a mother discussing her child's problems.
- Introduce the A–B–C of behaviour (see page 53) as a basis for discussion of *learning*.
- Repeat the video of Claire. Illustrate the A–B–C analysis for Claire and her mother and other family members.
- Talk on *rules, priorities, obedience, giving commands*, followed by group discussion.

Homework: Record A–B–Cs of target problem behaviours; parents given record sheets (see page 28) and an example.

Session 3
- Greetings.
- Discussion of successes and difficulties of the previous week; discuss records.
- Collect records.
- Discussion of *differential attention* – planned ignoring, attention to good behaviour (see page 181). (Handouts on these subjects.)
- Practise being precise about *reinforcing specific behaviour*.
- Role play and rehearsal of making eye-contact, being close by when giving instructions; showing firmness and warmth.
- Discussion of the behaviours that cannot be ignored.

Homework: Try out these methods, continue A–B–C recording.

Session 4
- Greetings.
- Discussion of successes and difficulties of previous week.

- Small groups–looking at the records.
- Collect the records.
- Discuss incentives, star-charts, and time-out (see pages 50 and 180 respectively).
- Video on time-out; role play and rehearsal of use of time-out.
- The importance of consistency.

Homework: Try out these methods, continue A-B-C recording.

Session 5
- Greetings.
- Discussion of successes and difficulties of previous week.
- Small groups–looking at the records.
- Collect the records.
- Discussion of coping strategies – self-talk, relaxation and self-reinforcement (see pages 146, 172 and 171).
- Problem-solving (discussion and exercises) (see page 188).

The remaining three sessions include revision of learning principles and management techniques. There is a thorough discussion of individual problems (e.g. disobedience, tantrums, etc.) also a discussion of expectations re. developmental norms for children. Methods rehearsed include response cost and over-correction:

- *Fading out* the programme is planned on an individual basis during the final (eighth) session.
- A further session is arranged for a *debriefing* and *evaluation* of the programme. Home visits are made for observations of parent-child interactions and repeat testing on the questionnaires used in the introductory home visit.

APPENDIX 3

Treatment Options In Cases of Child Abuse And Neglect

kely target problems (of the excess/deficit/inappropriate categories) which cur in relation to:

Characteristics of the parents (e.g. alcohol abuse; deficits in bonding and child-rearing skills; faulty expectations of the child).

Characteristics of the child (e.g. non-compliant aggressive problems; incontinence; inappropriately inflexible responses to different situations).

Unique interaction of the child and his/her parents (e.g. coercive/aversive communications; mutual avoidance; inappropriate, inconsistent (perhaps non-contingent) reinforcement/punishment).

Significant others in the family (interference, subversion of maternal authority by grandparent; sexual/physical abuse by relative/lodger, etc.).

Environmental factors (poverty, overcrowding, social isolation).

Social workers are likely to be faced with any of the following *specific blems* when child abuse cases are referred to them.

Specific Areas of Intervention

Deficits

- Skill deficits (poor problem-solving skills; ineffective communication skills; ineffective reinforcement skills).
- Social isolation.
- Witholding attention (ignoring) until there's a crisis (i.e. very annoying activities).
- Failure to *track* minor incidents before they blow up in major confrontations (e.g. fighting).
- Failure to acknowledge/notice/reward prosocial behaviour.
- Few family recreational activities together.
- Low self-esteem/low perception of self-efficacy.
- Less positive emotional expression.

Excess/surplus problems

- Use of *aversive* (negative, coercive, punitive) means of influencing/changing others (criticism/physical assaults).

- Parental yelling, shouting, nagging, threats, complaints.
- Punishment of prosocial behaviour.
- High parental stress/distress (marital discord/inadequate income, poor housing, lack of emotional/social support).
- Alcohol/drug abuse.
- Acting out, anti-social, conduct problems.

3. *Inappropriate beliefs/attitudes/knowledge/behaviour*

- Faulty attributions (cause-and-effect inferences).
- Reinforcement of inappropriate/deviant actions.
- Unpredictable/inconsistent.
- Mutual avoidance.
- Faulty expectations due to absence of basic knowledge about child development.
- Inflexible in response to child-disciplinary situations.

Potential Treatment Strategies

1. Systemic Level
(*Family*)
- Written contracts.
- Negotiation training.
- Conflict resolving (settling differences).
- Contingency contracting (exchange theory).
- Communication enhancement.
- Clarification of roles and rules.
- Enhancement of social contacts.
- Improvement of physical environment, resources (e.g. child-minding/day care).

2. Dyadic Level
(*Interactions/relationship*)
- Enhancing positive interactions.
- Operant programmes (increasing positive reinforcement – 'catching the child out in good behaviour').
- Decreasing threats, criticism, negative injunctions.
- Play.
- Increasing consistency.
- Negotiating fair/few/clear rules.
- Marital work.

3. Individual Level
Parents:
- Training in more effective child-rearing practices.
- Developmental counselling to improve knowledge/decrease faulty

expectations/attributions.
- Cognitive restructuring.
- Decreasing inappropriate anxiety/anger reactions
  (i) Relaxation
  (ii) Self-talk
  (iii) Self-control training.
- Improving Skills
  (i) Social Skills
  (ii) Problem-solving skills.
- Addiction/substance abuse.
- Self-esteem, self-efficacy enhancement (performance accomplishments).
- Depression/learned helplessness.

Children:
- Training/therapy as in Chapter 11.

APPENDIX 4

A case vignette to illustrate behavioural casework with a family referred for child abuse: failure to thrive in a two year old.

The names are fictitious, the identities disguised. The case is paraphrased (with permission) from the one reported by Dr Dorota Iwaniec (the key worker) and the author (co-therapist) in *The Australian Journal of Child and Family Welfare*.

❝Jimmy and Wayne Grant are twins. To see them on one of our home visits is to understand something of what the terms 'child abuse' and 'failure to thrive' mean. Jimmy is a chubby, rose-cheeked boisterous two year old. He appears to be a happy, mischievous boy, running, playing, talking and laughing. He comes to his mother for help and comfort and cuddles up to her spontaneously. He responds readily to her attention and affection. She smiles at him, picks him up, sits him on her lap, plays with him, answers his questions, watches his movements, warns him when he is in danger.

On the edge of the room, like a stranger, stands Wayne – posture rigid, staring fixedly at us. He is a sad, lethargic-looking child, very small and extremely thin. His pale face throws into relief the dark shadows under his eyes. He remains in one spot, as if at attention; by now he is gazing unswervingly at his mother. She takes no notice of him. When asked to call Wayne over to her she looks in his direction; as she does so her face hardens and her eyes are angry. She addresses him with a dry command; when he hesitates she shouts at him.

Our observations of his interactions with his mother (several visits over four weeks), which gave us base-line data, indicated that she *never* smiled at him, *never* picked him up, *never* sat him on her knee, *never* played or read to him. The only physical contact came about when she fed, bathed or dressed him, and at such times, her handling was rough and silent. When she approached him he appeared to be frightened and occasionally burst into tears. He would never come to her for comfort or help and she never approached him except to carry out the bare essentials of care and control. The children were both meticulously clean and well-dressed.

Home-based observations allowed us to see that when his father returned from work, Wayne brightened a little; he became somewhat more alert and lively, especially when his mother was out of sight. When she entered the room he stiffened up. Jimmy and Wayne didn't play together. Jimmy frequently pushed his brother and smacked him; Wayne's cries were largely ignored by his mother.

Looking at Wayne and Jimmy it is hard to believe that they were of the same weight at birth. Wayne's small stature was now reflected in a height and weight that were below the third percentile curves of normal growth. Wayne had been hospitalized several times because of his failure to gain weight. During the latest hospitalization Wayne's mother refused to visit him and requested his reception into care; she appeared to be very depressed and said that she could no longer cope with trying to feed him (he would refuse food, or spit it out screaming loudly). She added that she could no longer tolerate his behaviour ('defiance', whining and crying) and her hostile feelings towards him. At the stage of our entry into the case Wayne had to be fed by a combination of the health visitor, father or a neighbour.**"**

Failure to thrive

Failure to thrive has become a popular term to describe infants and children whose growth and development are significantly below expected standards. It is thought of as a pattern (syndrome) of severe retardation of growth which is frequently associated with a specific disturbance of parental (often maternal) behaviour and family disorganization. Certainly, in Wayne's case, it was clear (after the essential, exhaustive, medical tests) that his retarded growth at this stage of his life was not due to physical (organic) disease. Research findings suggest that organic abnormalities cause such failures to thrive in only a minority of children.

Studies of such children and their families have shown that the most commonly identified forerunners to these problems are emotional disturbance and environmental deprivation – with the wide range of psychological and social disorganization that these concepts imply. The deprivation often involves rejection, isolation from social contacts and neglect. Occasionally, physical abuse enters the picture. On several occasions Wayne showed severe bruising. The health visitor had placed him on the 'at risk' register.

The association of poor growth with adverse environmental factors has often been pointed out in the context of the maternal deprivation and child abuse literature. The mechanisms of the growth failure, in fact, are not clear. It is suggested that maternally-deprived infants can be underweight because of undereating (which is secondary to being offered inadequate food), *or* because of the refusal of the adequate nourishment offered, rather than as a result of some psychologically-induced defect in absorption or metabolism.

Assessment: Behavioural psychotherapy approach

To return to the Grant family – now in acute crisis – they were referred to the authors for a form of assessment and a broadly-based form of behaviour therapy which we call 'behavioural psychotherapy'. This family-orientated approach, which combines behavioural methods of assessment and modification with family-casework methods is being used (and evaluated) at the 'Centre for Behavioural Work with Families' (formerly the 'Child Treatment Research Unit') attached to the University of Leicester Clinical Psychology Department.

Wayne was hospitalized five times during his two years and three months of life. Altogether he had spent 68 days in hospital. The first admission was at the age of four weeks. He had been a difficult baby to feed from the word 'go'. He vomited frequently and seemed to cry or scream incessantly for the first few weeks of life. He was suffering from pyloric stenosis. After the operation he improved a little. His sucking became more vigorous although he took a long time to feed. The situation deteriorated when solids were introduced at the age of five months. He persistently refused to take them and gradually stopped taking liquids as well. From that time onwards, feeding time became a battle.

Wayne was 14 months old (weight 6 kg, height 69 cms) when his mother finally found it impossible to cope with his reluctance to eat. She screamed at him, smacked him, shook him, getting angrier and more frustrated each day. When she forced him to eat, he screamed, vomited immediately and then had diarrhoea. Soon Wayne began to scream at the sight of his mother. She could not touch him or come near him. In anger and helpless despair she would take him up upstairs and leave him there for hours. Wayne took some food from his father and next door neighbours and was fed only when they were available. Because he was losing weight rapidly, he was admitted to hospital for investigation.

In hospital, Wayne cried a lot, was at first unresponsive to nurses and movements around him. When not crying he looked blank and lethargic. Gradually he began to take food and became more alert and lively, doing well enough in the end to be discharged. This pattern of 'failure to thrive', improving in hospital, and deteriorating soon after going home, was to be repeated several times. All of this increased his mother's feelings of hostility and rejection towards the child, not to mention her feelings of inadequacy as a mother. He seemed better all round when he was in different places with different people. In the end she refused to have Wayne back home from the hospital.

Our work, after some initial sessions in the hospital, was carried out in the home with both parents and children. In order to be able to institute a full programme of assessment and treatment, we had to teach Mrs Grant to relax and to structure small, manageable daily tasks to counter her tension and her inertia and apathy. We diagnosed her depression as learned helplessness (see page 76). So as not to exacerbate her feelings of helplessness and demoralization, we underlined the point that we were not there as 'experts' to take over the burden of the child's problem from the parents, but that we would be partners in a co-operative venture with a major part of the responsibility rightfully in their hands. A period of counselling and support-giving and relaxation-training was embarked upon and covered seven weeks. We arranged for full-time attendance by the twins at a day-nursery.

Looking at the history we took at this time, it seems likely that the child learned to avoid food by associating feeding with painful experiences, e.g. forcing, hurrying, shaking, smacking, scolding and throwing. Finally, mother's person became a stimulus to evoke fear which (in proximity) brought physical symptoms like vomiting and diarrhoea, if she was angry. He expressed fear at the sight of his mother approaching him. Being reared in social isolation and lacking stimulation it is not surprising that Wayne manifested serious delay in the development of his speech. His brother was more generally advanced but also showed speech retardation.

Treatment programme
A variety of measures is used in the provision of services. This provision of methods and resources falls into two categories.

(i) *Immediate*. A variety of methods play their part. During the early stages of the Centre's involvement, attention in this sort of case is paid to immediate needs (crisis intervention) of the child and family. This has involved, in general:

(a) ensuring that the child was safe, fed and stimulated;
(b) arranging attendance at a day nursery (in part a safety measure). This allowed us to monitor the child for a substantial part of the day. It provided mother with a 'break' and the space to work on her problem with the social worker. It also gave the child some much needed social stimulation.
(c) arranging for health visitors, home-start volunteers and neighbours to assist mothers with feeding and child-care and to provide moral support;
(d) assisting parents with problems of housing, financing, welfare rights, etc. where and when appropriate;
(e) providing supervision by regular visits and phone calls (also emotional support);
(f) placing children on the 'at risk' register because of extreme rejection and/or abuse (failure to thrive);
(g) beginning and supporting self-help parents groups (composed of earlier clients) which parents could attend;

(h) desensitizing (where necessary) the mother's tension, anger and resentment when in the child's company. It was almost always necessary for the mothers of these children to learn to control and resolve feelings of anger and resentment and to deal with high levels of anxiety. This was sometimes achieved (before any formal feeding programme could be initiated) by training in relaxation, stress management and self-control.

(ii) Longer term. After the attention to the immediate safety and needs of child and family, the intervention focuses on critical issues such as the mother's relationship with her infant, her ability to feed her child and his to receive (and benefit from) sustenance; the depression and or anxiety she so often suffers from; the parents' relationship, and so on.

During this phase the treatment of failure to thrive cases consists of a 'package' of psychosocial methods ranging from 'talking' (personal and developmental counselling) to behaviour modification. This family-oriented approach combines behavioural methods of assessment and modification with family casework methods (including discussion, clarification of problems, task-setting and support giving). It is carried out in the home with both parents (generally speaking) and the child, but mother–child transactions become the main focus of therapy because of the acute crisis we meet in most cases. This *was* the case for Mrs Grant and Wayne.

Before we could initiate a programme dealing with the interactions between Mrs Grant and her child, we had to cope with the crisis issue of the mother's feeding her child. After all, Wayne was wasting away.

Phase I: This was tackled in a highly structured (and thus, directive) manner. At first we had to make the mealtimes more relaxed. She agreed (albeit reluctantly and sceptically) to desist from screaming, shouting and threatening the child over his meals. The period of eating was made quiet and calm. Mrs Grant was asked to talk soothingly and pleasantly to him.

This was extremely difficult for her. (The social worker joined the family for a few meals, helping to reassure Wayne, prompting the mother to help him eat in a gentle manner when he was in difficulties). Mrs Grant was encouraged to look at him, smile, and occasionally touch him. If Wayne refused his food she was to leave him. We encouraged her to coax him by play or soft words. The food was arranged to look attractive.

This aspect of the programme (lasting several weeks) was purely 'symptomatic' in the sense of encouraging the child to eat by creating less fraught circumstances. As long as the mother kept to this schedule,

Wayne would eat (not much, but sufficient to sustain life). If she broke the rules because she was moody or unstable, Wayne would not sit in his high chair. We added another rule (on the basis of this observation), that she never fed the twins when feeling acutely angry or tense. There should be a period of quiet relaxation (using the relaxation tape and the training we had given her) if this was difficult to achieve.

Phase II: This phase (as with earlier stages of treatment) was discussed in detail with both parents. A contract was drawn up specifying the mutual obligations and rules for the family and ourselves.

Objectives

1. To deliberately, and in planned fashion, increase positive interactions and decrease negative interactions between mother and child.
2. To desensitize Wayne's anxieties with regard to mother's caregiving (and other) activities.
3. To desensitize mother's tension, anger and resentment when in Wayne's company.
4. To increase and make more general the interactions with other members of the family (e.g. as a group, between Wayne and his brother, etc.).

Methods

Mrs Grant agreed to play exclusively with Wayne every evening after her husband returned from work, for 10 minutes during the first week; 15 minutes during the second week, 20 minutes during the third week and 25 minutes during the fourth and subsequent weeks. The father took Jimmy for a walk, or to another room, while Wayne had this period of play. Afterwards they would join in for a family play session. The mother was asked to play with Wayne on the floor – this was demonstrated and rehearsed – and she was encouraged to talk to him in a soft reassuring manner, encouraging him to participate in the play.

She was also instructed to smile at Wayne, look at him, touch him briefly, or praise him for each positive response she detected from him. (His tentative approaches toward her were 'shaped' by just such a series of successive approximations (see page 176).) After a period of weeks she was guided to seek proximity to him by hugging him briefly and then holding him on her lap for increasing intervals of time, eventually holding him close, but gently, while reading him a story.

There is no doubt that Mrs Grant found these times difficult, and, at times, distasteful; but they became gradually less so as time passed and especially as Wayne began to seek her out shyly and to smile and chat to her. We had to provide a good deal of support and encouragement to both parents during frequent visits or by phone calls. (Reinforcing the reinforcer is critical in this work.) Three months were occupied by this stage of the intervention.

Phase III: The final phase took two weeks and deliberately involved an intensification of Mrs Grant's interactions (now much improved) with Wayne.

1. She was to take him (as far as possible) everywhere she went. She was instructed to chat as much as possible to him in a soft measured way, smiling and cuddling him at appropriate times. These had to be discussed as Mrs Grant frequently put Wayne in a double-bind by giving contradictory verbal and non-verbal cues.)

2. She was asked to read to him and Jimmy, encourage them to play together, and read to them both at bedtime. *Their* positive interactions were to be reinforced socially.

The formal programme was faded out gradually (over a period of several weeks) after discussing with both parents the importance of a stimulating environment and a rich reinforcement schedule (see page 52) for the maintenance of the improvements they both detected in the family interactions and mother's feelings and attitudes (these were monitored for us by herself). Our assessment of Wayne's improved health, weight and height (and indeed his general psychological well-being) were confirmed by the assessments of the paediatrician, the dietary consultant, and a health visitor. Mrs Grant's sense of attachment (bonding) to Wayne had returned; what is of interest is that although we discussed her feelings and attitudes with her they were not the primary focus of treatment. She found it difficult, and in the end, refused to discuss them. We hoped that old feelings of affection and nurturance would return if we countered the avoidance situations (and sense of helplessness) which stood in the way of her learning to love him again. Feelings (and insights) *followed* actions.

■ ■ ■ ■

APPENDIX 5

Table 12. *Relative importance of screening characteristics for child abuse* (As determined by step-wise discriminant function analysis)

	Abusing families (n=62) %	Non abusing families (n=124) %
1. parent indifferent, intolerant or over-anxious towards child	83.9	21.8
2. history of family violence	51.6	5.6
3. socio-economic problems such as unemployment	85.5	34.7
4. infant premature, low birth weight	24.2	3.2
5. parent abused or neglected as a child	43.5	6.5
6. step-parent or cohabitee present	35.5	4.8
7. single or separated parent	38.7	8.1
8. mother less than 21 years old at the time of birth	40.3	23.4
9. history of mental illness, drug or alcohol addiction	61.3	21.8
10. infant separated from mother for greater than 24 hours post delivery	17.7	5.6
11. infant mentally or physically handicapped	1.6	0.8
12. less than 18 months between birth of children	22.6	15.3
13. infant never breast fed	46.8	40.3

From Browne, K. D. (1988) The naturalistic context of family violence and child abuse, Chapter 8 in Archer, J. and Browne, K. D. (ed.). *Human Aggression: Naturalistic Approaches*, Beckenham, Kent: Croom Helm. (With permission.)

REFERENCES

Anastasi, A. (1976) *Psychological Testing* (4th edn). New York: Collier Macmillan. [See chapter on projective techniques]

Aponte, H. (1978) 'The anatomy of a therapist.' In P. Papp (ed.), *Full Length Case Studies*. London: Gardner Press.

Argyle, M. and Henderson, M. (1985) *The Anatomy of Relationships*. Harmondsworth: Penguin Books.

Aries, P. (1973) *Centuries of Childhood*. Harmondsworth: Penguin Books.

Axline, V. M. (1947) *Play Therapy: The Inner Dynamics of Childhood*. Boston: Houghton Mifflin.

Bandura, A. (1977) *Social Learning Theory*. Englewood Cliffs, N. J.: Prentice-Hall.

Bannister, D. and Fransella, F. (1980) *Inquiring Man*. Harmondsworth: Penguin Books.

Barlow, D. (1981) *Sexually Transmitted Diseases – the Facts*. Oxford: Oxford University Press.

Benjamin, A. (1974) *The Helping Interview* (2nd edn). New York: Houghton Mifflin.

Bigner, J. J. (1979) *Parent–Child Relations: An Introduction to Parenting*. New York: Macmillan.

Biller, H. B. (1971) *Father, Child and Sex Role*. Lexington, Mass.: Heath.

Bowlby, J. (1980) *Attachment and Loss. Vol. I: Attachment*. London: Hogarth Press.

Brown, G. W. and Harris, T. (1978) *Social Origins of Depression*. London: Tavistock.

Cahill, M. M. (1984) *The Aids Epidemic*. London: Hutchinson.

Carter, E. A. and McGoldrick, M. (1981) *The Family Life Cycle*. New York: Gardner Press.

Clarke, A. and Clarke, A. D. B. (1976) *Early Experience: Myth and Reality*. London: Open Books.

Dominian, J. (1968) *Marital Breakdown*. Harmondsworth: Penguin Books.

Egan, G. (1986) *The Skilled Helper*. Monterey: Brooks/Cole.

Erikson, E. (1965) *Childhood and Society* (rev. edn). Harmondsworth: Penguin Books.

Fiske, M. (1979) *Middle Age: The Prime of Life?* London: Harper & Row.

Forward, S. and Buck, C. (1981) *Betrayal of Innocence: Incest and Devastation*. Harmondsworth: Penguin Books.

Freud, S. (1974) *Introductory Lectures on Psychoanalysis*. Harmondsworth: Penguin Books.

Frude, N. (ed.) (1980) *Psychological Approaches to Child Abuse*. London: Batsford.

Gale, A. and Chapman, A. J. (ed.) (1984) *Psychology and Social Problems*. Chichester: John Wiley.

Gelles, R. J. and Cornell, C. P. (1985) *Intimate Violence in Families*. London: Sage Publications.

Ginnott, H. (1969) *Between Parent and Child*. London: Staples Press.

Gittelman, R. (ed.) (1986) *Anxiety Disorders of Childhood*. Chichester: John Wiley.

Gorell Barnes, G. (1984) *Working With Families*. London: Macmillan.

Gottlieb, B. H. (1981) *Social Networks and Social Support*. Beverley Hills California: Sage Publications.

Guerney, B. C. (1977) (ed.) *Relationship Enhancement*. San Francisco: Jossey-Bass.

Haley, J. (1976) *Problem Solving Therapy*. New York: Harper Colophon.

Herbert, M. (1974) *Emotional Problems of Development in Children*. London: Academic Press.

Herbert, M. (1986) *Psychology for Social Workers*. (rev. edn). London: British Psychological Society/Macmillan. [Note chapters by Don Bannister on personal constructs; Neil Frude on the family; Barrie Hopson on transition and change/counselling; Peter Coleman on ageing.]

Hinde, R. (1978) *Towards Understanding Relationships*. London: Academic Press.

Hollin. C. R. and Trower, P. (ed) (1986) *Handbook of Social Skills Training: Applications across the Life Span. Vol. I*. Oxford: Pergamon Press.

Holmes, T. H. and Rahe, R. H. (1967) The social adjustment rating scale. *Journal of Psychosomatic Research*, **11**, 213–218.

Hopson, B. and Scully, M. (1980) *Lifeskills Teaching: Education for Self-empowerment*. New York: McGraw-Hill.

Hudson, A. (1987) [Personal communication.]

Kazdin, A. E. (1978) *History of Behaviour Modification*. Baltimore: University Park Press.

Kelly, G. A. (1955) *The Psychology of Personal Constructs*. New York: Norton.

Kempe, R. S. and Kempe, C.H. (1978) *Child Abuse*. London Fontana/Open Books.

Kennedy, E. (1981) *Crisis Counselling*. Dublin: Gill and Macmillan.

Lask, B. (1980) 'Evaluation. Why and How'. *Journal of Family Therapy*, 2, (2), 119–210.

Lee, S. G. and Herbert, M. (ed.) (1970) *Freud and Psychology*. Harmondsworth: Penguin Books. [Note chapter by C. Rycroft.]

Lewin, R. (ed.) (1975) *Child Alive*. London: Temple Smith.

Lidz, T. (1968) *The Person*. London: Basic Books.

Meichenbaum, D. H. (1974) *Cognitive Behaviour Modification*. New York: Plenum.

Maddox, B. (1975) *Step-parenting*. London: Unwin Paperbacks.

Madge, N. (ed.) *Families at Risk*. London: Heinemann Educational Books.

Minuchin, S. (1974) *Families and Family Therapy*. Cambridge, Mass: Harvard University Press.

Minuchin, S. and Fishman, C. (1981) *Family Therapy Techniques*. Cambridge Mass: Harvard University Press.

Morgan, R. (1984) *Behavioural Treatments with Children*. London: Heinemann Medical Books Ltd.

Mothner, I. and Weitz, A. (1986) *How to Get off Drugs*. Harmondsworth: Penguin Books.

Novaco, R. H. (1975) *Anger Control*. Lexington, Mass.: Heath.

O'Connor, R. D. (1969) 'Modification of social withdrawal through symbolic modeling'. *Journal of Applied Behavior Analysis*, **2**, 15–22.

O'Connor, R. D. (1972) 'Relative efficacy of modeling, shaping and the combined procedures for modification of social withdrawal'. *Journal of Abnormal Psychology*. **79**, 327–334.

Ollendick, T. H. and Cerny, J. A. (1981) *Clinical Behaviour Therapy with Children*. New York: Plenum.

Open University Course Organizers (1982) *Parents and Teenagers*. London: Harper and Row.

Parke, R. D. (1981) *Fathering*. London: Fontana/Open Books.

Parkes, C. M. (1972) *Bereavement*. London: Tavistock.

Patterson. G. (1982) *Coercive Family Process*. Eugene, Oregon: Castalia.

Price, R. H. (1978). *Abnormal Behaviour: Perspectives in Conflict* (2nd edn). New York: Hall, Rinehart & Winston.

Rapoport, R. N., Fogarty, M. P. and Rapoport, R. (ed.) (1982) *Families in Britain*. London: Routledge & Kegan Paul.

Richards, M. and Dyson, M. (1982) *Separation, Divorce and the Development of Children: A Review*. Cambridge: Child Care and Development Group.

Rogers, C. R. (1951) *Client-Centered Therapy*. Boston: Houghton-Mifflin.

Rutter, M. (1972) *Maternal Deprivation Reassessed*. Harmondsworth: Penguin Books.

Rutter, M. (1975) *Helping Troubled Children*. Harmondsworth: Penguin Books.

Rutter, M. (1981) 'Stress, coping and development'. *Journal of Child Psychology and Psychiatry*, **22(4)**, 323–357.

Rutter, M. and Madge, N. (1976) *Cycles of Disadvantage*. London: Heinemann.

Schaefer, E. S. (1959) 'A circumplex model for maternal behaviour'. *Journal of Abnormal and Social Behaviour*, **59**, 226–235.

Schaffer, H. R. (1971) *The Growth of Sociability*. Harmondsworth: Penguin Books.

Schaffer, H. R. (1977) *Mothering*, London: Fontana/Open Books.

Seligman, M. E. P. (1975) *Helplessness*. San Francisco: Freeman.

Sluckin, W. Herbert, M. and Sluckin, A. (1983) *Maternal Bonding*. Oxford: Basil Blackwell.

Sluckin, W. and Herbert, M. (ed.) (1986) *Parental Behaviour*. Chichester: John Wiley. [Note chapters by W. Sluckin, on bonding; C. Lewis on fathering.]

Spivack, G., Platt, J. J. and Shure, M. B. (1976) *The Problem-Solving. Approach to Adjustment*. San Francisco: Jossey-Bass.

Stern, D. (1977) *The First Relationship. Infant and Mother*. London: Fontana/Open Books.

Sutton Smith, B. and Rosenberg, B. (1970) *The Sibling*. London: Holt, Rinehart & Winston.

Treacher, A. and Carpenter, J. (ed.) (1984) *Using Family Therapy*. Oxford: Basil Blackwell.

Visher, E. B. and Visher, J. S. (1979) *Step families*. New York: Brunner Mazel.

Walczak, Y. (1984) 'Divorce, the kid's stories'. *Social Work Today*, 18 June, pp. 12–13.

Wallerstein, J. S. and Kelly, J. B. (1980) *Surviving the Breakup*. London: Grant McIntyre.

Watzlawick, P., Weakland, P. and Fisch, R. (1974) *Change: Principles of Problem Formation and Problem Resolution*. New York: Norton.

Winnicott, D. (1958) *Collected Papers*. London: Tavistock.

Walvin, J. (1982) *A Child's World*. Harmondsworth: Penguin Books.

Yelloly, M. A. (1980) *Social Work Theory and Psychoanalysis*. London: Van Nostrand Reinhold.

FURTHER READING

Part 1

Bruner, J. et al. (ed.) (1976) *Play: Its Role in Development and Evolution.* New York: Basic Books.
An invaluable guide to theoretical and other issues of value to those who wish to work through (and therefore understand) children's natural mode of self-expression – play.

Cunningham, C. and Davis, H. (1985) *Working with Parents: Frameworks for Collaboration.* Milton Keynes: Open University Press.
Drawing upon George Kelly's personal construct theory the authors provide valuable guidance in elaborating the necessary framework and practical skills which will enable professionals to work more harmoniously, more perceptively, and more effectively with parents of children with special needs.

Fransella, F. and Bannister, D. (1977) *A Manual for Repertory Grid Technique.* London: Academic Press.
A superb do-it-yourself guide to Repertory Grid work.

Herbert, M. (1987) *Behavioural Treatment of Children with Problems: A Practice Manual,* (*2nd edn*). London Academic Press.
A 'how-to-do-it' manual (with many caveats) for the helping professions. Illustrated with flow charts and case studies.

Herbert, M. (ed.) (1986) *Psychology for Social Workers.* London: Macmillan/The British Psychological Society.
This book has become a standard recommended text for many social work training courses. It includes a section on bonding and a practical guide to behavioural casework with children and adolescents. Also included are chapters on the family, transition and change, counselling, personal constructs, psychopathology and ageing.

Risk, R. (1987) 'Puppet Therapy', *Association for Child Psychology and Psychiatry Newsletter* 9 (3) July, 18–21.
How to make and use puppets in cases of *inter alia* sexual abuse, elective mutism and school refusal.

Sutton, C. (1987) *A Handbook of Research for the Helping Professions.* Routledge & Kegan Paul.
Members of the helping professions need ready access to the research literature in an increasingly wide range of fields. This Handbook draws upon empirical research from wide-ranging international sources, such as psychology, psychiatry, social work, social policy and sociology.

Vetere, V. and Gale, A. (1987) *Ecological Studies of Family Life.* Chichester: John Wiley.
An unusual and illuminating look at what happens within families. A useful review of theories and methods of studying family life is provided.

Part 2

Barber, D. (1978) *One Parent Families*. London: Hodder & Stoughton.
An anthology of experience – conveyed in personal accounts by parents and children – of life in one-parent families. It covers bereavement, lone mothers, lone fathers, decisions, politics and other themes.

Bell, R. Q. and Harper, L. V. (1980) *Child Effects on Adult Behaviour*. Lincoln, Nebraska: Univesity of Nebraska Press.
It is vital to understand the effects parents have on their children. This goes without saying. But what of the reverse? This important book elaborates the ways in which children are the products *and* the architects of the rearing process.

Caldwell, B. M. (1966) 'The effects of infant care'. In M. L. Hoffman and L. W. Hoffman (ed.) *Review of Child Development Research, Vol. I*. New York: Russell Sage Foundation.
One of a series of excellent volumes containing reviews of child development research.

Clarke, A. M. and Clarke, A. D. B. (ed.) (1976) *Early Experience: Myth and Evidence*. London: Open Books.
The authors challenge the widely held assumption that the child's social experiences in the first few years of life exert a disproportionate influence on later development. The book provides a stimulating antidote to the pessimism and fatalism that can overtake even the most robust professional at times.

Feldman, P. and Orford, J. (ed.) (1980) *Psychological Problems: The Social Context*. Chichester: John Wiley.
Note chapters by Jim Orford on 'the domestic context'; Martin Herbert on 'vulnerability and resistance to problems'; Phil Feldman on 'offenders'; Stephen Duck on 'intimate relationships'. this is a valuable book as it presents aspects of social and community psychology in dealing with psychological problems.

Herbert, M. (1985) *Caring for Your Children: A Practical Guide*. Oxford: Basil Blackwell.
A practical guide for dealing with and preventing the difficulties – normal or otherwise – that children are likely to experience from infancy to the onset of adolescence.

Herbert, M. (1987) *Conduct Disorders of Childhood and Adolescence: A Social Learning Perspective*, (2nd revised edn). Chichester: John Wiley.
An account of the development of social and antisocial behaviour in children and adolescents, with practical guides to the treatment of conduct problems.

Herbert, M. and Sluckin, A. (1985) 'A realistic look at mother-infant bonding'. In M. L. Chiswick (ed). *Recent Advances in Perinatal Medicine No. 2 Edinburgh: Churchill Livingstone*.
Examines issues such as stillbirth, twins, bonding in utero, infant death.

Herbert, M. (1987) *Living with Teenagers*. Oxford: Basil Blackwell.
This book carries on the task described in Herbert (1985), but now taking the child (and his or her difficulties) into the 'teenage' years.

Maddox, Brenda (1980) *Step-Parenting: How to Live with Other People's Children.* London: Unwin.
'Reconstituted' families are on the increase. Here is a step-parent describing the rights, duties, myths, dilemmas and joys of step-parenting.

Rapoport, R., Rapoport. R. N. and Strelitz, Z. (1977) *Fathers, Mothers, and Others.* London: Routledge & Kegan Paul.
A comprehensive review of the role, tasks and needs of parents through history and in modern times.

Sluckin, W., Herbert, M., and Sluckin, A. (1983) *Maternal Bonding.* Oxford: Basil Blackwell.
A critical, but sympathetic, look at the concept of maternal bonding – how mothers become attached to their babies.

Stoppard, Miriam, Herbert, M. and Ivimey , G. (1983) *Your Growing Child: The Complete Guide to Child Care from 3 to 11 Years.* London: Octopus Books.
A guide packed with information on health, diet, common childhood illnesses, stages of growth and development, schooling, hobbies and much else.

Topping, K. J. (1986) *Parents as Educators: Training Parents to Teach their Children.* London: Croom Helm.
A full and detailed review of the literature on training parents, plus a strongly argued case for working with parents.

Part 3

Barber, D. (1978) *One Parent Families.* London: Hodder & Stoughton.
An anthology of experience – conveyed in personal accounts by parents and children – of life in one-parent families. The book covers bereavement, lone mothers and fathers, decisions, politics and many other themes.

Barker, P. (1986) *Basic Family Therapy*, (2nd edn). London: Collins.
The basics of the subject. You cannot learn family therapy from a book but here is a valuable introduction to the subject.

Bornstein, P. H. and Bornstein, M. T. (1986) *Marital Therapy: A Behavioural-Communications Approach.* Oxford: Pergamon Press.
This book integrates the use of behavioural and systems models in treating the problems of distressed couples, allowing therapists to bridge the gap between systems theory and clinical practice. Its focus is on couples, their interaction and relationships.

Cartledge, G. and Milburn, J. F. (ed.) (1986). *Teaching Social Skills to Children* (2nd edn). Oxford: Pergamon.
A practical helpful and generally readable book. Contributions are from recognized experts in the field.

Cotler, S. B. and Guerra, J. J. (1976) *Assertion Training: A Humanistic-Behavioural Guide to Self-dignity.* Champaign, Illinois: Research Press.
This is mainly a 'how-to-do-it' book on procedures of assertiveness-training. The book is primarily concerned with anxiety reduction and social skills training. The goal is to encourage the skills that allow clients to establish close, interpersonal relationships, protect themselves from being taken advan-

tage of by others, make decisions and choices, recognize their own needs and rights . . . without violating the dignity and rights of others in the process.

Erwin, E. (1979) *Behaviour Therapy: Scientific, Philosophical and Moral Foundations*. Cambridge: Cambridge University Press.
Unsurpassed (in my opinion) exposition of the philosophical and ethical basis of behavioural work. The book examines critically the claim of behaviour therapy to be 'scientific'.

Ferber, R. (1986) *Solve Your Child's Sleep Problems*. London: Dorling Kindersley.
An invaluable practical guide to a vexing problem.

Forehand, R. (1977) 'Child non-compliance to parental requests'. In M. Hessen, R. M. Eisler and P. M. Miller (ed.) *Progress in Behavior Modification, Vol, 5* . New York: Academic Press.
A useful source for those giving advice or constructing programmes for that perennial problem – disobedience. The same applies to the book below.

Forehand, R. and McMahon, R. J. (1981) *Helping the Noncompliant Child: A Clinician's Guide to Effective Parent Training*. New York: Guildford Press.

Gittleman, M. (1965) 'Behavior rehearsal as a technique in child treatment'. *Journal of Child Psychology and Psychiatry, 6,* 251–55.
An important technique described and discussed in detail.

Hudson, B. L. and MacDonald, G. M. (1986) *Behavioural Social Work: An Introduction*. London: Macmillan.
Here are clear guidelines for the use of behavioural work in social work settings.

Kanfer, H. and Goldstein, A. P. (ed.) (1986) *Helping People Change*, (3rd edn). Oxford: Pergamon Press.
An eclectic review of methods of behaviour change.

Murgatroyd, S. (1985) *Counselling and Helping* (Psychology in Action Series). London: The British Psychological Society/Methuen.
An excellent introduction to counselling for the helping professions. Simple but not simplistic, practical, as well as readable, collection of practice guides.

Nelson-Jones, R. (1982) *The Theory and Practice of Counselling Psychology*. London: Holt, Rinehart & Winston.
Humanistic, behavioural and psychoanalytic models of counselling are analysed in this comprehensive introduction to a complex field of helping.

Rowan, D. and Eayrs, C. (1987) *Fears and Anxieties*. London: Longman.
A clear and practical guide to contemporary theories about fears and anxieties – how they come about and how they can be managed.

Thouless, R. H. (1974) *Straight and Crooked Thinking*. London: Pan Books.
The ideal of straight thinking is (*inter alia*) the application of the scientific habit of thought to practical problems. This book deals with situations in which cool, unemotional thinking is required, e.g. controversial, emotive issues. It lists 38 dishonest tricks which are commonly used in argument, with the methods of overcoming them.

Treacher, A. (1983) 'Family therapy with children: the structural approach'. In G. Edwards (ed.), *Current Issues in Clinical Psychology*, *vol. 4*. London: Plenum Press.
   This chapter throws light on a sometimes confusing, often complex subject.

Acknowledgements

It is impossible to acknowledge by name all those to whom I am indebted for ideas and research findings which appear in the book. However, I must express my thanks to publishers and authors for guidelines, ideas and lists adapted, elaborated or paraphrased in my book (and for permission to reproduce tables and figures):

Chapter 1

Page 6 Cunningham, C. and Davis, H. (1985) *Working With Parents: Frameworks for Collaboration*. Milton Keynes: Open University Press. (With permission.)

Page 8 Figure 1a from Schaefer, E. S. (1959) 'A circumplex model of maternal behaviour.' *Journal of Abnormal and Social Psychology, 59*, 226–35.

Page 8 Figure 1b paraphrased and adapted from Becker, W. C. (1964) 'Consequences of different kinds of parental discipline.' In M. L. Hoffman and L. H. Hoffman (ed.) *Review of Child Development Research, Vol. 1*. New York: Russell Sage Foundation.

Page 10 Table 1. Life tasks' list from Open University Course Organizers (1982) *Parents and Teenagers*. London: Harper & Row. (With permission.)

Page 13 Figure 2 from Herbert, M. (1987) *Living with Teenagers*. Oxford: Basil Blackwell. (With permission.)

Chapter 2

Page 20 Flow chart adapted and elaborated from Herbert, M. (1987) *Behavioural Treatment of Children with Problems* (2nd edn). London: Academic Press.

Chapter 3

Page 41 List of parenting skills adapted from Hopson, B. and Scully, M. (1980) *Lifeskills Teaching: Education for Self-empowerment*. New York: McGraw-Hill.

Chapter 4

Page 53 Figure 5. Layout for a preliminary analysis of a problematic classroom situation. From Herbert, M. (1987) *Living with Teenagers*. Oxford: Basil Blackwell. (With permission.)

Page 57 Method of eliciting constructs (Repertory Grid) based on George Kelly as described in Bannister, D. and Fransella, F. (1980). *Inquiring Man*. Harmondsworth: Penguin Books.

Page 58 Example of a completed Repertory Grid from Kelly, G. A. (1955) *The Psychology of Personal Constructs*. New York: Norton.

Page 64 Quotation from Rycroft, C. (1970) In S. G. Lee and M. Herbert (ed.) *Freud and Psychology*. Harmondsworth: Penguin Books.

Page 65 Guidelines to faulty family functioning from Lask, B. (1980) 'Evaluation. Why and How'. *Journal of Family Therapy, 2*, 119–20.

Chapter 5

Page 75 Developmental Tasks. List adapted from Erikson, E. (1965) *Childhood and Society*. Harmondsworth: Penguin Books.

Page 76 Quotation from Seligman, M. (1975) *Helplessness*. San Francisco: Freeman.

Page 89 Data on sexual encounters comes from Kinsey, A. C. *et al.* (1953) *Sexual Behaviour in the Human Female*. Philadelphia: Saunders

Chapter 6

Page 103 Winnicott, D. (1958) *Collected Papers*. London: Tavistock. This is the source of some of the ideas on the theme of emotional attachment/rejection in this chapter.

Chapter 8

Page 124 Figure 7 adapted with permission from Sutton, C. (1987) 'The evaluation of counselling: A goal-attainment approach'. *Counselling*. May issue, pp. 14–19.

Page 127 Table 10. Event recording of parent-child interactions: adapted with permission from Iwaniec, D. (1983) *An investigation of non-organic failure-to-thrive*. Unpublished PhD thesis. Psychology Department, University of Leicester.

Chapter 9

Page 142 Quotation from Treacher, A. and Carpenter, J. (1984) *Using Family Therapy*. Oxford: Basil Blackwell.

Page 147 Self-talk example from Novaco, R. H. (1975) *Anger-Control*. Lexington: Heath. (With permission.)

Page 151 Contract from Herbert, M. (1987) *Living with Teenagers*. Oxford: Basil Blackwell. (With permission.)

Chapter 10

Page 162 Groupwork guidelines paraphrased from Johnson, D. W. and Johnson, F. R. (1975) *Joining Together*. New York: Prentice Hall.

Page 167 The section on settling differences is elaborated from an idea described in Herbert, M. (1987) *Parents and Teenagers*. Oxford: Basil Blackwell.

Page 171 The stress management items are based upon (and adapted from) methods suggested by Reg Beech (1985) *Staying Together*. Chichester: John Wiley. (With permission.)

Chapter 11

Page 174 Some of the ideas on rules and routines here draw upon an unpublished manuscript and discussions with a colleague, Alan Hudson, from the Philip Institute of Technology, Melbourne.

Page 176 Case material in this and subsequent pages from cases (heavily disguised) at the 'Centre for Behavioural Work with Families' with thanks to Brenda O'Driscoll, Dorota Iwaniec, Annie Holmes – co-workers.

Chapter 12

Page 185 These ideas on social skills are discussed in more detail in Herbert, M. Social Skills Training with Children. In C. R. Hollin and P. Trower (ed.)

(1986) *Handbook of Social Skills Training. Vol 1: Applications Across the Life-Span*. Oxford: Pergamon Press.

Page 186 Argyle, M. and Henderson, M. (1985) *The Anatomy of Relationships*. Harmondsworth: Penguin Books. This book is the source of some of the information and ideas in this section on social skills.

Page 190 Spivack, G., Platt, J. J. and Shure, M. B. (1976) *The Problem-solving Approach to Adjustment*. San Francisco: Jossey-Bass. This book provides many innovative ideas and data on problem-solving training for children.

Appendices

Frude, N. (ed.) (1980) *Psychological Approaches to Child Abuse* London: Batsford; K. Browne, C. Davies and P. Stratton (ed.) (1988) *Early Prediction and Prevention of Child Abuse*. Chichester: John Wiley; and the IMPACT Workshops conducted by Martin Herbert and Dorota Iwaniec, are the sources for the various lists of signs and symptoms and behavioural indicators of child abuse. The case vignette and options for child abuse treatment are drawn from the IMPACT workshop handouts (Herbert and Iwaniec). Many of the ideas and research data which form the rationale of this material are derived from Gambrill, E. D. (1983) Behavioural intervention with child abuse and neglect. In M. Hersen et al. (ed.) *Progress in Behaviour Modification. Vol. 15*. New York: Academic Press.

Index